THE PROPHETIC VOICE IN PROTESTANT CHRISTIANITY

THE PROPHETIC VOICE IN PROTESTANT CHRISTIANITY

BY

RALPH G. WILBURN
Professor of Theology, Graduate Seminary
Phillips University

WIPF & STOCK · Eugene, Oregon

Wipf and Stock Publishers
199 W 8th Ave, Suite 3
Eugene, OR 97401

The Prophetic Voice in Protestant Christianity
By Wilburn, Ralph G.
ISBN 13: 978-1-62032-682-4
Publication date 12/15/2012
Previously published by The Bethany Press, 1956

To My Wife

Whose Loving Devotion

Has Inspired Much of

My Labor

PREFACE

This volume grew out of a series of lectures which I delivered in the N. C. C. New Testament Lectureship at Northwest Christian College in Eugene, Oregon, January, 1953. As they appear in this volume, the lectures have been revised and considerably expanded.

The book is written out of a conviction which I share with most leaders in ecumenical Christianity—the conviction, namely, that there is an urgent need to restudy our basic Christian beliefs critically and constructively, in the light of our total Protestant heritage. Such an enlargement of theological perspective, in our denominationally and confessionally differentiated forms of Christianity, offers substantial hope of bringing us closer to one another in our understanding of the Christian faith.

At the center of the Protestant type of the Christian faith stands the prophetic spirit which demands continuous reform of the empirical church and the forms which she assumes in the course of her realization in history. The motif of this book is its concern with the redemptive power of this prophetic voice in Protestant Christianity, and its implications and bearing on the outer forms of church life and thought.

Two fundamental and pressing problems in the contemporary scene have been singled out for critical restudy in the light of the prophetic voice in Protestantism. These are the problem of revelation and the problem of unity. The method adopted for this book is thus, first, to analyze and differentiate the major principles and values of the Protestant mind, traditional and modern, which appear to be of perennial worth, as aspects of its prophetic character. On the basis of this analysis, I then proceed to rethink critically first, the problem of revelation, and second, the challenge of the ecumenical movement.

For several years the conviction has been growing in my mind that the emergence in the church of numerous sectarian split-off groups stems from a tragic ambiguity in the Protestant doctrine of religious authority or revelation. In general, Protestants have not come to grips with this problem of authority frankly and courageously and adequately. As a result, the fictitious and historically unsound blueprint concept of the New Testament has served the purposes of various Protestant leaders who felt moved to organize Christianity rigidly about their peculiar interpretations of the New Testament, often under the battle cry of "restoring New Testament Christianity," even if a sectarian schism became necessary to achieve this end. And biblicistic absolutisms of one sort or another are still giving rise to heresy trials within the framework of Protestant Christianity.

Furthermore, an inexcusable prejudice against theology is still evident in many of our Protestant groups. This prejudice has fostered a sufficient degree of theological obscurantism (often naïvely called a plea for the "simple" gospel) and ambiguity to make it possible for such sectarian leaders and heresy-hunters to perform their evil work of fostering schism and division in the body of Christ.

It therefore seems high time that we come to grips more adequately with the problem of revelation and authority. For unless we do so, our theological vagueness will continue to furnish only too ample opportunity for many a twentieth-century Diotrephes.

It must be humbly confessed also that, for the most part, Protestants have failed to think through the problems of authority and unity, *in the light of our total Protestant heritage.* We have been too content to restrict our horizon to the perspective that has obtained in our own denomination or confessional group. In fact, most of Protestantism has only recently become tradition-minded, in this broad and critical sense. This book represents the growth of this broad, historical realism in the theological outlook of Protestantism. It has as a subsidiary purpose to augment the development of this realism.

Hence it is my desire that the book further the development of the ecumenical cause. For I share very deeply the conviction that this movement represents an inspiring fruition of the prophetic spirit of Protestant Christianity.

I hope also that the book will serve to stimulate and encourage numerous critical discussions of the issues with which it deals, among all Christian groups, Protestant and Catholic. For the contemporary ecumenical reformation of the church will be successful only to the extent that we penetrate to the heart of the Christian message and think our way, together, toward a more adequate understanding of its meaning.

Needless to say that, for whatever insights I have, I owe much to my teachers, formerly of the University of Chicago, to my colleagues on the faculty of the seminary at Phillips University, and to my students, who are a source of constant stimulation to my thought.

RALPH G. WILBURN.

Graduate Seminary
Phillips University

CONTENTS

PART ONE

Perennial Values of Protestantism

PART TWO

Protestantism and the Problem of Revelation

PART THREE

Protestantism and the Contemporary Challenge of Christian Unity

PART ONE

Perennial Values of Protestantism

CHAPTER ONE

The Dynamics of Undenominational Protestantism

The cause of non-Catholic Christianity,[1] since the Reformation inaugurated by Luther, has gradually become aware that, despite its divisions, it cherishes certain common principles which give it a distinct unity and identity in contrast to the Catholic type of the Christian faith. Thus, while non-Catholic Christians cherish, or should cherish, their total Christian heritage (including Catholicism), they treasure in an even more profound way their common non-Catholic heritage. We have come to refer to this as our Protestant heritage. In its wholeness, it is the heritage of transconfessional and undenominational Protestantism.

The term "Protestant" originated from the Protestation which was read in the famous Diet of Speyer, April 19, 1529. It was a protest in response to the Emperor's decision to repeal the recess of the Diet of 1526, which had granted permission to Saxony to live, rule, and conduct its religious affairs in keeping with their "obligations to God and the Emperor." In the Diet of 1529 the Emperor also ordered the Catholic estates to enforce the Edict of Worms (thus suppress-

[1]It is regrettable that in the thinking of the common man the term "Catholic" has come to be almost inseparably associated with Roman Catholicism. It is to be hoped that the term "ecumenical" will come to embody all of the truly universal meanings of the term "catholic" and eliminate the peculiar, sectarian meanings which Romanism has read into the term "Catholic." In this book we shall follow the customary usage, for the sake of expediency, and use the term "Catholic" to mean Roman Catholicism.

ing Lutheranism), and he demanded that no one in the Lutheran estates be prevented from hearing mass, if he so desired, and also that the Lutheran estates should cease making any further changes in the religious *status quo*.

That the Catholic clergy should be permitted to maintain its authority, even in Evangelical territories, meant, as the Evangelicals viewed it, not only that the Catholics would be able to secure their actual position, but also eventually the restoration of the entire medieval episcopal jurisdiction. That the Catholic mass was to be restored appeared to the Evangelicals to constitute a direct attack on the concept of Christian political authority which they had developed.

Jakob Sturm, the stalwart Evangelical mayor of Strassburg, voiced the reply of the Evangelicals: that in secular matters, the emperor rightly possessed supreme authority; but that in matters of conscience, one is to be ruled by the higher authority of God. When, on April 19, the Imperial Commission announced that it had accepted the conclusions which the majority from the area of Saxony had sanctioned, and that these conclusions would shortly be issued as the official decree of the Diet, five princes and fourteen cities[2] registered their Protestation.

In this historic Protestation (1) the Evangelicals *affirmed* that they had acted, since the Diet of 1526, in all good conscience and had remained true to the Diet's decree; (2) they *affirmed* that the Edict of 1526, which was based on the unanimous decision of all representatives, could not now justly be nullified by only a majority of the present Diet; (3) they said, "we protest *and testify*[3]. . . because these demands are

[2]The princes were: Johann, Elector of Saxony; Duke Philip of Hesse; Duke Ernst of Lünenberg; Prince Wolfgang of Anhalt; and Duke George of Brandenburg-Ansbach. The fourteen imperial cities were: Strassburg, Nürnberg, Ulm, Constance, Lindau, Memmingen, Kempten, Nördlingen, Heilbronn, Reutlingen, Isny, St. Gallen, Waissenburg, and Windsheim.

[3]*Wir protestieren und bezeugen.*

against God and His holy commandments and against the unanimous Edict of the Diet of 1526"; they declared that until the promised general council of the church was forthcoming, "in matters pertaining to the honor of God and the salvation of the soul each person in Saxony must stand for himself before God and render account."

At first glance, this protestation might not seem to be of profound historical significance. But in the particular context in which it was delivered, it was indeed a dramatic symbol of Christian liberty, comparable to Luther's burning the papal bull. As one lonely monk had protested against the hierarchical order of the church, so now a group of territories and cities protested against the authoritarian secular-priestly order of the Roman Empire.

One must not overlook the fact (as some have done) that this was considerably more than a mere negative protest. As the Evangelicals themselves put it, it was also a *positive affirmation;* it was a *religious witness* of their faith. From the outset, therefore, Protestantism has never been a mere negative protest, as some Roman Catholics erroneously contend. It was, and has always been, a positive affirmation of faith, in the presence of its enemies. Instead of the traditions and the authority of the hierarchical church, it *affirmed* the clear and simple meaning of holy Scripture, and the liberty of the Christian man.

From 1529 on, the supporters of Luther's cause came thus to be known as Protestants. Few of the non-Catholic Christian groups have used this term exclusively, however, as a term of self-designation. This has perhaps been due to the seemingly negative import of the term. Nevertheless, the term "Protestantism" has acquired new and additional positive meaning through the years. It has come to mean a fairly definite type of Christian piety.

In this first chapter, it will be our aim to describe the positive spiritual dynamics of this Protestant type of Christianity. Eight enduring values or perennial principles of the Protestant spirit include:

1. a prophetic spirit calling for continuous reform,
2. the kind of faith-relation which guards against idolatrous attachment to human programs and dogmas,
3. the lure of the Eternal which incites love of, and loyalty to, truth,
4. the final authority of "The Word" which evokes man's increasingly valid response,
5. the experience of the divine *agape* which fulfills man's longing for religious certitude,
6. a profound reverence for the individual conscience which guarantees its liberty,
7. a personal encounter which elicits the response of authentic individuality,
8. a radical laicism which erases hierarchical distinctions and closes the gap between the sacred and the secular.

A discussion of these principles may perhaps help derogate from the persistent blight of denominationalism and confessionalism, and strengthen the realization that there is in fact a dynamic inner unity whereby all Protestants are one, despite wide variation in confessional and denominational theory and practice.

The urgency of our task would seem to be evident in the face of a militant, united Catholicism, on the one hand, and a secular culture which is in grave danger of disintegrating by virtue of its own autonomy, on the other.

1. *A Prophetic Spirit Calling for Continuous Reform*

At the heart of Protestantism stands a dialectical principle, characterizing the relation of the human to the divine. This principle calls for the *affirmation and negation* of every particular temporal fulfillment of eternal values. By this prophetic principle, Protestantism views all historical structures, through which the spirit of eternal love seeks to express and realize itself, in terms of judgment as well as fulfillment, in terms of negative as well as positive worth.

In a particularly illuminating paragraph, Paul Tillich has written:

> What makes Protestantism Protestant is the fact that it transcends its own religious and confessional character, that it cannot be identified wholly with any of its particular and historical forms. . . . Protestantism has a principle that stands beyond all its realizations. It is the critical and dynamic source of all Protestant realizations, but it is not identical with any of them. It cannot be confined by a definition; it is not identical with the structure of the Reformation or of early Christianity or even with a religious *form* at all. It transcends them as it transcends *any* cultural form. On the other hand, it can appear in all of them; it is a living, moving restless power in them.[4]

The Protestant understanding of the inner reality of Christianity forbids one to identify this reality with its historical development. The Protestant believes that Christianity is more than the forms of doctrine, church order, and moral codes which it has produced in the course of its history. As Wilhelm Pauck says, "Protestantism possesses resources that transcend its historical forms."[5]

This prophetic refusal to equate the spirit and the form, or "the letter and the Spirit" to use the Apostle Paul's terms,[6] does not mean that the Spirit ever exists apart from historical forms. Distinction here does not mean separation. To believe that it does is

[4] Paul Tillich, *The Protestant Era*, trans. James Luther Adams (Chicago: The University of Chicago Press, 1948), pp. 162-3. Copyright 1948 by the University of Chicago.

[5] Wilhelm Pauck, *The Heritage of the Reformation* (Boston: Beacon Press, 1950), p. 148.

[6] See 2 Corinthians 3:6, KJV.

the fatal error of thoroughgoing mysticism. The distinction means, first of all, that the Spirit of the Eternal is not dependent upon *any particular historical form* for its self-realization; it expresses itself in ever-new forms of fulfillment, often abandoning forms which were once significant but which, due to cultural change, have become inadequate and obsolete.

This creative adaptability to the ongoingness of historic process means that the spirit of reform remains continually alive in the Protestant type of Christianity. The Reformation must continue if the church remains true to its Protestant heritage. The spirit of reform is of the essence of the dynamic of the Christian faith. Whenever the church loses this dynamic, she forfeits the essential prophetic principle of her life.

Protestants thus feel that there is an abiding truth in the statement of the greatest of all Reformers who said: "I have not come to bring peace, but a sword."[7] Whenever religion ceases to be a prophetic sword whose judgment cuts through and transcends all human structures and ideologies, including the historical forms of the church, it is conquered by historical absolutism, its perennial foe. The Protestant view of historical existence, to borrow Tillich's phrase, looks forward to "a continuous revolutionary shattering and transforming of the existing situation."[8]

2. *The Kind of Faith-relation Which Guards Against Idolatrous Attachment to Human Programs and Dogmas*

The prophetic spirit of Protestantism is closely correlated with a principle which furnishes a safeguard against man's seemingly universal inclination

[7]Matthew 10:34.

[8]Tillich, *op. cit.*, p. 172.

toward an idolatrous attachment to relative religious forms. In the name of the New Testament gospel, undenominational Protestantism issues a call to make the sovereign Lord of all history and life the only object of absolute religious devotion. It protests against the view which regards the historically relative as absolute. It protests against all tendencies toward self-sufficiency in human life and thought.

In the days of Israel's prophets, this idolatrous tendency manifested itself in attachment to the priestly system, which intervened between the people and God. This system became that in which the people placed their religious trust, that upon which they relied supremely, that, therefore, which became their god.

In Jesus' day, this same persistent tendency showed itself in devotion to the legalistic system of the Pharisees and their tradition. Indeed, Israel's leaders were so completely devoted to this idol that when Jesus threatened to destroy their idolatry, they crucified him.

In the Middle Ages, the idol was the hierarchical church, submission to which was equated with salvation. The institutional church was regarded as an object of absolute religious devotion and trust, thereby idolatrizing the Eternal. This idolatry inspired its devotees to torture and kill the heretics, those who for reasons of conscience refused to bow to the idol of church authority.

It is part of the glory of undenominational Protestantism that it continually reminds us that the creative Lord of all life, and he alone, is the *only* worthy object of religious devotion and trust. It says that when the human spirit is bound to any structure of reality, to any system, to any earthly form, and this binding assumes the proportion of absolute devotion, idolatry has triumphed. For idolatry is nothing else but the directing of religious devotion to something other than the living God. The first commandment is therefore still the first: "You shall have no other gods before me."

Protestantism is a vigorous protest against any view which holds that the historical forms through which life's ultimate meaning is realized are absolute; and it is an equally vigorous affirmation that only the living Lord is to exercise absolute lordship over our lives. To him, to his way of life, to his spirit we are to yield ourselves completely. But devotion to the organized church, to a system of doctrine, or *to anything else in this world* is to be qualified by the extent to which this something else makes possible the fulfillment of God's creative love, opened up in Jesus Christ. Such is the judgment which undenominational Protestantism passes upon all religious traditions, institutions, ceremonials, and doctrines.

The distinction involved in this Protestant judgment is of fundamental significance. It is the distinction between the unconditional character of ultimate, creative Love and the relative nature of the historical structures through which this Love is expressed. Eternal Love reaches infinitely beyond all historical forms, yet its redemptive power is fulfilled in and through them.

This distinction brings to light most clearly the basic difference between the Catholic and the Protestant understanding of the faith-relation. The tragic error of Catholicism lies in its attempt to regard some of the ecclesiastical and doctrinal forms through which faith expresses itself as permanent, fixed, and indispensable to salvation. This turns out to be an idolatrous distortion of the faith-relation, for it generates an absolutism which inevitably tends to enslave the human spirit; it demands a kind of relationship in which the self is ruled by another in an authoritarian way. The Protestant view of faith abolishes all absolutes except personal trust in Christ, and it thereby escapes the idolatrous distortion of the faith-relation which is generated and perpetuated by Roman Catholicism.

On the other hand, Protestantism also stands opposed to the autonomous character of our modern, self-sufficient culture. Such a culture is demonic, for it ignores or denies the fact that the human spirit is created by and grounded in the divine. It forgets that man is under the rule of God. As a result, our modern culture suffers the blight of mediocrity; it becomes insipid, dull and pointless; it holds no great meaning, is sustained by no inspiring vision, and is vivified by no relation to the Eternal, to ultimate reality. Hence our culture vainly tries to escape into the cults of aestheticism, statism, social reformism, social revolution, scientism, or some other idolatrization of the divine. These secular cults, however, do not suffice; for creative human talents dedicated supremely to any end less than the Eternal inevitably become debased.[9] An autonomous, secular culture inescapably disintegrates into a collection of warring interests and loyalties, each of which is jeopardized by the others.

Prophetic Protestantism thus saves the human spirit from two deadly perils: the idolatrization of the religious relationship in Catholic authoritarianism, and the atheistic autonomy of secularistic humanism. For central in the Protestant view is the theonomous (being under the rule of God) understanding of the relation of faith, which avoids both the error of ab-

[9]Cf. Leroy S. Loemker's excellent analysis of secularism in *The Christian Faith and Secularism*, ed. J. Richard Spann (New York: Abingdon-Cokesbury Press, 1948), pp. 15-16.

solutizing the historically relative, and also the equally fatal mistake of secular autonomy.

3. *The Lure of the Eternal Which Incites Love of, and Loyalty to, Truth*

It is because Protestantism makes the faith-relation with life's ultimate mystery central that it greatly enhances the lure of truth and places a supreme value on a personal apprehension of, and devotion to, a growing love of the truth, and to a love of a growing knowledge of the truth.

The spirit of the sixteenth-century Reformation was, in a way, comparable to the spirit of the Renaissance; although the two struggles for freedom operated on different levels. Nor should it be forgotten that the former was a struggle which operated in a God-centered perspective, while the latter was fundamentally man-centered in outlook. Yet both movements represented the human struggle for freedom. The entire scientific enterprise was indeed stirring, in embryonic form, in the Renaissance. This was, in part at any rate, a rebirth of love for truth.

In the scholastic period of the church's history, thinking had been *obliged* to proceed within the prescribed limits of the creedal dogmas of orthodoxy. This dogmatism dominated the process of thinking, and indeed included the whole of man's life and his world, thanks to the all-inclusiveness of papal control. It is a matter of common knowledge that the shackles of this absolutism unduly retarded the development of the scientific enterprise.

Poor Galileo got his neck caught in the wringer for daring to think beyond the prescribed limits. He came out at first with a few bold statements. He threw into the teeth of the Scholastics the statement: The

Ptolemaic system is no more reconcilable with the theory of Joshua and the sun than the Copernican; what are you going to do about it? Another one of his famous sayings, by which he objected to the church's dogmatic control of intellectual inquiry, was: The Holy Spirit aimed to show us how to go to heaven, not how the heavens go. The Jesuits got him, however, in the early twenties of the seventeenth century, and Galileo promised to remain silent; he had no hankering for martyrdom. But he proved unable to quiet the restless spirit of inquiry in his mind. Ten years later (1632) he published his *Dialog of the Two Systems*. The Inquisition then laid its firm hand upon him and forced him into silence—a broken old man. Yet Galileo's sole aim was to get at the truth, an aim which Roman Catholic absolutism squelched.

The Reformation was an expression, in the dimension of religion, of a similar rebellion against this enslaving absolutism and of a demand for truth. John Wyclif, for example, argued that true Christianity had been smothered beneath a vast array of nonsensical tenets and dogmas: indulgences; confessions; the worship of saints, images, and relics; pilgrimages to holy places; special masses for the dead; and so forth. Wyclif demanded plainness of speech and intelligibility in religion. Let the priests speak in the language of their country, he urged, and let there be real piety in worship!

A similar love for truth moved Luther to nail the Ninety-five Theses to the door of Castle Church in Wittenberg. These were meant to be simply propositions for academic debate, published according to medieval custom. Luther wanted the dirty business of indulgences brought out into the light of day; he believed that in the light of free and open investigation, truth would win out. Luther introduced the theses by saying that he would like to debate the following propositions out of love for truth and in an endeavor to bring it to the light.[10]

This same lure of truth was graphically illustrated also in Luther's stand at the Diet of Worms in 1521. The Pope finally felt forced to declare that Luther was a troublesome heretic who must be destroyed, "a wild boar" who was devastating the vineyard of the Lord.[11] Evidence indicates that in obeying the summons to the Diet of Worms, Luther felt that he was going to his death.[12] Yet he calmly finished some literary work and left for the Diet on April 2, telling Melanchthon that if his enemies won the battle and he failed to return from Worms, Melanchthon should faithfully continue his teaching. If you do this, said Luther, my death will be of little consequence.[13]

The proceedings of the Diet are most interesting to read. Johann von Eck, the official delegate of the Archbishop of Trier, who presided over the hearing, attempted to force Luther to retract his writings, which Luther's integrity forbade him to do. Eck finally shouted to Luther, urging him to let his conscience alone, and to recant. Luther replied by repeating his former offer, namely, that he would gladly recant if one could show him in what way specifically his writings contradicted holy Scripture. Inasmuch as his doctrines were based on the Word of God, he could not recant; on this he would finally stand. Then, according to the records of the Diet, Luther uttered

[10]See Heinrich Bornkamm, *Luthers Geistige Welt* (Bielefeld: Ernst Gieseking, Deutscher Heimat-Verlag, 1953), p. 50.

[11]As it was expressed in the papal bull *Exsurge Domine* of June 15, 1520.

[12]See Thomas Martin Lindsay, *A History of the Reformation* (New York: Charles Scribner's Sons, 1906-07), I, 273.

[13]*Ibid.*

the words: "God help me to do this."[14] Eck replied that the church councils had not erred. Luther responded: "I should be glad to prove that they have."[15]

In this heroic stand of Luther at Worms, the Protestant cause holds a moving example of *profound loyalty to the truth, as one sees it,* whatever the cost. It was the *lure of truth* which rescued the human spirit from the shackles of Catholic dogmatism and authoritarianism.

The lure of truth in Protestantism was equally pronounced in the Campbellian Reformation of the nineteenth century, to cite another significant example. Throughout the seventeenth and eighteenth centuries, the Protestant cause had actually developed in a way which falsified its own true nature. It also was getting bogged down in a doctrinaire authoritarianism which was similar, in some ways, to that which enslaved the medieval mind. Freedom of interpretation was once again being curbed. By way of protest, the lure of truth incited several men of goodly stature to look once again beyond the creeds, to broaden the vistas of their intellectual horizon, to fix their gaze upon and quest vigorously for new and undiscovered aspects of the full truth of the gospel. Such men as Thomas and Alexander Campbell, Barton W. Stone, and others thus initiated a liberating impulse in American Christianity which helped greatly to loosen the shackles of Protestant creedalism. And Disciples of Christ, the church grouping in American Christianity generated by this impulse, throughout their history have made a unique contribution in their continuous

[14] "*Das helff mir Gott*" (*D. Martin Luthers Werke,* bearbeitet von G. Buchwald, P. Drews, J. R. F. Knaacke, P. Pietsch, E. Thiele [Weimar: Hermann Böhlaus Nachfolger, 1897], VII, 886).

[15] "*Ich erbiete mich das zu beweren*" (*Ibid.*).

plea for a noncreedal type of Christianity. They have helped materially to inspire the Christian cause with the lure of the Eternal.

It must not be forgotten that this liberty to follow the lure of religious truth is never fully won. Eternal vigilance is the price of liberty in this area as well as in the political realm; for the intellectual and religious Hitlers who tyrannize the mind of man are subtle and dangerous foes. If Christians are to guard their religion from trailing off into the vagaries and uncertainties which always obtain where prejudices reign and where the method of church authority holds sway, thoughtful minds must always be on the job, carefully and critically examining the content and presuppositions of our religious beliefs, with unbiased minds and hearts, dedicated to the lure of the Eternal.

4. *The Final Authority of "The Word" Which Evokes Man's Increasingly Valid Response*

One way of clarifying the Protestant conception of religious truth is to say that in Protestant Christianity, the final authority rests not in anything human, but in "the Word of God." As Luther put it, "the life and substance of the church is in the Word of God, as Christ said, 'Man lives by every word that proceeds from the mouth of God.' "[16] This living Word of God is finally nothing else but Christ the Lord, the Word which "became flesh and dwelt among us."[17]

It is true that Protestantism has repeatedly misconstrued this basic principle of authority and fallen into the trap of biblical absolutism, sometimes called bibliolatry. But repeatedly also it has been

[16] "Tota vita et substantia ecclesiae est in verbo Dei, sicut Christus dicit 'In omni verbo quod procedit de ore vivit homo' " (*D. Martin Luthers Werke*, *op. cit.*, VII, 721).

[17] John 1:4.

saved from this idolatrizing tendency in the realm of doctrine by a new discovery that the living Word in Christ is not a legalistic truth, that the living Christ is infinitely greater than any of our feeble doctrines about him, and that it is by *him* finally that we are redeemed, not merely by ideas about him, even biblical ideas, important and vital as these are in leading us to Christ. Protestantism is thus in line with primitive Christianity which, beyond all doubt, centered in trust in and loyalty to the person of Christ, not merely in belief in a set of propositions about him.

Let us say, then, that Christ the Lord is our absolute, but that our human response to his divine call, however vigorous our response may be, remains ambiguous, fragmentary, and incomplete, both in terms of holiness of life and apprehension of truth. Or put it this way: in the experience of faith we do know the Absolute, but not absolutely. We have a knowledge of the Absolute, but we have no absolute knowledge. We do hold this treasure, but in earthen vessels, and in such a way, said the Apostle Paul, as "to show that the transcendent power belongs to God and not to us."[18] We do see, through Christ, a saving glimpse of the Eternal, but "in a mirror dimly."

Humility keeps us aware of the gap between the *Logos* of God and our growing apprehension of it; we can never fully comprehend it. Such is the fate of our finitude. As Nels Ferré says, "A little of the that and a little of the how man seems to know; less he knows of the what and the why. Dim is the distance beyond the life of man. His knowledge is touched with all the contingency of experience."[19]

Undenominational Protestantism thus maintains that the religious knowledge which grows out of man's

[18] 2 Corinthians 4:7.

[19] Nels F. S. Ferré, *The Christian Fellowship* (New York: Harper and Brothers, 1940), p. 17.

response to the Word, through the Bible, must be kept open, growing, and dynamic. It must not be permitted to become closed, completed, and static. The lure of truth springs eternal in the Protestant breast. It continually inspires new discoveries of Christian truth and truer perspectives on truth already partially perceived. As the saying goes, "God still has new light to break forth from His holy Word." The Protestant conception of religious truth is virile, developmental, and dynamic, as over against the deadening fixation of religious truth in Scholasticism.

Futhermore, the Protestant *method* of pursuing the truth of the divine Word is empirical and experiential,[20] as opposed to the creedal and dogmatic method of Catholicism. The lure tends to depart in Catholicism, for the claim is made that the body of Catholic truth is absolute, infallible, and complete, and that the church actually *possesses* this truth. In Protestantism, the lure remains to inspire the quest. Catholics believe themselves to have arrived. Protestants, like Paul, are certain that they are as yet only on the way, pressing toward the goal. It would be difficult to cite a more inspiring aspect of Protestantism than its invigorating quest for truth, a quest rendered significant and fruitful by the impact of God's self-revelation to us.

5. *The Experience of the Divine Agape Which Fulfills Man's Longing for Religious Certitude*

Does the Word of God, in the Protestant view, say anything of which one can be absolutely sure? Finality there must be, if religion is to perform one of its fundamental functions, namely, provide the spirit of man with a point of inner personal stability. Does Protestantism, then, offer any final resting place

[20]As I shall attempt to show in the following chapters.

for the human spirit? Is there anything which the Word *actually gives,* whereby one can maintain his spiritual equilibrium in life's process? "Yes!" says Protestantism. "The impregnable rock of God's Word" does fulfill man's longing for certitude. The Word, incarnate on Calvary, says that sinful man stands under judgment, but that at the cost of infinite inner suffering, God pronounces the free, sovereign judgment of forgiveness over our lives of selfishness and sin.

In a way, Protestantism was born when Luther, reared in the monastery on the idea of God the Judge and the works-scheme of salvation through penance, discovered the gospel of forgiveness, through the writings of Paul. Prior to this discovery, the New Testament phrase "the righteousness of God" had meant to Luther merely a designation of one of the divine attributes. It signified the righteousness which belonged to God. At that time, Luther believed God to be the great Judge, whose rules of righteousness are the norms by which all men shall be judged. The reality of Christ, for the young Luther, was simply a clear and emphatic declaration of this norm: by "Christ" all will be judged! The saving light of grace, which radically altered Luther's thought about God and the religious relationship, generated the discovery that the genitive of this Pauline phrase does not signify a righteousness which *belongs to God* in his transmundane perfection, but rather a righteousness which is *bestowed by God* out of the free creativity of his grace. The "gospel" therefore is the free gift of God's grace. "God justifies the ungodly," as the Apostle Paul put it.

Luther thus discovered that acceptance by God is not something which is attained through human effort. On the contrary, it is *freely given,* through divine forgiveness, appropriated by faith. He believed therefore that the Christian gospel is unique among the religions of the world. They all say that one must actually become godlike in order to become acceptable before God. Christianity's offense is that it boldly announces that God justifies the sinner, that his love finds the sinner acceptable. The mystery and free sovereignty of this love are evident in that it finds the sinner acceptable *in spite of his sins;* and its creativity is seen in that, through it, one receives the power to become godlike. But basically, godlikeness is a consequence, not the ground of fellowship with God.

Standing in this personal relationship of faith, Luther, in humility and profound honesty, boldly faced up to the ambiguities and contradictions of his own heart. He recognized that truth was diluted and polluted with falsehood, that the other-regarding impulse of altruism was weakened and corrupted by a sinful kind of self-regarding motivation, and that goodness was strangely intertwined with evil. The religious greatness of Luther lies in the fact that, standing in this situation of soul-shaking, personal tension, he boldly rejected the lame safeguards which his own Catholic tradition had offered him; for he realized that it is only out of the anxiety of this concrete situation that one can hear the saving Word of God's forgiveness over the whole of one's life, a saving Word which in no sense is won from God by any human effort or good works, but which is rather the free gift of God's sovereign will.

In Luther's experience of grace, the creative and redemptive depth of the divine *agape* was opened up. The gospel was recovered from the ashes of penance and sacerdotalism. It was rediscovered that grace is not a metaphysical *habitus*, a *something*, as Thomism had taught, but rather a relationship, the relation namely of being in the favor of God, of being the recipient of the *agape tou Theou.* In this relation of faith, there is solid ground for triumphant certainty, in a faith which responds affirmatively to the "Yes" which the divine *agape* pronounces over our lives of finitude and sin. "Faith," says Luther, "is a living daring confidence in God's grace, so sure and certain that a man would stake his life on it a thousand times."[21]

Luther's experience of "justification by faith" enabled him to rise above the level of religious experience where one finds a sense of security only in external authorities, such as monastic disciplines, church dogmas, and sacramental, hierarchical orders. All of these had left Luther anxious and terror-stricken. He was able to find peace of soul only by rising above all of these and *by laying hold of God himself, through Christ.* In this new Christocentric faith Luther found a spiritual strength, joy, and security which were unknown to the medieval Christian.[22]

One thinks of the similar response of the Apostle Paul to the divine *agape* revealed through Christ: "If God is for us, who is against us? He who did not spare his own Son, but gave him up for us all, will he not also give us all things with him?"[23]

In its blindness, the human heart often attempts, in vain, to satisfy its deep longing for certitude with the idols and false gods of church authority, mechanical inspiration, and creedal absolutisms. What greater certainty, however, can finite man ask than this spiritual certainty of personal trust in Christ, a certainty which bestows "the peace that passes all understanding"? What more certainty could one want than the stabilizing assurance of the spontaneity and boundlessness of God's forgiving goodness? Is

---

[21]*The Works of Martin Luther* (Philadelphia: A. J. Holman Co., 1915-32), VI, 452.

[22]Cf. Adolf Harnack, *History of Dogma,* trans. Neil Buchanan (Boston: Little, Brown and Company, 1900), VII, 184.

[23]Romans 8:31.

not this divine *agape* the absolute for which the human heart really yearns, in the personal depth of its being?

6. *A Profound Reverence for the Individual Conscience Which Guarantees Its Liberty*

Prophetic Protestantism has incessantly demanded a continuous rebirth of individual liberty from authoritarianism, either in the form of an ecclesiastical hierarchy or in the form of authoritatively imposed doctrinal interpretations.

Protestantism raises the Pauline cry that one of the Christian's inalienable rights is his individual freedom. Judaizers who "spy out our freedom which we have in Christ Jesus" and seek to destroy it are not to be tolerated "even for a moment," Paul argued.[24]

There is an old proverb which says that "each tub must stand on its own bottom." This proverbial truth is especially relevant to religion, for religion is too sacred and personal a matter to be realized adequately by submitting to the demands of an established institution, in an external way. Such behavior is insufficiently inward.

The drift of the spirit of reform has always been in the direction of individual liberty. Jeremiah and Ezekiel are the best representatives of it in the Old Testament. Jeremiah stood alone, against all the representatives of national religion: kings, priests, prophets, and even his own kinsmen. In contrast to modern collectivisms, Jeremiah learned that the individual, in communion with God, possesses the reality of religion; and that this reality would remain, though the nation and all institutions of religion perish.

Socrates was the first martyr among the Greeks to academic and religious freedom.

---

[24]Galatians 2:4-5.

With the Apostle Paul, of course, there was an especially powerful breakthrough of individual freedom from the shackles of Jewish legalism. Augustine recovered this freedom for the Christian cause in an ambiguous way. He clung to it with his double-jointed Neo-Platonic-Pauline hand; but with the other, he held firmly to the ecclesiastical system of Rome, and became one of its leading exponents.

Luther once again recovered the true liberty of the Christian man, in his union with Christ through faith. "God and faith belong together," said Luther; so that "the Christian is lord over everything, yet in love is servant of all."

Luther's achievement of individual liberty has been praised by historians as the birth of modern history. When Luther, a lowly monk, excommunicated by the Holy Roman See, surrounded by a group of professors, students, and townsfolk, burned the papal bull against himself, a new period of history indeed began. Papal bulls had been burned before, of course, but by political rulers who had armies of soldiers to protect them. This time it was by a poor monk with nothing but his own faith to defend him. The entire incident was symbolic: the individual soul had discovered its true value; authentic individuality and personal liberty were reborn that morning in Wittenberg, at 9 o'clock, December 10, 1520, when the assembly watched the papal bull go up in flames.

This Protestant principle of individual liberty eventually led also to a loosening up not only of the authority of popes and church councils, but also of the authority of the creeds. Many Protestant leaders came to see that to be loyal to this principle, the individual conscience would have to be liberated from any and all authoritative use of the creeds, Catholic or Protestant. Thomas Campbell, for example, wrote:

> That although inferences and deductions from Scripture premises, when fairly inferred, may be truly called the doctrine of God's holy word, yet are they not formally binding upon the consciences of Christians farther than they perceive the connection, and evidently see that they are so; for their faith must not stand in the wisdom of men, but in the power and veracity of God.[25]

Similarly, Isaac Errett wrote that liberty of course involves certain risks; but, said Errett,

> Free and kind discussion will soon correct them. There is not a hundredth part of the danger from an occasional outcropping of error as the result of free investigation, that must accrue from the murderous stifling of free thought and free speech.[26]

Protestantism pleads that the individual *must remain free* to understand and follow the gospel, as *he sees it;* and that such freedom must not only be *tolerated* by the church; it must be vigorously *supported* and *guaranteed.* It is part of the main business of the church to keep the fires of freedom burning brightly.

Individual liberty must not be misconstrued, however, as radical individualism. It does not mitigate the value of or need for community. The Protestant Reformers of the sixteenth century clearly taught that Christian truth can be found and realized only in the close bonds of the fellowship of believers.

The difference between the Protestant and Catholic views of the church, however, is that Protestants think of the church as a fellowship of faith and love; whereas the main mark of the Catholic conception is the aspect of the institution, whose authority dominates and rules the individual members. The difference between the Protestant and Catholic conceptions

[25]Thomas Campbell, *Declaration and Address* (The Bethany Press, 1955), p. 46.

[26]*The Christian-Evangelist,* Vol. 89, No. 48, p. 1143.

of the church is precisely individual liberty. The former preserves this value at all costs; the latter hedges it in, subjects it to external controls and tends therefore to stifle it.

This conclusion follows inevitably from the dogma of papal absolutism and infallibility, a dogma which is made quite clear by the bull *Quanta cura* issued by Pope Pius IX, December 8, 1864. In this bull, the Pope stipulated eighty errors which Catholics everywhere must join the Pope in anathematizing. Article fifteen of this famous Syllabus pronounces anathemas upon the proposition that "every man is free to embrace and profess the religion which guided by the light of reason, he believes to be true."[27]

The principle of papal domination of the individual conscience, in a totalitarian way, could scarcely be made plainer. Pope Leo XIII followed, and on April 21, 1878, declared that the utterances of the bull *Quanta cura* possess the authority of infallibility.

Over against this absolutization of the authority of the church in Catholicism, Protestantism regards the authority of the church to be the relative authority of corporate, Christian experience. It is a kind of authority which not only is not incompatible with individual liberty, but which actually stimulates and supports it.

Nor is the Protestant ideal of individual liberty opposed to systematic theological statements of the corporate faith. These are exceedingly important for intelligent religion. Every Christian group which has neglected the task of critical theological explication of the meaning of the faith has fallen, inevitably, into the clutches of theological vagueness and obscurantism. It must be humbly confessed that numerous Protestant groups have succumbed to such vagueness. The

[27]Henrici Denzinger, *Enchiridion Symbolorum*, Edito 29 (Barcinone: Herder, Friburgi Brisg., 1953), p. 485. Trans. R.G.W.

desire for a simple, pietistic, Jesus-centered faith seems easily to result in such theologically vague religious sentimentalism. The Protestant plea for individual liberty must never be confused with such pietistic vagueness.

The principle of individual liberty is threatened not when the church thinks through and states her beliefs clearly, systematically, and forcefully, but when she ceases to do so; for the cessation of creative theological statements brings the authoritarian principle into play, and the creed is thereby established. The Protestant plea for individual liberty opposes simply absolutistic interpretation of theological statements which turns them into creeds. It opposes that kind of church authority which binds them upon the individual conscience, in an arbitrary way. The Protestant struggle has been a struggle to build a kind of Christianity which leaves the individual free to understand and to worship, as the saying goes, "according to the dictates of his own conscience."

The Protestant type of individual liberty, therefore, is a liberty which avoids both dogmatism and theological vagueness, both authoritarianism and pietistic sentimentalism. It is a liberty which guarantees the individual conscience freedom from external authorities, but which also inspires the individual conscience with a serious concern for meaningful theological explication of the corporate faith of the Christian community.

7. *A Personal Encounter Which Elicits the Response of Authentic Individuality*

Closely correlated with the plea for individual liberty (one might even say the positive side of it) is the Christian challenge which calls for a meaningful, personal response to the presence of God in Jesus Christ. Protestantism, that is, refuses to streamline members of the church; its gospel calls for the creation of *authentic* individuality, as opposed to the *inauthentic* mode of religious being which characterizes thousands who blindly conform to and whose individualities are submerged in the religious masses. True individuality is swallowed up by religious collectivisms of various sorts. Protestantism demands the continuous recovery of faith and the personal dimension in religion.

Here again, Protestantism proves itself to be a true heir of prophetic religion. Micah, for example, insisted that true religion consists not in the routine performance of external rites, such as sacrifices and ceremonies, but in a personal realization of spiritual values: doing justly, loving kindness, and walking humbly before God. The tithing of mint and dill and cummin is proper, said Jesus, but real religion lies finally in the spiritual qualities of the individual soul: justice, mercy, and faith. In the name of this personalism of spirit, Paul contended that no one can be justified by works of law; redemption is an affair of the heart. In the name of this personal authenticity, the medieval predestinarians and the mystical brotherhoods raised their voices of protest against the mechanism of Roman institutionalism.

Protestantism brings this perennial need for authentic individuality into sharp focus. It says that there is nothing so despicable as a secondhand religion. It would apply especially to religious values what Goethe said about cultural values in general: Appropriate personally what you have inherited from your fathers that you may *possess* it as your very own. Schleiermacher undoubtedly had this demand for authentic individuality in mind when he argued, against the rationalistic religion of the Enlightenment, that if everyone had the same religion no one would have the right religion. And Kierkegaard also was partially correct in his revolt against the organized Christianity of his day, in the name of existential integrity. Distorted though it was, this represents a fundamentally Protestant element in the theology of Kierkegaard.

The continuous need for an *experientially real and personally valid* Christianity is paramount, for Christianity is a profoundly personal matter. The verities of the faith have to be won anew, not only by each generation, but also by each individual.

It is interesting that this aspect of Protestantism is in accord with one of the basic insights of the Enlightenment. Whatever may be the one-sidedness of the rationalism of the eighteenth century, of lasting value was its contention that even a true belief is really not truth for anyone, unless and until he himself sees it to be true; and that even a morally right act is in reality amoral for a person, unless and until one perceives it to be right. In the area of man's religious experience, this is especially true. There can be no genuine Christianity apart from individual *perceptions* of truth and *convictions* of righteousness, however elaborate may be the external paraphernalia of organized religion.

Christianity, to be sure, has its ordinances of baptism, assembly for worship, and the Lord's Supper; it does include a high ethical code of behavior; it does treasure deeply the New Testament witness to the truth of the gospel. But the externality of all these does not suffice. Real Christianity exists only where there is an internalization and subjectification of the verities of the gospel.

All of these forms, to be sure, are important—the ordinances, the code, the doctrine. One should not in any way detract from their true value; he should rather (as the New Testament itself does) point out that the *essence* of Christianity lies in something deeper still. The essence of Christianity does not consist in the performance of ordinances, conforming to ethical commands, giving assent to doctrinal statements. It lies in the creative and redemptive love of God, the faith and love in our hearts which it begets and nourishes, and the anticipation which, as a result, stirs in the human breast. The forms of worship, the codes of behavior, and the doctrinal formulations are only means whereby the life and love of the Eternal are realized in our hearts and lives.

In the light of this Protestant demand for authentic individuality, it must be said that the Calvinistic idea of irresistible grace is an aberration. The idea of a grace of divine election which moves in a straight line, achieving its goal, is inconsistent with the high personalism of Christianity. Futhermore, it is simply a fact that God's grace does not operate in this way. As persons, we cannot be helped to the good life in any such atomistic, mechanical fashion. Because God has made us persons, he has limited himself and defined the manner of dealing with us. We are constantly being made aware of the impossibility of helping people, except through themselves. To develop a religion of authentic individuality everything external to self is irrelevant, unless it is able to approach us through some personal relation. An individual may of course be irresistibly helped, as when a helpless child is picked up by an adult and snatched out of danger of an oncoming automobile; or as the mother cat seizes the kitten by the nape of the neck and carries it out of danger. But no really *personal* aid can be of such purely external operation; it must call forth a personal response from within. That is, the *only* way that God can help us, as persons, is through faith and the personal dimension.[28]

The faith that redeems, says Protestantism, is a personal encounter with God which elicits authentic individuality.

8. *A Radical Laicism Which Erases Hierarchical Distinctions and Closes the Gap Between the Sacred and the Secular*

A democratic society such as ours in America, which rests upon the conviction that opportunity for life, liberty, and the pursuit of happiness should be offered to all men equally, is Protestant in spirit. For it was the idea of "the priesthood of all believers" that inspired Luther's associates to take up the cause of the Reformation. Modern political philosophy, to be sure, is in grave danger of losing the dynamics of its belief in human rights whenever it attempts to secure them without any reference to the Eternal, which is the ultimate ground of their validity. Insofar as democratic political theory is guilty of this attempt, it is considerably less than Protestant. But there is a definitely Protestant element in its emphasis on the ideal of equality.

It is difficult for a modern democratic mind to imagine the paralyzing fear which the Roman priesthood inspired in medieval hearts. The enslaving power of ecclesiastical control reached out its tentacles in every direction and fastened them to the life of

[28]Cf. John Oman, *Grace and Personality* (Cambridge: University Press, 1928), pp. 16, 68-71; also John Baillie, *The Interpretation of Religion* (New York: Charles Scribner's Sons, 1928), p. 342.

the average man. And its power was greatly extended by the multiplication of the sacraments to seven in number. Through them, the priesthood stood between the infant and the sacramental grace which was believed by all to be bestowed at baptism; between the dying man and the final grace of extreme unction; between the common people and daily worship; between them and the supreme grace of the Eucharist; between a Christian and his burial in consecrated grounds; between a dead Christian and his release from the fires of purgatory.

It was believed also that the Pope, by one stroke of the pen, could issue an interdict whereby an entire nation was cut off from any access to God. The medieval man regarded such an interdict as more deadly than the plague of the Black Death.[29]

Luther graphically described this tyranny of the Roman priesthood thus:

> The sacrament of orders has been and is a most admirable engine for the establishment of all those monstrous evils which have hitherto been wrought, and are being wrought, in the church. In this way Christian brotherhood has perished; in this way shepherds have turned into wolves, servants into tyrants, and ecclesiastics into more than earthly beings . . . when I see how far this sacrosanct sanctity of these orders has already gone I expect that the time will come when the laity will not even be allowed to touch the altar, except when they offer money.[30]

To say these things is barely to hint at the evils fostered by the development of the hierarchical distinction between clergy and laity, in the structure of

[29]Cf. Lindsay, *op. cit.*, p. 440.

[30]Martin Luther, *First Principles of the Reformation or the Ninety-five Theses and the Three Primary Works of Dr. Martin Luther*, trans. and edited by Henry Wace and C. A. Buchheim (Philadelphia: Lutheran Publication Society, 1885), pp. 232, 235.

the church.[31] The concentration of power in the hands of a few is always a menace. For power has a way of tending to corrupt those who hold it; and the greater the concentration of power, the greater the danger of worse corruption. When, therefore, such concentration of power received the absolutistic sanction of Roman sacerdotalism, the danger was immense, for it was thereby enabled successfully to prey upon and to exploit the religious fear and ignorance of the medieval mind.

Another of the evils which grew out of this clericalism was the cleavage which it precipitated between the cloister and the market place. It generated the baneful illusion that the men of the cloth were the only really religious members of the social order. And along with this mistaken idea, it fostered the pseudo-humility of monasticism, a humility which was actually only an appearance, concealing the worst kind of Pharisaic pride.

Thus a sharp line was drawn between the sacred and the secular realms, and the life of daily toil was divested, in large measure, of its fundamentally sacred character.

The thing which really broke the back of this clerical superiority and domination was Luther's conviction and teaching that the empirical experience of God's redemptive love in Christ is the heart of Christianity. Luther experienced the evangelical kind of religious certainty which stems from a faith-union with Christ. Standing in this relation, Luther argued that one can hurl defiance at sin, death, hell, the devil, and all of the enemies of God. This victorious faith which fears no ill, however cruel it may be, is significantly different from the faith of the medieval

[31]For a fuller treatment of the unique Protestant contribution to the understanding of the nature of the church see *infra* Chap. VIII.

man. To establish this direct relation with Christ, through faith, meant at once to abolish the entire order of priestly mediation. All Christians become priests equally.

This democratic doctrine of the priesthood of all believers means essentially three things:

(1) It puts an end to clerical domination, because there are now no priests in the medieval sense; all are laymen alike, yet all are also in a new way priests alike, equally worthy to appear before God, to pray for and to teach each other mutually;

(2) While this principle of laicism *denies* clerical control, it also *affirms* the Christian obligation to serve one another in Christlike love. One's vocation, as Luther put it, is the workshop of the love of neighbor; and hereby each Christian becomes a kind of Christ. Such service of mutual love is the real priesthood of our faith;

(3) Differences remain in the tasks of Christian service, but they are now regarded as functional in nature, not hierarchical. The peculiar *function* of the clergy is now the ministry of the Word. Protestantism would be untrue to its own genius should it ever forget that this does not set the clergy apart as a "holy order" of superior rank to other types of Christian life and work. All orders of Christian life and work are equally sacred. The "holy" or "divine" is not one value alongside secular values; it is a qualifying power appearing in all values and orders, indeed in the whole of life.

Protestantism has not always been consistently true to the principle of the priesthood of all believers. Anglicanism, for example, has never been able to become thoroughly Protestant at this point; for it still preserves a remnant of hierarchicalism in its doctrine of apostolic succession. Most Protestant groups, however, have organized their ecclesiastical structures in harmony with this basic principle of Protestantism.

Such is the spirit of creative community, such is the fellowship of love, such is the holy commonwealth signified by the Protestant principle of the priesthood of all believers. It describes the healing flow of creative love, unrestricted by the absolutistic control of Christian life and thought by artificial, priestly orders. Thereby the Spirit is free to foster and develop the values of appreciative consciousness and love, under only the inherent limitations of the finitude of human existence.

These, then, are eight fundamental principles which define the inner spiritual dynamics of undenominational Protestantism: (1) It is a prophetic spirit, demanding continuous reform; (2) It demands that kind of faith-relation which guards against idolatrous attachments to human dogmas, programs, and schemes; (3) It places dominant emphasis on the lure of the Eternal, which inspires man's continuous quest for truth; (4) It holds the final authority in religion to be "the Word of God," and insists that this authority evokes man's increasingly valid response; (5) It provides for the fulfillment of man's longing for religious certitude by the experience of the divine *agape* in Christ who inspires the subject of faith with absolute confidence and personal trust; (6) It holds the individual conscience in profound reverence and guarantees its liberty from arbitrary domination by external authorities; (7) It interprets the confrontation by the Lordship of Christ as a challenge which elicits the response of authentic individuality; (8) It calls for a radical laicism in its doctrine of Christian community, which erases hierarchical distinctions, closes the gap between the sacred and the secular orders, and provides the kind of community that promotes the values of equality and liberty, of brotherhood and unity.

CHAPTER TWO

A Critique of Liberal Protestantism

From our analysis of the dynamics of Protestantism in the preceding chapter, it should be evident to the reader that, as the typically Protestant mind sees it, Christianity is never to be identified absolutely with any of its historical forms of expression, denominational or otherwise. This means that growth is inherent in Christianity when it functions creatively within the historical orders of existence.

One of the most interesting chapters in the history of Christianity's growth is the phase of modern theological Liberalism. The liberal development is restricted mainly to Protestant Christianity. Catholicism has thus far prevented the flowering of Liberalism in its ranks. If Liberalism ever attains any vigorous growth in Catholicism, it will destroy the major blockage to effective ecumenical relations between Catholics and Protestants, namely, the idol of papal authority.

Our aim in this second chapter is to indicate briefly the historical development and to offer a critical evaluation of the theological Liberalism of modern Protestant Christianity. By "modern" is meant the Protestantism of the last one hundred fifty years or so.

In a way, this task seems formidable. There is so much variation and disagreement among those who place themselves within the group known as "liberals" that some think it utterly futile to describe theological

Liberalism with any significant degree of consistency. That this judgment is an exaggeration will be clear, I hope, when we have completed the argument of this chapter.

Liberalism as a Historical Movement

Liberalism, as a historical movement within American Christianity, represents a theological modification brought about by the impact of the humanism of modern Renaissance culture on Christian thought. The development of Liberalism revolved mainly about two foci: (1) a renaissance of faith in human goodness, freedom, and dignity, which led to a revolt against the orthodox, Calvinistic conception of man as totally depraved; and (2) increased confidence in the powers of reason, which led to the rejection of the traditional idea of religious knowledge in terms of supernatural revelation.[1]

The first of these, the renaissance of faith in human goodness and the correlative revolt against Calvinistic anthropology, began in the colonial days. It had its roots, to begin with, in a rising tendency in American Christianity to emphasize the positive value of the use of human *means* in salvation. A growing number of Calvinistic ministers in the first half of the eighteenth century gradually adopted this novel view regarding the means of salvation and admitted that, after all, certain "means" might be used *to put the soul in position to receive* the regenerating power of the Spirit.

This more liberal notion of man's native goodness was also augmented by the circulation in America of a rising tide of Arminian views, as expressed by certain

[1]For an excellent, more extensive survey of the development of Liberalism in American Christianity, see "Protestant Liberalism" by A. C. McGiffert, Jr., in *Liberal Theology*, ed. David E. Roberts and Henry Pitney Van Dusen (New York: Charles Scribner's Sons, 1942), pp. 106-120.

English writers, particularly Daniel Whitby, an Anglican, and John Taylor, a Presbyterian. Both writers inveighed heavily against Calvinism. Taylor was especially critical of the Calvinistic theories of original sin and a limited atonement. These diverging Arminian views were adopted by several New England ministers who, even before the middle of the eighteenth century, had begun to write in defense of what was termed "Liberal Theology."

In 1749, for example, Lemuel Briant published a sermon on "The Absurdity and Blasphemy of Depreciating Moral Virtue"—a direct attack on Calvinism. The response of the orthodox to such a liberal publication was of course voluminous. Sermons were preached and tracts were published, attempting "to put a stop to the prevailing contagion of Arminian errors and other loose opinions . . . which threaten to banish vital piety out of the land.'"[2]

Most of the liberals, at this time, were in and around Boston. Jonathan Mayhew, minister of the West Meeting House in Boston, in good liberal spirit, insisted that "total depravity is both dishonorable to the character of God and a libel on human nature.'"[3]

The appointment of Henry Ware, an avowed liberal, to the Hollis Professorship of Theology at Harvard in 1805 greatly furthered the liberal cause.

The renowned William Ellery Channing, who flourished in the first half of the nineteenth century, also pressed the liberal cause, stressing the recovery of the dignity of man and the liberal belief in human ability, freedom, and reason. Channing forcefully rejected "the theological fiction" of total depravity, arguing that a more irrational doctrine could not be contrived.[4] Worse still, said Channing, the doctrine

---

[2]William Warren Sweet, *The Story of Religions in America* (New York: Harper and Brothers, 1930), p. 196.

[3]As quoted by McGiffert in Roberts and Van Dusen *op. cit.*, p. 108.

[4]William Ellery Channing, *The Works of William E. Channing* (Boston: American Unitarian Association, 1900), p. 245.

is immoral, for it alienates men from God and from one another. "Were it really believed, . . . men would look up with dread and detestation to the Author of their being, and look round with horror on their fellow-creatures."[5] If men were to look upon one another as "wholly corrupt beings—incarnate fiends—," society would become as repulsive as "a den of lions or a nest of vipers."[6]

It is most instructive to compare Channing's emphasis on human dignity with Luther's position on this problem. Speaking of the nature of man, Luther wrote, " 'Tis as the man said who had young wolves to sell, when asked 'which of them was best?' he replied, 'If one be good, then are they all good.' "[7]

Another name of distinction in the liberal cause is that of Ralph Waldo Emerson. Emerson felt that Christianity was diseased with the ideas of original sin, depravity, predestination, and the like. These doctrines, Emerson wrote, "are the soul's mumps and measles and whooping coughs, and those who have not caught them cannot describe their health or prescribe their cure."[8]

This growing confidence in man's natural ability and goodness represented an expression and development of the philosophical spirit of the Renaissance and the Enlightenment. It was substantially strengthened also by the fabulous success of the great American venture; the pioneer spirit was proving, beyond doubt, that man does have considerable ability to build a new world. Some areas of liberal Protestantism were quite thoroughly transformed by the autonomous character of the culture of the Enlightenment and by

[5]*Ibid.*

[6]*Ibid.*

[7]Martin Luther, *The Table Talk of Martin Luther*, trans. & ed. William Hazlitt (London: H. G. Bohn, 1856), p. 115.

[8]H. H. Emmons (ed.), *Light of Emerson* (Cleveland: The Rex Publishing Co., 1930), p. 30.

the humanistic philosophy which stemmed from the Renaissance. As a result, some Christian leaders frankly became avowed humanists, eliminating all reference to any transcendental, suprahuman God, content to regard "God" solely as a personified symbol of man's social ideal. One thinks of such names as Frederick Harrison, A. E. Hayden, Edward Scribner Ames, and Walter Lippmann. Religion came to be conceived simply as *man's own effort* to adjust himself to the cosmos, or, more simply, to the human situation, and to make the most of it in terms of human values. Christian moralism was thereby severed from its ancient idealistic roots; and it attempted to live on in the newly discovered naturalistic climate.

Not all liberals, to be sure, permitted their theology to be so thoroughly determined by the autonomy of modern culture; but the drift in this direction was quite strong in the latter part of the nineteenth and the early part of the twentieth century.

It would probably be correct, however, to say that in the main the liberal faith was motivated by a stimulating sense of cooperating with God in the venture of building his kingdom on earth. Liberalism's prophetic-progressivistic philosophy of history gave it a mark of similarity with ancient Hebraic prophetism. The emphasis on divine immanence led to the belief that God is working in history for a progressive realization of the values of universal love, liberty, justice, and brotherhood. Liberalism thus construed the meaning of human existence to be the task of finding and fulfilling one's place in the creative order of the value-realizing process.

The prospects for the success of this stimulating "devotion to human values" were rendered highly plausible also by the spirit of sociological utopianism which electrified the atmosphere of the day, a spirit fostered by such men as Auguste Comte, and in the latter part of the nineteenth century by John Stuart Mill and Herbert Spencer.

Much of this utopian enthusiasm inspired the Social Gospel in the heyday of the movement, the second decade of the twentieth century. Walter Rauschenbusch, for example, wrote, "sometimes the hot hope surges up that perhaps the long and slow climb may be ending.... The swiftness of evolution in our own century proves the immense latent perfectibility in human nature. . . . Perhaps these nineteen centuries of Christian influence have been a long preliminary stage of growth, and now the flower and fruit are almost here."[9] In the second decade of our century, before World War I, the kingdom once again seemed to be at hand.

The second major focus of the Liberal Movement in Protestantism was an increased confidence in the powers of human reason. This led to the rejection, in the name of reason, of the traditional idea of religious knowledge in terms of supernatural revelation. This aspect of Liberalism also represents the impact of the rationalism of the Enlightenment on Christian thought.

One might say that, on this side, the liberals were in a sense deistic; that is, they placed supreme confidence in reason. They believed that man is essentially a rational being who has the ability to distinguish between truth and error. By developing a true, rational Christianity they aimed to supplant a false, irrational Christianity. Benjamin Franklin and Tom Paine in the latter part of the eighteenth century thus negated the orthodox Christianity of revelation and developed a positive natural religion, based on a ra-

[9]Walter Rauschenbusch, *Christianity and the Social Crisis* (New York: The Macmillan Company, 1913), pp. 421f. Used by permission of Lisa Rauschenbusch.

tional knowledge of God as the original, self-existing Cause, Providence, and source of Goodness, albeit non-personal. William Ellery Channing was equally vigorous in his refusal to be cowed by the Calvinistic debunking of reason in the name of revelation. Reason, Channing argued, is a greater authority than any book, the Bible included. Emerson and Theodore Parker, in the middle and latter parts of the nineteenth century, drawing heavily upon the philosophy of Schleiermacher and Spinoza, attempted to substitute religious intuition for the old method of supernatural revelation.

This rationalistic emphasis of Liberalism was of course many-sided. One aspect of it led Protestantism to monumental attempts to render Christianity intelligible and meaningful in the light of the thought-forms of modern philosophy and science. Hence the "modernistic" phase of Liberalism came into being. In principle, modernism is very ancient. Strictly speaking, "modernism" is a term which denotes a type of attitude and a method. It signifies the kind of thinking involved whenever any religious tradition comes to terms with the prevailing thought-forms of contemporary culture. The Apologists of the second century were modernists, because, as Christian theologians, they came to grips with the philosophy of Hellenism. Thomas Aquinas was a modernist, for he used the newly discovered Aristotelianism to explicate basic Christian beliefs. There have been, of course, numerous forms of modernism in liberal Protestantism, such as the intellectual adjustment of the faith to the philosophy of evolution, to Kantian moralism, to the philosophy of naturalism, and to absolute idealism. Names of a good company of great men, too numerous to mention, come to our minds here.

A particularly dominant scientific aspect of the rationalism of liberal Protestantism is concerned with the effect on Christianity of a rigorous application of the scientific method of historical and literary criticism to the Christian sources, especially the Bible. The fruits of this phase of liberal theological method are matters of common knowledge. Scientific method has so thoroughly demonstrated the involvement of the biblical manuscripts and messages in the relativities of history that for thoughtful Christians there can be no turning back to the scholastic concept of revelation in terms of textual, mechanical infallibility.[10]

On the whole, however, one must say that Liberalism's stout confidence in human reason is rather hard put to defend itself today, without serious qualification, thanks to the decline of humanism and the recent debunking of reason. Freudian psychology, epiphenomenological and biological theories of mind, and the demonic use of reason in modern totalitarianism have put the liberal faith in reason on the defensive.

Liberalism as a Philosophical Principle

It should be remembered that liberalism is not only a particular historical phase of modern Christianity; it is also a fundamental philosophical attitude which finds social, political, and scientific, as well as theological, expression.

This philosophical attitude of liberalism is one of intellectual curiosity and freedom.[11] The unfree man is of necessity bound to the demands of external authorities. He must do as they see fit and follow what they prescribe, unquestioningly. The liberal

[10]The following five chapters are devoted to a more thoroughgoing historical and constructive treatment of the problem of revelation in Protestant theology.

[11]See William Ernest Hocking's excellent statement in Roberts and Van Dusen, *op. cit.*, pp. 47 ff.

mind, however, is released from this restriction. He experiments with new possibilities for improvement. If someone desires to learn how many teeth there are in a horse's mouth, the medieval dogmatist goes to his authority to find the proper answer: he goes to Aristotle. The liberal breaks away from this method of authority; he decides to go catch a horse and count the teeth for himself. This indicates something of the spirit of the liberal. It is an inquiring, exploratory, creative outreach of the human mind.

Our contemporary liberal arts college preserves something of this initial impulse of modern liberalism. In receiving a "liberal" education, one is not tied down to a particular vocation. Instead, he inquires and searches after knowledge out of a sheer interest in truth. He roams about over all creation; he studies language, history, music, drama, philosophy, and psychology. Some even study theology. He indulges his creative talents; he delves into antiquity; he becomes appreciatively acquainted with the rich variety of ways in which the human spirit has sought attainment and fulfillment. He becomes liberalized.

When this flexible, exploratory attitude expresses itself in religion, it inevitably has a negative effect on the dogmatic attitude. Liberalism is essentially antidogmatic.

It was the power of Liberalism to undermine and destroy dogmatism which unsuccessfully perturbed John Henry Newman during his early theological development. He fought against it and finally was able to secure the principle of dogmatism in the realm of religious beliefs. Thus he became a cardinal in the Roman Catholic Church. In his sketch of a history of his religious opinions, Newman confessed that his main battle had been with liberalism. "By liberalism," he wrote, "I meant the anti-dogmatic principle and its developments."[12]

This antidogmatic aspect is, of course, not to be regarded as a complete definition of Liberalism, but no definition would be complete without it. For Liberalism refuses to equate Christianity with any of its historical forms, which dogmatism makes bold to do. Because of this refusal, Liberalism is fundamentally true to the genius of prophetic Protestantism.

As a result of adopting this antidogmatic attitude, the representative liberal Protestant finds himself rather hard put. He meets opposition from two major sources. On the one hand, the orthodox standpatters charge that he is forsaking the faith "once for all delivered unto the saints," that he is going too far in the free use of reason. Indeed, the central dilemma of the liberal position may be put in the form of a question: Why *should* one tolerate a belief which he honestly and deeply feels is false? Is this not treason to one's own convictions? Will not one who sets out on such a path become finally a pitiable jellyfish, believing everything, believing nothing?

On the other hand, the nonreligious liberals charge that our liberal theologian has sat down in a puddle in the middle of the road; that he has not gone far enough down the road to find the exercise of a reason completely liberated from obsolete ways of the past. To borrow E. E. Aubrey's apt portrayal, the humanist accuses the liberal theologian of "breeding obscurantism."[13] He charges that "by his sentimental attachment to the historic tradition, he is inhibited from clear-eyed thought about the modern world."[14] Per-

[12]John Henry Newman, *Apologia Pro Vita Sua* (London: J. M. Dent and Sons Ltd., 1921), p. 67.

[13]Crozier Quarterly, Vol. XXV, No. 1, p. 4.

[14]*Ibid.*

haps indeed, the humanist suggests, the liberal is not even wholly honest in his use of traditional terms.

Deeper still, criticism is directed not merely against the liberal's theories and ideas, but also against the ethical and emotional value of his position. To the irreligious atheist, the views of the liberal will seem to be "the opiate of the people"; to the conservative who absolutizes the *status quo* (Roman Catholics and Protestant fundamentalists, for example), Liberalism appears to be a pitifully thin substitute for the wonderful experience of salvation through the grace of the sacraments, or for the impregnable rock of the infallible Book. Hence the liberal theologian has his enemies too, on the right hand and on the left.

Enduring Values of Liberal Protestantism

Before we point out some of the ways in which we must revise Liberalism, as we have known it, let us enumerate some of the positive, enduring values of the liberal tradition. These values, we believe, must be preserved at all costs, whatever revision may be demanded in the interest of a truer and more adequate theology. History moves forward, not backward. Christianity has passed through the modern, liberal phase of its development. Whatever be its weaknesses and inadequacies, Liberalism has recovered and wrought out, through profound creative effort, certain values which are of perennial worth. Many of these were, in fact, part of the nascent creativity of primitive Christianity, but were lost or destroyed by the development of ecclesiastical and doctrinal absolutisms.

(1) *An Antidogmatic Attitude*

The Oxford dictionary defines a "liberal" as a person who is "free from narrow prejudice; open-minded.'"[15] The liberal is not bigoted in his attitude. He does not cling rigorously and blindly to traditional opinions and established institutions. Lying deep in the liberal heart is an antidogmatic attitude toward the traditionally determined *status quo* of our religious heritage.

The liberal refuses to accept our religious heritage as a mere legacy; he refuses to hold inherited beliefs in a doctrinaire, authoritarian manner. He insists on exploring, experimenting, and working his way into the inner heart of the faith, so as to make our religious beliefs an adequate truth about life and experience in the contemporary world. He personalizes the faith so that it acquires validity in terms of the experience of modern man.

(2) *A Receptive Attitude Toward New Ideas*

Closely correlated with this antidogmatic attitude toward tradition, stands the liberal's receptive and venturesome attitude toward new ideas. Unlike the dogmatist, the liberal is "open to the reception of new ideas or proposals of reform"[16] and improvement.

Most Christians, of course, are liberal in their moral theory; that is, they hold it to be part of the Christian ideal to be able to rise to increasingly higher levels of holiness. The liberal, however, is more consistent in that he also possesses the ability to grow in his religious knowledge. He is flexible and can adjust his set of beliefs to new visions of truth. Henry Sloan Coffin rightly says that the main characteristic of a liberal is his wholehearted response to truth, no matter where he encounters it.[17]

(3) *Historical Realism*

A third positive value of Liberalism lies in its *his-*

[15]*Oxford Universal Dictionary*, ed. C. T. Onions (Oxford University Press: Doubleday, Doran and Company, Inc., 1937), V, 1135.

[16]*Ibid.*

[17]Roberts and Van Dusen, *op. cit.*, p. 223.

torical realism. The liberal takes the present historical situation seriously. He knows that if life is to be lived to the fullest, it must be integrated with the contemporary historical situation. He is realistic also in the further sense that he recognizes the inescapably historical character of *all* human thinking. He is therefore appreciative of and sensitive to the scientific and philosophical thought-forms of modern culture, for he clearly recognizes that if the faith of our fathers is to exercise redeeming power *today,* it must be interpreted *in terms of the demands of modern life and thought.*

Liberalism is thus more than mere negative reaction to entrenched dogmas. It is positive in its resolve to keep the spirit of religion vital and dynamic by integrating it with the main current of modern life. Liberalism rescues religion from the stronghold of traditionalism and makes possible a continual renewal of religious life.

(4) *A Creative Synthesis with Modern Science*

The liberal's historical realism leads him to demand that the church humbly recognize its great debt to the liberal achievement in the realm of biblical scholarship. Thanks to Liberalism's thoroughgoing application of the modern science of literary and historical criticism to the Christian sources, the Bible has come alive today in a way of which the church of eighteen centuries was almost wholly ignorant. The liberal school of thought has given the church a more critical understanding of, and a truer perspective on, the *historical* character of the Bible. In this regard, Liberalism has enabled the church to become truly contemporary.

Much, of course, remains to be done in this general area; for beyond the application of historical and literary criticism to a study of the Bible, stands the more difficult theological problem of effecting a sound, meaningful, and fruitful synthesis of the modern thought world of science as a whole, and the abiding values of the Christian faith.

Too few have tackled this problem with requisite courage and thoroughness. Too many ministers and other church leaders are still talking solely in terms of traditional theology. As a result, the church's appeal to the modern, scientifically minded person is inexcusably lame and ineffective. Much, therefore, remains to be done in this task of developing a redemptively effective synthesis of the abiding values of the faith with the thought-forms of modern science.

(5) *A Broad Humanism*

A fifth positive value of the liberal spirit, a much greater measure of which is urgently needed in our day of international strife and cultural conflict, is the broad humanism of Liberalism's universal outlook. Liberalism is not narrow-minded and provincial. It shuns every form of sectarianism in religious thinking with skeptical suspicion. With Augustine, the liberal knows that God's acre is the whole world. Liberalism does not suffer from the delusion that any one group has a monopoly on religious truth. It has acquired an admirable humility which enables it to appreciate truth and goodness whenever and wherever they are found.

Liberalism is therefore not only willing but anxious to explore the entire range of the history of religious thought and experience, knowing that a broad historical approach to the pursuit of religious truth is the surest way for one to transcend religious sectarianism and provincialism.

The liberal is a Christian who has grown conscious of the dangers which lurk in an intellectually parasitic religion. He knows that segmented religious thought is as grave a danger, theologically, as segmented human behavior is, psychologically. He therefore is quick to recognize the danger and folly of driving one's stakes down too soon in man's quest for truth.

(6) *A Dominant Emphasis on Individual Liberty*

In its ardent plea for individual liberty, Liberalism represents Protestantism reaching a historically unique expression and creatively restoring a fundamental value of New Testament Christianity, albeit in a somewhat distorted way. Under this aspect of individual liberty, theological Liberalism must also be regarded as a particular expression of the basic philosophy of American democracy. And, although many liberals developed this emphasis on liberty in the framework of reference of an autonomy which ignored or denied the divine ground of human existence, there is nevertheless a point of agreement between the teachings of Jesus and that of the liberals in the belief in the inviolable dignity of the individual and in his inalienable rights. Liberals, like Jesus, recognize that every man has the right to go wrong, that every man has the right to go to hell, if he so chooses.

Liberalism demands also that we respect these rights. We must respect one another's differences in belief. We must not, for any reason whatever, violate the personal integrity of the individual by resorting to the use of pressure methods of any sort, as a means of dealing with differences in religious beliefs. Vigorous, but kind and courteous, persuasion, coupled with profound love and respect, is the only method which Liberalism will use in dealing with differences of belief.

This means that the liberal Protestant is aware of the fact that the principle of liberty is a two-edged sword; it cuts two ways. It demands that one give to others the same liberty which he claims for himself. The liberals therefore have often been heroic martyrs in the cause of freedom. They have fought valiantly to liberate the individual conscience from the cold, clammy hand of religious domination and oppression. The liberal heart is stirred to revolutionary depths by the ghastly specter of the totalitarian spirit in religion, in any of its numerous forms. It believes that nothing is more tragic and fatal than the traditional absolutisms which have choked out the good seed and stifled the creative spirit in the human breast.

Liberalism insists that whoever causes one of the little ones who believe, to fail in creative fulfillment and inward integrity, it would be better for him to have a great millstone fastened round his neck and to be drowned in the depth of the sea. The renowned Voltaire phrased this plea for liberty aptly when he said: "I do not agree with a word you say, but I will defend to the death your right to say it."

Here, then, is one answer to the conservative who asks: "Why *should* a person tolerate a belief which he honestly holds to be wrong? Is this not treason to one's own convictions? Will not one who sets out on such a pathway finally become a theological jellyfish, believing everything, believing nothing? Will he not lapse into the sheer negativism of complete religious indifference?" So Roman Catholicism affirms. J. Pohle, for example, insists that such indifference and tolerance in the realm of religious beliefs are inseparable. He writes,

Such a tolerance can only be the outcome of an attitude which is indifferent to the right of truth, and which places truth and error on the same level. In philosophy this attitude is briefly termed scepticism, in the domain of religion, it develops into religious indifferentism which declares that all religions are equally true and good or equally false and bad. Such an internal and external indifference toward all religions, especially the Christian religion, is nothing else than the expression of personal unbelief and lack of religious convictions.[18]

The liberal replies that this dilemma of the dogmatists is false. He claims that such tolerance does *not* necessarily mean that one thereby holds his own convictions with diminished force. It means, *in the first place,* that you, whom I believe to be wrong, have a *God-given right* to utter what you believe, and that it is my Christian duty to uphold your right of expression; all the while, of course, peaceably but vigorously contending with you to show that you are wrong.

In the second place, the tolerance of Liberalism means that the social welfare requires uninhibited expression of thought, even when the thought is perverse, for only by this open policy of freedom of expression can mankind benefit from those new insights into truth, whose birth is usually unwelcome to the established authorities of the day.[19]

In the third place, the tolerance of Liberalism means that the liberal heart is graced with the virtue of humility. The liberal possesses the ability to admit seriously that he might possibly be wrong, since he is only man and not God.[20] Hence the tolerance of the liberal is unlike the tolerance of the Roman Catholic dogmatist who feels that one can be tolerant of a different belief only if he is *absolutely certain* that he

[18]*The Catholic Encyclopedia* (New York: The Gilmary Society, 1912), XIV, 763-764. Used by permission.

[19]This was the argument of John Stuart Mill for individual liberty.

[20]For a detailed statement of the liberal plea for a combination of humility and conviction, see Ralph G. Wilburn, "The Skeptically Religious Student," in *Christian Education,* Vol. XXX, No. 3, September 1947, pp. 239-247.

himself is correct in his own belief.[21] This Roman Catholic type of tolerance is a looking-down-the-nose kind of tolerance with which the liberal will have nothing to do, for the tolerance of the liberal is thoroughly democratic; it is infused with the virtue of a humble wisdom which has learned that no human being knows the truth absolutely. One is morally obligated therefore to tolerate the beliefs of others with whom he differs, since in humility he recognizes the possibility that they might be right, though at this juncture he feels profoundly that they are wrong.

And in the fourth place, the tolerance of Liberalism stems from an awareness of the existential character of human truth. The particular formulations which will possess the stamp of truth for one individual in one situation will not necessarily apply to another individual in another situation, due to the different concrete factors which determine the different situations. Hence the liberal refuses to *impose* his theoretical beliefs upon others; they must come to perceptions of truth *for themselves.* That each individual possesses the inherent right to do so, is one of the profoundest beliefs of Liberalism.

(7) *The Primacy of Religion Over Theology*

The spirit of religious tolerance is reinforced also by Liberalism's appeal to *experience,* by its insistence on the primacy of religion over theology. All liberals

[21] J. Pohle argues, for example, that the only legitimate kind of religious tolerance is the attitude of "indulgence." Roman Catholics hold intolerance in the realm of religious belief to be a Christian virtue. Yet along with such intolerance they are able to maintain a forbearing or indulgent attitude toward those of other theological persuasions. Expressing the typical Catholic attitude, J. Pohle, for example, writes, "Absolutely unflinching in their fidelity to the Church as the sole means of salvation on earth, they will treat with respect, as ethically due, the religious convictions of others, and will see in non-Catholics, not enemies of Christ, but brethren. Recognizing from the Catholic doctrine of grace that the possibility of justification and of eternal salvation is not withheld even from the heathen, they will show towards all Christians, e.g., the various Protestant bodies, kindly consideration" (*The Catholic Encyclopedia, op. cit.,* p. 767).

are united in stressing the primacy of religion over doctrine, the primacy of experience of God over theologies about this experience. Liberal philosophies of religion are experience-centered, through and through.

This does not mean that Liberalism places a lesser value upon theology than did scholastic Protestantism.[22] It does represent Liberalism's sound effort to eliminate scholastic absolutism in modern Christianity. It does mean that Liberalism regards theology's role in a constructive, functional sense, and that it holds the primary and supremely important reality in religion to be something infinitely deeper than any of our human interpretations *about* this reality. It is to this supreme reality itself that liberal Protestantism would have us make an all-out commitment, not merely to someone's ideas about it.

This emphasis on the primacy of experience makes possible a kind of relativism in theology which furnishes a sound reason for respecting the personal experience of another, even if one cannot see eye to eye with him theologically. Such charitable respect toward those of different theological persuasions is manifest in our Lord's rebuke[23] of his disciples for the partisan spirit which caused them to hold in disrespect one who was casting out demons in the name of Christ, yet did not line up in the theological camp of the Twelve. Again, one thinks of Jesus' liberal respect for the centurion's faith. The centurion did not belong to orthodox Judaism. Yet Jesus made bold to declare that he had not found such great faith, no not in Israel.[24] The final appeal in liberal religion is thus to the experience of the divine which lies beneath and behind theological explication.

---

[22]Some liberals may have allowed the plea for tolerance to degenerate into the kind of relativism which amounts to theological indifference.

[23]Luke 9:49-50.

[24]Matthew 8:10.

(8) *A Demand for a Reasonable Religion*

A final positive value for creative religion is the liberal's demand for a reasonable religion. Much of the liberal confidence in reason was, to be sure, an unwarranted exaggeration. This was due to Liberalism's alliance with the false understanding of human life fostered by the autonomous character of modern culture. Yet there is in Liberalism at this point a fundamental value. Revelation, rightly understood, does not destroy or nullify human reason; it rehabilitates it and liberates it from a distorted self-centeredness and basic conflicts which seriously modified the validity of reason's function.[25]

It appears to the liberal to be the height of folly to say, in Tertullianic fashion, that Christ wishes his followers to believe something because it is absurd and nonsensical. On the contrary, it was Christ himself who said, "*You will know the truth,* and the truth will make you free."[26] It was Christ who said to his disciples, "Blessed are your eyes, *for they see,* and your ears, *for they hear.*"[27] It was Christ who said, "Blessed are the pure in heart, *for they shall see God.*"[28] And again, "And this is eternal life, *that they know thee* the only true God, and Jesus Christ whom thou hast sent."[29] And when the young lawyer asked our Lord bluntly, "Who is my neighbor?" Jesus did not answer in an authoritarian manner, demanding that the young man blindly accept his dictum. On the contrary, Jesus told the story about the good

---

[25]Tillich has given a penetrating analysis of these conflicts of the reason which is antecedent to faith. He says that there are three fundamental conflicts: (1) autonomy vs. heteronomy; (2) relativism vs. absolutism; and (3) formalism vs. emotionalism. Paul Tillich, *Systematic Theology* (Chicago: The University of Chicago Press, 1951), I, 83-94. Copyright 1951 University of Chicago.

[26]John 8:32.

[27]Matthew 13:16.

[28]Matthew 5:8.

[29]John 17:3.

Samaritan[30]; this reply *enabled the young man himself to perceive the truth and to answer his own question,* which Jesus returned to him.

What else, in the final analysis, do we have to safeguard religion from the rankest kind of obscurantism, except our God-given powers of reason and understanding? The wildest kind of superstitions have obtained in Christianity, down through years, parading under the banners of an irrational faith. Witches have been burned and heretics stretched on the rack, in the name of such a faith. Even yet today people are called upon, as good Christians, to believe in the bodily assumption of the Virgin Mary to heaven, the mysterious and sudden streaking of the sun across the sky at Fatima, and the miraculous appearance of the "Blessed Virgin" to peasant children on a hillside. If we do not grant any validity to the liberal's insistence upon a *reasonable* religion, one that *makes sense,* what, pray tell, do we have to protect the faith from such superstitious nonsense?

There is therefore, we contend, considerable validity in the liberal's confidence in reason. And there is validity also in his confidence that the Christian faith *can* come to terms with scientific and philosophical reason, without losing its integrity.

Weaknesses in Liberalism Calling for Revision

With all of its strength, however, there were some weaknesses in the theology of the liberal tradition. An honest assessment of these weaknesses leads to the demand that we revise theological Liberalism, as we have known it, and work out a more adequate theology in the light of our present situation. Having differentiated several values of the spirit of Liberalism which, we believe, are valid and of great worth if Christianity

[30] Luke 10:30 ff.

is to be redemptively effective in the contemporary situation, we must now describe some of the basic weaknesses of liberal Protestantism.

(1) *Tended to Render the Supreme Authority of the Lordship of Christ Irrelevant*

It must not be forgotten that Liberalism came to birth as a reaction to the *status quo* of scholastic dogmatism. And like most reactionary movements, Liberalism's reaction to the dogmatism of scholastic Christianity was also doubtless often extreme. For example, the liberals were not always sufficiently aware of the danger involved to creative religion whenever the plea for tolerance degenerates into indifference. As the term "tolerance" is popularly used, it is a democratic and Christian virtue; but a willy-nilly Liberalism, which implies that it really does not make too much difference *what* one believes, is a tragic fallacy. If Jesus was correct when he said, "you will know the truth, and the truth will make you free," a liberal indifference which takes the seriousness out of man's pursuit of truth is to be combated vigorously, "not with moral indignation but with therapeutic concern," to borrow a phrase from T. H. Greene.[31]

Furthermore, there can be no religion worthy of the name where there is no all-out commitment to a supreme authority, for true religion is grounded in man's relation to ultimate reality, in its essential character. And *that kind* of Liberalism which renders the demand for absolute commitment to the Lordship of God in Christ irrelevant represents a point of view which has diverged from the redemptive fountainhead of the Christian religion.

[31]A phrase which the author heard him use in his address at the Hazen Conference at Santa Barbara, California, in August, 1951.

With much of Liberalism's criticism of historic Christian traditions, prophetic Christianity is in agreement. But with much of Liberalism, prophetic Christianity is also in disagreement; for prophetic Christianity remains subject to the Word of God in Christ; and to this extent, it is bound to an authority which transcends all human interpretations of it.

(2) *Obscured or Denied the Relation of Man to the Eternal*

There is also too much anthropocentrism (man-centeredness) in the liberal movement as a whole. This is due, of course, to the profound way in which liberal Protestantism was affected by the autonomous character of modern culture.

Liberalism has freed us from the tyranny of Catholic and Protestant absolutisms. In this we rejoice. But in liberating modern man from these idolatrous objectivizations of the divine, Liberalism was too unaware of the other extreme, the equally grave danger of humanistic autonomy. Or to put it in another way, Liberalism delivered us from a slavish devotion to the Pope and from the creeds of orthodoxy; but in so doing it created the erroneous impression that now man is *absolutely free, dependent on and controlled by no one but himself*. It thus resurrected the fallacy of the ancient sophists which makes man the measure. It yielded too thoroughly to the lure of the freedom which was offered by the autonomous order of human life.[32]

Where now is that supreme religious principle of man's absolute dependence upon the Almighty? Where, indeed, is belief in the Almighty? The living

[32]Cf. Pauck, *op. cit.*, p. 249.

strength of vital religion has always been that it has taken its stand with Socrates, over against the subjectivism of the sophists. It has insisted that not man, but the *eternal God,* is the ultimate measure of all things.

Has Liberalism resurrected the adamic self-sufficiency of the sophists to plague the human race once again? Does not the disintegration which besets our modern Western world stem from the fact that it has yielded itself to the law of autonomy? Many of our greatest minds are now affirming that if our modern, occidental civilization is to be saved, we must recover the deep religious springs of life, from which we have allowed ourselves to be separated. We must find the eternal center or ground of life, beyond the little systems of man. This alone can redeem man from the disintegration which follows the structuring of human existence on the principle of self-sufficiency.

Another evidence of the irreligious man-centeredness of Liberalism is manifest in its exaggerated faith in human reason, which led it to reject the idea of revelation. Here again we must evaluate Liberalism both positively and negatively.

As we shall show more fully in following chapters in this book, Liberalism was correct in rejecting the old *idea* of revelation, construed as a body of infallible information about God. It is to the credit of Liberalism's integrity that it demonstrated conclusively and stated plainly that the historical facts regarding the texts and concepts of Scripture do not confirm such a theory of revelation. The fact is that *all* human thinking and endeavor are caught in the relativities of history, the text of the Bible included. Many fundamentalists are evidently either still ignorant of the facts about the Bible, or they lack the honesty requisite for facing these facts.

Too often, however, Liberalism hastily drew the conclusion that divine revelation therefore does not exist. Religion was thereby transformed into man's quest for, and discovery of, truth. Religious experience became a soliloquy. The dialogue of worship was lost. Too often, liberal Christianity gained its freedom from the dead hand of the past at the sacrifice of genuine religious conviction.

Too often the liberals failed to realize that their emancipation, too, was being effected by the same spirit which has brought on the sickness of modern secularism. Much of liberal Christianity allowed itself to become subject to the law of an autonomous culture.[33] And whatever the idea of revelation might or might not mean, it could never be fitted into any such autonomy, for basically the concept of revelation stands for a *God-centered* conception of human existence.

Say then that Liberalism was correct in rejecting an erroneous and antiquated *theory* of the meaning of revelation, but wrong in rejecting the *fact* of revelation, the supreme fact of prophetic religion. What was needed was a truer interpretation of this central fact, in the light of modern scientific knowledge. A wholesale rejection of it lands one either in deism or in a frankly humanistic philosophy of life.

Protestantism today is gradually recovering from this mistake of Liberalism. Yet at the same time, it is not being ensnared by the absolutism of the old Protestantism. It is coming to see that by the term "revelation" prophetic Christianity means not some

[33]Cf. Pauck, *op. cit.*, p. 251.

static, stultifying absolutism, but something very creative and dynamic, namely, the impact upon our life and thought of God's disclosure of *himself* in history. Revelation is not merely a set of doctrines; it is a dynamic event, a happening in history, the impact of which leads us to a new vision of God and to a new experience of his grace.

We say then that Liberalism's valid rejection of ecclesiastical and creedal absolutisms does not justify it in forfeiting the God-centeredness of genuine religion. Let us not throw out the religious baby with the dogmatic bath. The truly religious man can never submit to the principle of self-sufficiency, for the essence of religion lies in man's devotion to a reality which is infinitely greater than man.

To this unconditional and unconditioned reality, the God who dwells in the light that no man can approach unto, the Creator and Redeemer of our life, religion gladly submits its all. Religion is nourished in the human heart by its devotion to this suprahuman reality, the sovereign Lord of all life.

This is why Christianity must be forever opposed to any autonomous culture. Whatever revelation may mean, it stands in judgment upon the law of autonomy and points to the basic, theonomous (God-grounded) character of human existence.

Good Christian people who become confused sometimes by technical and precise terminology frequently sense, however dimly, the truth or falsity of the theologian's reasoning. And good Christian people have rightly sensed this fallacy of Liberalism. Some have reacted violently and mistakenly tried to call us back to the old scholastic orthodoxy. Yet they have rightly perceived that there is sometimes more of the spirit of genuine religion in the old fundamentalism than in some of modern Liberalism.

We are confronted here with a deep yearning of the human heart which all would do well to ponder at length. The contemporary reactions to Liberalism—the prophetic call of Karl Barth, Calvinistic fundamentalism, the revelation theology of Richard Niebuhr and Paul Tillich—all these are to be viewed as a valid indication of the inadequacy of traditional Liberalism at the focal point of all genuine religion, namely, man's relation to the Eternal.

(3) *Magnified Man's Dignity to the Neglect of his Misery*

A third basic weakness of Liberalism is evident in the inclination of many liberals to eliminate the term "sin" from our modern theological vocabulary. This tendency was the result of the liberal's neglect of the idea of divine transcendence. The God of Liberalism was too exclusively immanent. The biblical dualism of man's sin and God's holiness was obscured or more frankly denied.

To be sure, maladjustments, immaturity, and imperfection due to ignorance and finitude were recognized. But the embarrassing term "sin" was discarded. This, of course, was quite logical, for a humanistic liberal can make no room in his philosophy for the concept of sin. As one whom Reinhold Niebuhr calls "a particularly vapid modern social scientist" put it, "the sense of sin is a psychopathic aspect of adolescent mentality."[34] "Sin" is a theological term which can embody a meaningful interpretation of human failure only in a theological framework, where

---

[34]Reinhold Niebuhr, *The Nature and Destiny of Man* (New York: Charles Scribner's Sons, 1943), I, 94.

the eternal God is the ultimate referent, where the significance of human failure is interpreted against its cosmic framework of reference, and not merely against the immediate societal background. But it is just this cosmic reference which, in Liberalism, was watered down and sometimes eliminated.

Further, there is a strange blindness in the liberal's evasion of the tragic, personal character of sin's guilt. The cause of evil was found in man's finite nature, or in sociological conditions which determined the act, or in anything else but a tragic personal abuse of man's metaphysical freedom.

Accordingly, Liberalism's strategy in dealing with human failure was solely to use methods of education and Socratic persuasion. Liberalism clung stubbornly to its confidence in the goodness of man. It relied too heavily and too exclusively upon man's fundamental goodness; and it therefore argued, consistently, that *education* is all that man needs to attain the good life. "Only tell man the truth, and he will act in the proper way"—so many a liberal felt, and felt very deeply.

Twentieth-century history, however, has painfully revealed the somewhat superficial character of this optimism. The liberal belief that all that man needed was a knowledge of the true meaning of his existence, does not appear to be empirically grounded. But so deeply rooted was this liberal confidence in man's goodness that many liberals even yet find it difficult to face up boldly to the fact that insight into the nature of human life—psychological, biological, sociological, and so forth—has *not* enabled man to actualize his potentialities for good. Evil is more deeply rooted in human nature than the liberal thought. In an illuminating paragraph, Pauck writes:

The autonomous man is always inclined toward self-sufficiency, individualism. He acts not according to the dictates of his insight, but according to the dictates of his *power,* and he uses his insight for the sake of expressing and increasing his power. It is this power of free men which constantly destroys the harmony of humanity. And it is the recognition of this element of power in all freedom which invalidates the liberalist interpretation of life. Rationality, harmony, unity, continuity, cannot be the key words of a philosophy which claims to interpret life truly, for as long as life is dominated by the element of power, there is irrationality, disharmony, disunity, discontinuity in life.[35]

Pauck is correct in saying that "it is the power of free men which constantly destroys the harmony of humanity" if by "free" is meant "autonomous," i.e., life divorced from any recognition of dependence upon God. It would be saying too much, however, to affirm that all power, all effective assertion of self, all historical vitalities are in contradiction to the divine demand of love. Reinhold Niebuhr seems to say this, although he nowhere comes right out and says that power, *qua power,* is evil. Exerting power in some form, however, is obviously essential to be a self, a person. And it is an exaggeration to say that to possess influence as a person is sinful; this would be tantamount to saying that to be a person is to be a sinner.

Furthermore, as Daniel Williams points out,[36] a conflict of powers, of interests, of life with life can and often does function constructively in the growth and good of life. A conflict of selves seems to be inherent in God's personal creation. This is not itself evil, nor does it necessarily create evil. On the contrary, it is frequently productive of great good, as in sports, for example.

It remains true, however, that this aspect of human selfhood, the capacity for power, like all other

[35]Pauck, *op. cit.,* p. 267. Used by permission.

[36]Cf. Daniel Day Williams, *God's Grace and Man's Hope* (New York: Harper and Brothers, 1949), p. 88.

aspects, is caught in a profoundly deep self-centeredness which is productive of an amazing amount of cruelty, brutality, and inhumanity. It is, therefore, painfully evident today that the liberal category of education must be revised, extended, and altered so as to do justice to the highly relevant category of redemption or grace.

Say, then, that it is the glory of Liberalism that it recovered for Christianity an awareness of the fundamental goodness of man, at a time when Calvinism had unduly obscured this great biblical truth regarding the image of God in man. Realism demands, however, that we recognize how paradoxical a creature man is. We must recognize, with equal clarity, man's sinful self-centeredness. We must face up to the fact that the divine image has been blurred, distorted, and marred. The glory of man's dignity must not hide from our eyes the tragedy of his misery.[37]

Perhaps with Augustine we might chart a revised course, in our conception of man, between Pelagianism, on the one hand, and Manicheism, on the other. We shall thus avoid that Pelagian view of man which so construes his goodness and dignity that the relevance of the gospel of redemption becomes problematical. Yet at the same time, we shall not get caught in that Manichean pessimism, which reads the life of man in such somber, dualistic terms that the relevancy of redemption again becomes problematical, for man is so conceived that a basic phase of his being (the flesh, corporealness) is incapable of being redeemed.

(4) *Lacked Realism in Its Somewhat Utopian Philosophy of History*

Correlated with Liberalism's concept of man is

[37]For a thoughtful, recent study of the doctrine of the *imago Dei*, see *The Image of God in Man* by David S. Cairns (New York: The Philosophical Library, 1953).

its philosophy of history. Most liberals conceived of the relation between the kingdom of God and history in terms of continuity. Their philosophy was essentially the progressivistic moral gradualism which was popular in the nineteenth century.

Cooperating with God, Liberalism hoped to build a better world. It represented an all-out effort to see to it that God's will, revealed in the ethical principles of Jesus, is done *on earth,* as it is in heaven. Liberals insisted that world-bettering is kingdom-building. Hence, they have labored and are laboring tirelessly in doing what needs to be done to clear the way for a social order of justice, peace, and brotherhood.

Liberals were not always agreed on their method of attacking social evils. But most of them held that ethical, social action finds its meaning and the ground of its support in religious truth, which gives sound hope for success.

Liberals emphasized the doctrine of the immanence of God. They insisted on holding the "sacred" and "secular" together by the dynamic of the ideal of the kingdom of God. They believed that when we actually seek to order human life, individually and socially, in harmony with the demands of love and justice, we are "working together with God," God's will is being done by us on earth, and his kingdom thereby moves toward fulfillment.

It must be conceded that, in many ways, this liberal hope was and is glorious. Surely no one today would fail to recognize how superior it is to that distorted kind of otherworldliness frequently encountered in Christian history, where the ethical, social aspects of the Christian way were almost totally neglected, as monastic ideals prevailed. There is a power, a depth, and a prophetic rigor in Liberalism at this point which should be evaluated positively. In the main, the liberal hope of "the progressive transformation of all human affairs by the thought and spirit of Christ"[38] must constitute a permanent element in any Christianity worthy of the name of prophetic religion.

Yet here, too, we must confess that Liberalism often overshot the mark. Closely allied with the cultural spirit of the nineteenth century, it was affected by the enthusiasm of sociological utopianism. Hence some liberals held the fantastic notion of inevitable progress. Others were more realistic. In 1918, for example, E. W. Lyman wrote that probably none of his contemporaries would deny "that social progress is . . . not a swiftly unfolding and self-operating movement, but a tragically complicated and baffling problem."[39] Yet prior to World War I, the intellectual climate was such that the idea of inevitable progress had a strong appeal.

It is probably true that no liberal today any longer clings to such a hope. Penetrating theological criticism of this position, combined with the stern realities of recent history, has effected a significant modification of the liberal hope at this point. Yet in evaluating the movement of liberal Protestantism as a whole, one must once again briefly characterize this eschatological weakness.

The utopian character of the old liberal hope has been painfully exposed in our day. Twentieth-century history scarcely vindicates the hope of an evolutionary transformation of the orders of history into the king-

[38]Walter Rauschenbusch, *Christianizing the Social Order* (New York: The Macmillan Company, 1919), p. 458.

[39]E. W. Lyman, *The Experience of God in Modern Life* (New York: Charles Scribner's Sons, 1918), p. 25.

dom of God. Human nature is more recalcitrant than many liberals thought. War is devastating human civilization. Gigantic historical forces seem to sweep all individuals before them. Individuals seem to be embedded, like bits of rock, in the glacial forces of historical process. Death—stark, cold, and calculating—is stalking the earth. The path of the past three decades is strewn with the wreckage of teeming thousands of victims of man's barbaric selfishness.

Is there, as Reinhold Niebuhr and Karl Barth contend, a basic, ineradicable conflict of powers and interests everywhere in human life? Is such conflict the *abiding essence* of man's historical existence? Could it be that war is not an isolated problem? that it is symptomatic of the *whole historical plight of man*? Could Erich Frank be right when he argues[40] that Christ's kingdom is not of this world, that it belongs to the spiritual realm? Is it true that in *this* world Caesar will always be victorious, while Christ is forever crucified?

The line of thought suggested by such questions as these constitutes a valid criticism of the liberal philosophy of the late nineteenth and early twentieth centuries. *It did not take man's need for redemption with sufficient seriousness!* Yet it would seem to be clear also that the Barthian teaching of a radical discontinuity between the kingdom and history is equally unsatisfactory, for it leads to a kind of Neo-Calvinism that borders too closely on the ancient Gnostic heresy, a heresy which found no meaning for the grace of creation.

Say, then, first of all, that the traditional liberal philosophy of history failed to come to grips ade-

[40]Erich Frank, *Philosophical Understanding and Religious Truth* (New York: Oxford University Press, 1945), p. 128.

quately with the basic fact of man's need for redemption. Sigmund Freud had not yet made his psychological contribution, and the liberals were insufficiently aware of the nonrational factor in human life, the surd which must ever be taken into account in the formulation of an equation that would estimate the limitations of man's rational powers. The liberal concept of man was unrealistic in failing to face up to the concrete fact of sin and to the stubborn persistence of evil in all structures of human history.

Reinhold Niebuhr has rendered the Christian cause a notable service in his penetrating insights which have exposed the unrealistic character of the traditional liberal philosophy of history. Niebuhr argues convincingly that there is sin on every level of moral and spiritual growth. The self-centeredness of pride, he finds best illustrated, for example, in the life of the church itself.

Niebuhr's more realistic insight into the human situation is, however, somewhat distorted. He exaggerates man's ineradicable sinfulness in such a fashion that he fails to do justice to redemption *as an accomplished fact*. He says that we are redeemed in "principle" but not "in fact."[41] He thus fails to realize that redemption is not only the assurance of forgiveness, but also an actual gift, an accomplishment. Niebuhr's theology tends toward the eschatological view of the Hebrew prophets and somewhat away from the New Testament teaching of what C. H. Dodd has called "a realized eschatology." Nevertheless, his vigorous theological realism does strike at a point where Liberalism needed correction and modification.

This means that Liberalism had an inadequate appreciation of the basic Protestant principle which

[41] Niebuhr, *op. cit.*, II, 49.

draws a distinction between the inner, eternal Spirit of Christianity and the historical forms, moral and otherwise, through which the Spirit finds expression. It failed to recognize that the creativity of divine love is never fully and finally embodied in history, that *in a fundamental sense* the kingdom will always transcend history. There is no social order which is not corrupted by exploitation and injustice, and it would now seem to be utopian to expect such.

Secondly, the traditional liberal philosophy of history was inadequate, for its staunch opposition to the old Calvinism led to an unwarranted arbitrariness in its doctrine of man's freedom. Reinhold Niebuhr has also eloquently exposed this arbitrariness.[42] If, as the liberal insisted, man has absolute freedom to guide his own life, by virtue of what can we joyfully affirm (as Liberalism did) that he will progressively use this freedom for good instead of evil? Real freedom is always freedom also to rebel against the good, as the biblical story of the Fall eloquently declares. The conclusion is inescapable: so long as man is genuinely free, evil as well as good will be an immanent possibility.

Thirdly, several critics have pointed out yet another weakness in the liberal philosophy of history. It is concerned with the fact that the flowing character of the temporal process jeopardizes the enduring significance of a person's experience of value. As John Locke said, "Time is perpetually perishing." The liberal view of history, with its gaze fixed upon a kind of millennial terminus of the process as the goal, failed to discern adequately the meaning of fulfillment for the individual, here and now. The individual got lost in the shuffle of the process. The *end* was

[42]Niebuhr, *op. cit.*, I, 24, 110; II, 95, 240, 245.

the important thing. The late Nicolas Berdyaev insisted that this liberal doctrine of progress is "an entirely illegitimate deification of the future at the expense of past and present, in a way that has not the slightest scientific philosophical or moral justification."[43]

In the theology of contemporary Protestantism, we need a revised teleology and eschatology.[44] We need a world view in which the Eternal can be conceived as interpenetrating, transforming, and transfiguring the temporal throughout; yet all the while, preserving an awareness that the finite limitations which inhere in historical existence, coupled with man's self-centeredness, render this process of transfiguration paradoxical and problematical. But as the late A. N. Whitehead said, "Throughout the perishing occasions in the life of each temporal creature we must find some sense in which those occasions live forevermore."[45] If the ultimate value of our human life is to be secured, we must find some sense in which the value-experiences realized in cosmic process are not forever wasting away, but are conserved eternally, in that they incarnate the Eternal.[46] Then, and only then, can we attain the blessedness of life everlasting.

---

[43]Nicolas Berdyaev, *The Meaning of History* (Goeffry Bles, The Centenary Press, 1945), p. 187; cf. Williams, *op. cit.*, p. 114.

[44]For an excellent recent critical study of the different Christian interpretations of this problem, see H. Richard Niebuhr, *Christ and Culture* (New York: Harper and Brothers, 1951).

[45]Alfred N. Whitehead, *Process and Reality* (New York: The Macmillan Company, 1930), p. 533.

[46]*Ibid.*, p. 529.

APPENDIX TO CHAPTER TWO

It is appropriate here to indicate some of the basic principles which enter into the formulation of an adequate Christian view of history.

The Christian outlook on the future is unique. It is different, for example, from the outlook of the ancient Greek mind. The Greeks thought that the process of history followed the law of the circle, and that we therefore get nowhere in history: we come out exactly where we went in and inherit a spiritual zero. Nor was the Greek mind able to see any way in which the fatalistic control of this vicious circle could be broken; so that every deed was thought to carry irrevocable consequences. If a father, for example, rose up in a fit of anger and slew his son, the deed was *done,* and to all eternity it could never be undone. This father's future was very black indeed! This is the view of history which lies behind the tragedy of the Greek drama; it is what makes the tragedy so terribly tragic.

The Christian ideas of repentance, forgiveness, and redemption are utterly foreign to this typically Greek way of thinking about man's future. Hence Celsus and other Greek philosophers regarded Christianity as foolishness, for it ran counter to their basic assumptions regarding the nature of history and the future of man. The good news of repentance and redemption broke the vicious circle of Greek fatalism and offered hope to mankind.

Similarly, the Christian outlook on the future must be viewed in sharp contrast to the Hindu outlook, which is found, for example, in the ancient writings of the Upanishads. The Hindu concept of human life was centered in the idea of an eternally revolving wheel, the spinning of which is regulated by the principles of karma (the inexorable law of cause and effect transformed into a cosmic principle) and the transmigration of souls. The typically Hindu mind sees no purpose whatever in the dizzy spinning of the wheel of existence. Historic process is utterly without meaning. Hence the escapist mysticism of the Hindu religion. The goal is to find and realize the absolute identity of God and the soul, and thereby escape the tragic illusion of phenomenal existence on the dizzily spinning wheel. Christianity boldly rejects this negative attitude toward man's historic existence. In contrast to the negative view of the Hindu idea of Nirvana, Christianity clings to a deep-rooted faith in life, life that is abundant and free. Christianity's attitude toward historic life is essentially positive.

There is also the ancient Jewish, apocalyptic view of the future, which enabled ancient Israel to tolerate the evils of their situation by looking forward to a future "day of the Lord," a day when the Lord would rise up and show his hand, and in sweeping judgment destroy the enemies of the covenant people and also members of the covenant people who had failed to keep their covenant relationship with God. At that time, God would establish the Messianic age of righteousness and peace. This ancient Jewish view of the future did offer some religious hope to the human heart. And it did contain a partial, prophetic truth. Unqualified, however, it turns out to be a kind of opiate, a compensatory idealism which glorifies the future at the expense of the present, in a way that cannot be theologically justified.

By way of contrast to these views of history, we list here and discuss briefly four basic principles which enter into an adequate Christian view of history.

(1) *The Christian View of History Is Dramatic in Nature; It Has as Its Basic Motif the Concept of Crisis, or the Challenge-Response Motif.*

The dramatic character of the Christian view of history is due first of all to the fact that it is based upon the cross and resurrection of Christ. This is Christianity's basic premise. The central Christian affirmation about history is that this supreme event of Jesus Christ, though genuinely historical, is nevertheless not wholly drowned in the forces of historical relativism, but constitutes a final revelation of the meaning of all history. Here, the Infinite is reflected in the finite, the Eternal in a temporal moment, the love of God in the form of a human servant. Here is one event in history which lights up the meaning of all history.

To put the cross of Christ at the center of our view of history is to make the element of dramatic struggle predominant. And the struggle of Christianity, in our century, with numerous other ways of life which are making challenging bids for the primary loyalty of the human heart, has greatly deepened our understanding of the New Testament dramatic character of the fulfillment of the inner meaning of history. We have come to view this fulfillment in terms of judgment and deliverance, in the bright white light of the cross and the resurrection.

That history is a profound spiritual drama means also that the fulfillment of the kingdom of God in history is no smooth and easy victory. We must frankly face up to the fact that "in the ancient homelands of Christianity the forces of evil have been gaining ground."[47] The battle between Christ and culture, between the kingdom of God and the kingdoms

[47] F. R. Barry, *Recovery of Man* (New York: Charles Scribner's Sons, 1949), p. 99.

of this world, between the sons of the kingdom and the "principalities and powers in the heavenly places" —this battle by no means involves an inevitable or even gradual progress of a Christian victory over the cultural forces which are at work. The future of history, from this point of view, remains uncertain. The fulfillment of the ultimate meaning of history, *at any particular time in history,* remains always uncertain and problematical, because man's metaphysical freedom is real, and freedom is freedom also to rebel, because the drama of redemption is no sham battle, but a fearfully genuine struggle, because the struggle of the human heart with the forces of evil is a deadly serious affair. Christianity says that the dramatic conflict between good and evil in the human heart constitutes the very stuff of man's historical existence.

(2) *The Christian View of Man's Future Maintains an Awareness that the Dimension of Sin Runs Through the Whole of Human Existence.*

The cross of Jesus Christ means that Christianity takes the facts of sin and death in bitter earnest. One reason why some philosophers dislike the Apostle Paul's thought is that Paul stubbornly refused to slur over the fact of man's sinfulness and idealize it as somehow good—all for the sake of a monistic hypothesis.

The roots of self-centeredness in the human heart are so deep that there has never been a community in history which has not been marred and corrupted by it. And it would now seem to be utopian to expect such. That is, it would be utopian to conceive of the relation of the kingdom of God to history, *at any time,* in a way in which the motif of dramatic conflict would no longer be relevant.

Modern man's education regarding the selfishness of the human heart has been so profound and thoroughgoing that we feel at times that we have actually seen "the man of sin," the spirit of antichrist personified in diabolical twentieth-century supermen, who have drenched the earth with the blood of our brothers. Through these power-thirsty demigods, we have seen, with tragic clarity, how what is best in man can be corrupted and enslaved to evil ends.

The whole of human history seems to be almost infected with a sinful kind of self-regarding attitude. We are learning to appreciate the truth of the great Pauline doctrine of the reign of the tyrant sin. Subjection to this tyrant of self-centeredness seems indeed to be the perpetual, historical predicament of the human heart. It would now appear that history has not only always been the kind of place where Christ is crucified and where the good is stretched on the scaffold, but that it may always be the kind of place where such tragedy occurs.

We are now aware also that the eschatological outlook of the writers of the New Testament was apocalyptic in nature, and that they did not look forward to a long, gradual development and progressive realization of the kingdom in history.[48] The Christians of the New Testament period, of course, had no incentive to look forward in any such fashion, for their historical perspective was violently abbreviated by the hope of the imminent return of the Lord.

Futhermore, sin has a curious way of blinding its victims. One of the most illuminating passages in the teachings of Jesus is the portrayal of the judgment scene, with the assembly divided on the right hand

[48]See, for example, 2 Timothy 3:13.

and on the left.[49] One of the profound principles at the heart of this teaching is that when the sentence of damnation was passed on those on the left, they affirmed their blissful ignorance regarding their sinfulness; they actually thought that they were righteous. Whereas those on the right, who were invited to enter into eternal life, were unaware that they had fulfilled the demands of God's righteousness. This evidently means that the righteous are aware of their failure; while those who *regard themselves* as righteous thereby become blind to their missings of the mark.

Many respectable churchgoing people, therefore, who consider themselves to be among the right-wingers and who hold a contemptuous attitude toward "those sinful people out there in the world" will probably find themselves among the left-wingers, in that great day. Indeed, "the time has come for judgment to begin with the household of God."[50]

In humility, therefore, we are now beginning to realize that there *is* sin at every level of moral and spiritual development, and that the church itself is by no means free from it. The pharisaic attitude in religion stems from an erroneous conception of the relation between the church and the world. Reinhold Niebuhr feels that we have an eloquent and clear expression of sin in the attitude of complacent, self-righteous church members, who consider themselves as "saints," as set apart from "the sinful world." The sin of self-centeredness stands out, in bold relief, in these pharisaic "come-outers." These "saints" are the chief of sinners. So, says Niebuhr, the publicans and sinners must come to the aid of Christianity and "rescue an important aspect of truth about life."[51]

---

[49]Matthew 25:31-46.
[50]1 Peter 4:17.
[51]Reinhold Niebuhr, *op. cit.*, I, 122.

The "saints" had forgotten "that sainthood is corrupted whenever holiness is claimed as a simple possession," for then the church is betrayed into "new forms of self-righteousness."

Niebuhr's realism appears to be empirically sound when he contends[52] that a fundamental contradiction between self-will and the new life in Christ always remains, in history. If we maintain a keen awareness of this truth, we shall be able to avoid any utopian illusions regarding the future of man.

(3) *The Possibilities of History for Good Are Immeasurably Great Due to the Redemptive Power of the Living God.*

Christianity takes the fact of sin in dead earnest, yes. But it would be only a partially Christian view, if this were all. The Christian truth about history is a double truth. It affirms *both* the cross *and* the resurrection. It affirms that human existence is always under God's judgment, but also that it is always being redeemed by his power and grace. It affirms that history is at once both tragic and glorious. All of us, at all times, are sinners, and stand in need of redemption. By keeping this truth before us, we escape the heresy of Pelagianism and the equally untenable view of ethical perfectionism, the erroneous belief that Christians can actually live lives totally free from sin. But lest we fall into the equally grave mistakes of esoteric mysticism and Manicheism, we must remember also that all men and the whole of human existence are capable of being redeemed.

Hence Christianity is not simply "optimistic." Yet neither is it "pessimistic," for it affirms that all men are capable of being redeemed; and the doctrine

---

[52] *Ibid.*, p. 121.

of the resurrection means that the whole of human life—body, soul, and spirit—is capable of being redeemed.

If, therefore, we must reject the philosophy of progressive moral gradualism, which affirmed that, year after year, the influence of Christianity will grow and expand, and the world will become better and better, till finally the kingdom of God will be fully and completely realized *in history;* if we can no longer say, "nearer and nearer draws the time, the time that shall surely be"; if we must now set aside this outmoded, liberal philosophy of history as utopian, we must be on guard not to get caught in a new form of the old Gnostic heresy, which held the category of redemption to be utterly irrelevant to history, and which therefore developed an escapist mysticism, offering a privileged and private exit, by which the initiated could escape the frustrations of history, and, leaving this evil world behind, could secure a one-way ticket on an esoteric flight to the superworld of Eternal Light.

These kinds of "come-outers" are not the saints of New Testament Christianity. On the contrary, they have suffered from the disease of moral and spiritual defeatism.

Christianity is not a failure of nerve by which we take flight from the world. It is a faith and hope which gives us the courage to wrestle valiantly with "the principalities and power in the heavenly places"; it is a power by which we can overcome the world. It does not offer man a way of *dodging* the evil world; but it puts him in contact with an ultimate power and meaning which enable him to conquer and transform the world (though the victory always remains fragmentary and ambiguous).

The strength and truth of the liberal view of history is that, when confronted by what it (erroneously) conceived to be the mutually exclusive alternatives of ethics or apocalyptic, it refused (and rightly so) to abandon the ethical content of the gospel. There *is* a moral meaning to be realized *in* history. If the doctrine of inevitable progress is fallacious, so also is the doctrine of cynicism and despair. God give us the wit to distinguish between "belief in progress" and "belief in the possibility of progress," by the power of the living God.

For history to be genuinely creative, the future must remain open. The dice are not rigidly loaded either way. The challenge is genuine and the moral struggle is profoundly real. Christianity is not "optimistic," in the old liberal sense of the term. It gives no encouragement to any secular utopianism. Its view of history is too realistic for such optimism. But neither is it pessimistic and defeatist. For through faith in God and his infinite power to redeem, Christianity looks forward to the future with a hope that inspires, strengthens, and sustains.[53]

Say, then, that the challenge confronting us is tragically profound, but by the power of "God, Father, Almighty," the future *can* become an immeasurably glorious fulfillment of the kingdom; if we are supremely dedicated to the kingdom ideal, if we perform wisely and well the immediate tasks which it lays upon our hearts and lives, and if we remain penitently under the overarching sky of God's forgiving graciousness.

The cross is, therefore, not the final word about history. "Resurrection" is the final word. And resurrection means that sin is defeated and death is

[53]Cf. Robert Lowry Calhoun, *What Is Man?* (New York: Association Press, 1939), p. 68.

destroyed. As F. R. Barry aptly puts it,[54] the resurrection is the "guarantee" that all history belongs not to blind fate, nor to the Devil, but to the living God. "At the centre of history there is a 'living hope.'"[55] The recuperative capacity of history is immeasurably great because the living God is at work in it. If our world is always under God's judgment, it can always be redeemed and restored by his love and grace.

(4) *The Christian View Holds that the Risen and Eternal Christ Is Always Confronting Us, in His Kingdom, and that Therefore Every Time in History Is Equally a Time of the End as Every Other Time.*

The Christian view of history is purposive; but the relation between historic process and the "end" of history is vertical, not horizontal. The end or purpose of history is not temporal; it is spiritual and transcendental. Though, to be sure, it must be presented to the popular mind in temporal symbols and images.

The doctrine of a literal end or terminus of historic process at some specific time in the future is not a particularly Christian doctrine, though many Christians have doubtless clung to such a belief. The end of history has nothing to do with any such notion of a temporal terminus of the world. Whether there will or will not be such a terminus is a purely scientific problem, which does not affect the Christian faith one way or the other. The end of history is not temporal, but spiritual. The end of history is its goal, its ultimate meaning, its final, inner truth of Christlike love.

---

[54]Barry, *op. cit.*, p. 107.
[55]*Ibid.*

Eternal life, for example, an aspect of the doctrine of the end things, is misunderstood when construed as mere temporal interminability. Eternity is not merely time but a lot more of it. Eternity is essentially qualitative in meaning, not quantitative, as is clearly implied in the statement of Jesus when he assured his followers that "he who believes in the Son" already "has eternal life," here and now.[56] One does not have to wait to go to heaven by and by in order to live eternally.

What is needed therefore is an incarnational eschatology, or what C. H. Dodd has called a "realized eschatology." We need a view of the end of all things in which eternity and history coalesce. A. N. Whitehead aptly wrote: "That religion will conquer which can render clear to popular understanding some eternal greatness incarnate in the passage of temporal fact."[57]

We must always see history in the light of the end; but the point is that *every* time is a time of the end. The end of history is the meaning of history, as it is determined by the purpose of God's creative love. We need to see that the end of history, which has been supremely revealed in Jesus Christ, is forever pressing in upon this world, interpenetrating, transforming, transfiguring it throughout. Yet all the while, we remain aware that the limitations of man's finitude and his radical self-centeredness render this process of transfiguration ambiguous, fragmentary, and problematical.

The Christian view of history is thus forever opposed to all secular philosophies of history, such as the dialectical materialism of Marxism. For Christianity reads history in the light of an eternal meaning, a

[56]John 3:36.

[57]Alfred North Whitehead, *Adventures of Ideas* (New York: The Macmillan Company, 1933), p. 41.

meaning revealed in the cross and resurrection of Christ. It is also opposed to the negative view of history found in escapist mysticism, such as the ancient Greek mystery religions and Buddhism, in which a sense of despair generated the ideal of radical flight from this world by means of a direct mystical union with the ultimate. On the contrary, the Christian analysis says that the end of history is to be realized *in* history, *in* the temporal process, even though the consummation lies beyond. But neither is the Christian view of history optimistic, in the evolutionary, nineteenth-century sense of the term. For Christianity sees history as at once both tragic and glorious. Christianity has learned the lesson that this world will always be a tragic place. It knows that there is no security *in history* against the final dissolution of all temporal existence. Its hope lies beyond, over yonder, in the power and grace of the living God.

PART TWO

Protestantism and The Problem of Revelation

CHAPTER THREE

The Idea of Revelation in Historical Protestant Thought

From our discussion in the preceding chapters, it should be evident that one of the most crucial theological problems which has confronted Protestantism throughout its development is the problem of revelation and authority. If contemporary Christianity is to recover from the weakening of its prophetic, redemptive power brought on by an alliance with the autonomy of modern culture, and if it is to achieve a more significant depth of unity, the concern to understand the meaning of revelation must become more widespread than it is at the present time. It is to the promotion of this concern that this second part of this volume is dedicated.

The Reformation was born when Luther gained the insight that all things human, the church included, must be subjected to the criticism of the Word of God. Luther refused to concede that the quality of absoluteness characterizes the offices of the church, from acolyte to pope. He recognized that the church possesses a relative authority; but he insisted that it does not possess an absolute authority. Luther repudiated the idea of an infallible papacy and the belief in an infallible church council.

The Doctrinaire View of Revelation in Roman Catholicism

A copy of Luther's ninety-five theses fell into the hands of Johannes Eck, a Catholic professor at Ingolstadt. Eck was among the first to perceive the implications of Luther's attack on indulgences, for the whole hierarchical system of the church.

After considerable correspondence between Eck, Carlstadt, Luther's colleague at the University of Wittenberg, and Luther himself, the issue came to a public debate at Leipzig, June 27 to July 16, 1519.

In the course of the debate Luther was led by Eck to repeat his affirmation that the authority of the Pope was only a human institution and was therefore not infallible,[1] and that the hierarchical order was neither biblically grounded nor supported by divine authority. He was also led to affirm more clearly and emphatically than he had done theretofore[2] that church councils could err, indeed had done so, being composed of fallible men, and that the Word of God in the Bible should be our only religious authority.[3]

Luther's public repudiation of the infallibility of church authority caused considerable uproar. Nor was it long before Luther's cause became a national issue. Long before Rome had reached any final decision regarding Luther, it was clear that Luther's cause had already become the cause of the German nation.[4]

The success of Luther's reform, however, did not weaken the adherence of the Roman leaders to the idea of infallibility. On the contrary, it evoked such powerful reaction from the papacy that it proved

[1]*D. Martin Luthers Werke,* bearbeitet von J.K.F. Knaacke (Weimar: Hermann Böhlaus Nachfolger, 1884), II, 279 f., 308, 379.

[2]Though he had already expressed this idea prior to this debate. See *D. Martin Luthers Werke,* bearbeitet von J.K.F. Knaacke (Weimar: Hermann Böhlaus Nachfolger, 1883), I, 656 f., 308, 583 f.

[3]Cf. Erich von D. Seeberg, *Luthers Theologie in Ihren Grundzügen,* Zweite Auflage (Stuttgart: W. Kohlhammer Verlag, 1950), p. 173; Roland Bainton, *The Reformation of the Sixteenth Century* (Boston: The Beacon Press, 1952), pp. 41-42; Harold J. Grimm, *The Reformation Era, 1500-1650* (New York: The Macmillan Company, 1954), pp. 124-125.

[4]Cf. Paul Joachimsen, *Die Reformation als Epoche Der Deutsche Geschichte* (München: Chr. Kaiser Verlag, Verlag von R. Oldenbourg, 1951), p. 68.

to be a major factor in helping to bring about the final crystallization of the idea of papal infallibility. This idea really did not actually become a dogma, however, until the great Vatican Council of 1870, a Council which was the crowning achievement of Pope Pius IX. This delay was due to the fact that the popes still had to fight through the battle with many bishops who even yet attempted to retain an episcopal (rather than papal) concept of the church. These conciliarist-minded bishops contended that their authority was derived directly from Christ and not through the Pope, and that the authority of the Pope should be subordinated to that of an episcopal council.

The papal concept eventually won out, however, and received its dogmatic formation at the Vatican Council of 1870. In making the dogma, it was stated emphatically that the dogma did not create something new. The Pope had been infallible since the days of the apostles. This decree of the Vatican Council merely gave *dogmatic recognition* to the ecclesiastical fact that the Roman pontiff is infallible "when he speaks *ex cathedra* . . . in defining doctrines of faith or morals."[5]

To this very day, Roman Catholic theologians are still clinging desperately to this absolutistic view of church authority and to the correlative concept of revelation as a body of infallible doctrines, to which one is asked to give intellectual (?) assent, even blindly, if necessary.

George D. Smith, a representative contemporary Catholic writer, for example, defines revelation as "a divine testimony." He feels that "it is man's bounden duty to accept it by an act of belief, by an act of faith."[6] Faith is "that act whereby . . . we give mental

[5]Denzinger, *op. cit.*, p. 508.

[6]George D. Smith (ed.), *The Teaching of the Catholic Church* (New York: The Macmillan Company, 1949), I, 11. Used by permission.

assent to a truth which he (God) has revealed." Smith adds that the motive for this assent "is not the intrinsic evidence of the statement itself, but the authority of God who makes it; in other words, I believe simply because God has said it."[7] This evidently means that in faith one accepts certain propositions as true not because he himself perceives their truthfulness, but *simply because another person tells him that they are true.* Smith's explication of faith clearly reveals the authoritarian character of the Catholic view of faith, which jeopardizes intellectual integrity.

The Catholic Encyclopedia similarly defines faith: "Objectively, it stands for the sum of truths revealed by God in Scripture and tradition, and which the Church . . . presents to us in a brief form in her creeds; subjectively, faith stands for the habit or virtue by which we assent to those truths."[8]

In such a doctrinaire theory of revelation, Christianity becomes intellectualistic without becoming rational. Faith becomes a kind of formal intellectualism which forfeits the demand for rational integrity and violates the truth of autonomy. The individual is no longer responsible for his beliefs.

In a similar vein, Karl Adam, a contemporary exponent of Romanism who holds forth at the University of Tübingen in Germany, contends that the Pope possesses a *plenitudo potestatis* "which comprises full doctrinal and disciplinary authority, the complete governance of the Church in the most comprehensive sense."[9] When the Pope speaks "as successor of St.

---

[7]*Ibid.*; see also Cardinal Newman's statement of acceptance of the Roman position, Newman, *op. cit.*, p. 215.

[8]*The Catholic Encyclopedia* (New York: The Gilmary Society, 1913), V, 753. Used by permission.

[9]Karl Adam, *The Spirit of Catholicism*, trans. Dom Justin McCann (London: Sheed and Ward, 1939), p. 109. Used by permission of The Macmillan Company.

Peter, then he speaks with a divine authority that demands the obedience of all the faithful. . .'"[10] Hence, says Adam, "the Church's preaching has an overwhelming power and an absolute validity.'"[11]

Adam freely admits the limited extent of papal infallibility. He bemoans the fact that even popes can be enslaved by worldly ideas and sinful ways, but he insists that they are nonetheless infallible in the pronouncement of doctrine in faith and morals.[12]

Adam does not explain *precisely how* the Pope can be infallible in one area of his thinking and behavior, while remaining fallible in other areas. Such a feat would seem to be a psychological impossibility. Because the thought of any individual is an interrelated whole, no part of it can be wholly unaffected by other parts.

When therefore the Pope proclaims the magical idea of transubstantiation to be a dogma, *how can one be sure* that this is infallible truth and not what it seems to the observing student of psychology and history to be, namely, a corruption of the Christian idea of grace by the Hellenistic notion of immortality and by medieval magic and superstition? There is obviously no intelligent way in which one can be sure that, *in the promulgation of the notion of transubstantiation and other dogmas,* the popes were not in reality "children of their age and slaves of its conceptions."

Nevertheless, Adam possesses the typically Catholic, emotional certainty which leads him to say that

> as the authorized preacher of the truth, the Church will never cease to give her authoritative witness to it *and to oblige all consciences to accept it.* . . . The Church does not supplicate or discuss terms with conscience; she makes a direct demand upon it, and requires that it surrender itself

[10]*Ibid.,* pp. 45-46.
[11]*Ibid.,* p. 231.
[12]*Ibid.,* pp. 255-257.

to the word of God *as proclaimed by her*. . . . When the Church speaks to conscience, *there can be no subjectivism or antinomianism, no doubt or scepticism*.[13]

The idea that in the reception of the doctrinal affirmations of the church, "there can be no subjectivism," no careful weighing and testing of propositions which are set forth as truth, no personal evaluation, is foreign to the mature conception of faith reflected in the New Testament. In the days of the New Testament, people accepted Christ and the gospel *because they listened to preaching with critical ears and hearts.*

The author of Acts, for example, commends the Beroean Jews above those of Thessalonica. The former, he says, "were more noble than those in Thessalonica, for they received the word with all eagerness, *examining the scriptures daily to see if these things were so. Many of them therefore believed.*"[14] To be sure, the early Jewish Christians were still wedded to their "Scriptures" (the Old Testament) as authority. But the experience of Christ gradually liberated the Christian conscience from this external authority, as the Christian principle of faith grew to maturity. This maturity found clearest expression in the thought of Paul and John. For both Paul and John there could be no thought of coercion or "obliging" of conscience, but rather a personal appeal. Unlike the Pope, the Apostles and Christ himself[15] refused to ride roughshod over the individual conscience. They would not violate the sanctity of personal freedom and intellectual integrity!

The representative quotations cited above suffice to render explicit and clear the objectivistic character of the Roman Catholic concept of revelation and its

---

[13] *Ibid.*, pp. 235-237. Italics mine. R.G.W.

[14] Acts 17:11-12.

[15] See, for example, the nonauthoritarian manner in which Jesus led the lawyer to perceive the truth, who inquired as to who his neighbor was, whom he was to love as himself. Luke 10:29 ff.

demonic quality, that is, its attributing to something relative and conditional an unconditional or absolute significance.

The Ambiguous Attempt of the Reformation to Transcend the Medieval Principle of Church Authority by Developing a View of Revelation as a Redemptive Dynamic

With admirable clarity, Martin Luther perceived the demonic character of the Catholic view of revelation. And he sought to rescue the church from it by directing the Christian conscience to the Word of God in the Bible. Luther was deeply aware of man's basic need for a religious absolute. Unlike the humanists, Luther did not use the principle of rational autonomy to destroy this external church authority and restore individual liberty. Instead, he contended against the idol of church authority *in the name of prophetic Christianity.*

One of the most moving examples of Luther's struggle against this idolatry was his reply at the Diet of Worms. The question had been raised as to the fact that Luther, in some of his writings, had denied the decisions of ecclesiastical councils. Would he now reaffirm this denial? Or would he recant? The Emperor demanded an unequivocal answer.[16] To this, Luther replied:

> Unless I am proved to be wrong by the testimony of Scripture or by evident reasoning, it is impossible for me to recant. I can trust neither the decisions of Popes nor councils, for it is clear that they have erred and that they have contradicted each other. My conscience is held captive by the Word of God, and it is neither safe nor honest to act contrary to conscience.

[16] "Ohne Hörner und Zähne", as the presiding Johann Eck expressed it.

I can do naught else, here I stand. God help me. Amen.[17]

Luther thus sought to liberate the Christian conscience from the clutches of the papacy by the power of prophetic Christianity. He raised his courageous protest against the absolutistic authority of the papacy, and the Reformation was born.

At the heart of this protest lies a principle which is basic in prophetic Christianity, the principle, namely, that we must not absolutize *the finite response* of man to the creative call of the infinite Word of God; the Word of God always transcends and judges the words of men.

The Reformation, *at this central point of prophetic religion,* however, was carried through ambiguously. For it was but a generation or two until the terrible blight of Protestant scholasticism set in, the phase of Protestantism which we associate with creedalism and denominationalism. Alexander Campbell correctly argued that "creeds and manuals, synods and councils, soon shackled the minds of men, and the spirit of reformation gradually forsook the Protestant church. . . ."[18]

However, the sixteenth-century reformers themselves did not aim to establish another external authority which would operate in the same manner as church authority, robbing the Christian conscience of its liberty. Luther's famous treatise "On the Liberty of the Christian Man" represents a vigorous blow against all external authoritarianism. The Christian conscience, Luther insisted, knows an inner certainty; its freedom means that it is not subject to any other authority than "the inner testimony of the Holy

[17]"Ich kann nicht anderst, hie stehe ich, Gott helff mir. Amen" (*D. Martin Luthers Werke, op. cit.,* VII, 838). Trans. R.G.W.

[18]Alexander Campbell, *The Christian System,* p. 3.

Spirit" which enables one to perceive the truth of the apostolic witness.[19]

It is a matter of common knowledge that Luther's distinction between the Word of God and the Bible enabled him to handle the Bible with considerable freedom. One cannot find in Luther's writings the doctrine that every single word of the Bible is inspired by the Holy Spirit. In the name of the gospel (justification by faith), Luther proceeded to measure and evaluate all biblical writings.[20]

Luther contended that Moses used many different sources for his writings. The Book of Revelation is really not apostolic; it is a Jewish book.[21] James argued erroneously that Abraham was justified by works of obedience, and that one can know a man's faith by its fruits.[22] This shows that James did not understand the doctrine of justification; hence Luther felt that the Book of James is an epistle of straw.

In one passage[23] Luther distinguished between the moment of prophetic inspiration and the secondary level of inspiration where the prophetic sayings are collected and written down in a book and included in the Bible. The Bible thus draws its life and support from prophetic inspiration, but, by implication, it cannot be said to be inspired in the same sense that the prophet is inspired.

Whether or not we find ourselves in agreement with Luther in his theology about the Bible, it is clear

[19]Cf. Edgar P. Dickie, *Revelation and Response* (New York: Charles Scribner's Sons, 1938), p. 127.

[20]Cf. Seeberg, *op. cit.*, p. 141; also Rupert Erich Davies, *The Problem of Authority in the Continental Reformers: A Study in Luther, Zwingli and Calvin* (London: The Epworth Press, 1946), p. 34.

[21]*D. Martin Luthers Tischreden* (Weimar: Hermann Böhlaus Nachfolger, 1912), I, 121, 364.

[22]*D. Martin Luthers Werke,* bearbeitet von O. Bremer, K. Drescher, R. Reichert (Weimar: Hermann Böhlaus Nachfolger, 1912), XLIII, 213-214.

[23]*D. Martin Luthers Tischreden* (Weimar: Hermann Böhlaus Nachfolger, 1913), II, sec. 1839, p. 234.

that Luther never intended to institute a paper-pope in the place of the Roman Pope. As Roland Bainton aptly puts it, "Luther treated Scripture with royal freedom but not at whim."[24]

The inclination to fashion out of the Scriptures an external authority was more prominent in the reformed theology of Zwingli and Calvin than it was in Luther. For Luther, the Bible was the Word of God because it contained the gospel of God's forgiving grace in Christ. For Zwingli, the Bible was the Word of God because it revealed the will of God. Zwingli believed that we learn what God would have us to do and to be from the Bible. Hence the Bible, in reformed theology, came to be regarded "as our only rule of faith and practice." In the Zwinglian view, the distinction between the Bible and the gospel almost disappeared. In reformed theology, the tendency thus easily developed to treat Scripture as equally authoritative in all of its parts, to regard the Law and the Gospel as identical in principle, and to hold Scripture itself to be the actual content of revelation.

Furthermore, there were impulses even in the thought of Luther which indicate that he had not thought through the problem of revelation with complete adequacy. When his opponents got him in a corner, he too could take refuge in biblical literalism. At the Marburg colloquy on the Lord's Supper in 1529, for example, Luther would march into the conference room, take a piece of chalk and write on the conference table the words, *hoc est corpus meum,* and say to Zwingli, "On these words of Scripture I take my stand; where do you stand?"

Seventeenth-Century Protestantism Engulfed by the Scholastic Distortion of Revelation

In the main, however, Luther did steer clear of

[24]Bainton, *op. cit.,* p. 45.

bibliolatry. But the same cannot be said of all the children of the Reformation. The liberation of the Christian conscience by the sixteenth-century reformers was not successfully carried through. For in the latter part of the sixteenth and in the seventeenth centuries, other external authorities and absolutes were set up in the house of Protestantism itself, namely, the creedal interpretations of Scripture. These became the authoritative basis of membership and unity in the different national Protestant groupings. Thus the cause of Protestant Christianity became nationalistically and, eventually, denominationally differentiated.

The internal theological disputes of the followers of Luther in Germany resulted finally in the "Formula of Concord" in 1580. This creedal statement represented an irenic attempt to settle the seemingly interminable debates which threatened the Lutheran reform with disintegration. It received the approbation of fifty-one German princes, thirty-five cities, and some nine thousand pastors. Many, of course, refused to sign. But it did represent a goodly majority of Lutheran Germany.

The "Canons of the Synod of Dort" were drawn up by the extreme Calvinists of Holland in 1609, as an attempt to arrest the development of Arminianism in the reformed tradition. Its five articles represent direct replies to the five basic articles of the Arminians' *Remonstrance*. Needless to say, the "Canons of the Synod of Dort" did not stop the growth of Arminianism. It did help to divide and separate the cause of reformed Christianity.

Similarly, the adoption of the "Thirty-Nine Articles of the Church of England" in 1563 did not unify the Christian cause in Great Britain. It was an official statement of the "middle way" of Anglicanism. It proved troublesome to the Catholics, for it was more Protestant than the English Book of Common Prayer, the universal use of which had been required by Parliament's "Act of Uniformity," January 21, 1549. Yet it was equally unacceptable to the Puritans and other dissenters. The net result for England was that it enabled the majority (Anglicans) to label all dissenters as "sectarian nonconformists," thereby extending and deepening rather than healing the cleavages in the church.[25]

The wilderness of sectarian antagonism and division which resulted from the creedal crystallization of Protestantism was painfully eloquent proof that the creative development of the Protestant cause itself was seriously arrested by a scholastic distortion of the concept of revelation.[26] The principle of external authority was now eloquently exemplified in Protestantism itself. Church dogmas, in the form of Protestant creeds, took on the quality of the absolute. The evil of such external authority is evident in that creedalism has always proved itself to be *essentially divisive.* True revelation, however, is *unitive* in its working. The author of the Ephesian epistle says the purpose of the revelation in Christ is "to unite all things in him."[27] Historically, it is plain that the authoritative use of creeds has functioned to exclude and divide; while Christ came to include and to unite.

Nevertheless, the divisive authoritarianism of Protestant creedalism lives on, to this very day. Liberalism has diminished its force, but it has not yet wholly destroyed it. How long will it take denominationally minded Christians to see, humbly and clearly, the tragic divisiveness of creedalism? How long, O

[25]The creeds of Protestantism multiplied into a great number. We have mentioned specifically here only a few of the more significant ones.

[26]Cf. B. A. Abbott, *The Disciples, An Interpretation* (St. Louis: The Bethany Press, Christian Board of Publication, 1924), p. 9.

[27]Ephesians 1:10.

Lord, until thy church manfully raises itself out of the quagmire of sectarianism and sees no creed but Christ?

The Precarious Status of the Idea of Revelation in the Rationalistic Christianity of the Enlightenment

As scholastic Protestantism inclined to find its life more and more in such externals as doctrinal and creedal formulae, the inner life of the Spirit tended to depart. By the middle of the seventeenth century one could hear the rattling of the dry bones of Protestant orthodoxy. And it must be frankly admitted that it was not the theologically ineffective attempt of seventeenth-century Pietism within Christianity itself which rescued the human spirit from this deadening externalism. On the contrary, it was one of the most powerful expressions of rational autonomy in history; it was the Enlightenment of the seventeenth and eighteenth centuries, which brought forth a renaissance of philosophy.

Philosophy was now no longer content to serve as the handmaiden of theology. It wrenched itself free and asserted its independence, claiming an ability to stand on its own two feet. The whole of Western culture was shortly overawed by this resurrection of the spirit and outlook of the ancient Greeks. Once again, philosophy reigned supreme.

Ere long Christian thought began to feel the pressure and to be significantly affected by the attractive lures of rationalism. John Tillotson, Archbishop of Canterbury (d.1694), set the fashion for nearly all Christian thought, for a number of generations, by popularizing the view that revelation is simply a *supplement to* natural reason, and that it is nevertheless *to be validated and verified* by natural reason.

Tillotson's emphasis on the rational evidences of miracle and prophecy, and his insistence on the harmony between Christianity and natural reason, helped materially to create a theological outlook which appealed to cool, intellectual common sense, while the more mystical idea of an "inner light" or the divine presence in the soul was viewed, with suspicion, as ill-founded superstition.[28]

Tillotson's younger contemporary, John Locke, also moved a long way in the direction of rationalism. Locke, too, cherished a negative attitude toward the element of mystery in religion. He held a kind of contempt for people who, for want of sound thinking, allowed themselves to be dominated by religious "enthusiasms." With a touch of humor, Locke admired the person who holds that his belief is true because it is a revelation from God; but, Locke wrote, it is amusing that the same person will add that he knows it to be a revelation "by the light it brings with it which shines in the mind," that is, because he believes it to be true. Such a person lacks rational grounds for his beliefs; he therefore reasons in a circle: he believes it to be true because it is a revelation, and he believes it to be a revelation because he regards it as true. Wishful thinking *par excellence,* said Locke.[29]

Locke's rationalism and liberalism made him theologically offensive to the orthodoxy of his day. He affirmed the sovereign right of reason to determine the truth of revelation. He did admit that the truths of revelation are in a sense "above reason," and that such truths, when revealed, are the proper matter of faith.[30] Yet he hastened to add that "faith can never convince us of any thing that contradicts our knowledge."[31] What God reveals is of course true; and such

[28]See John Locke, *Essay on Human Understanding* (London: George Bell and Sons, 1903), Book IV, Ch. 19. Sec. 11. Used by permission.

[29]*Ibid.,* sec. 11.

[30]*Locke Selections,* ed. Sterling P. Lamprecht, The Modern Student Library Philosophy Series (New York: Charles Scribner's Sons, 1928), p. 315. Used by permission.

[31]*Ibid.*

revelation is the proper object of faith. "But," Locke argued, "whether it be a divine revelation or no, reason must judge."[32] It belongs to reason, he wrote, "to judge of the truth of its being a revelation, and of the signification of the words wherein it is delivered."[33] "Indeed, if any thing shall be thought revelation which is contrary to the plain principles of reason and the evident knowledge the mind has of its own clear and distinct ideas, there reason must be hearkened to. . . ."[34] One must not blindly accept a teaching merely because it lays claim to being revealed. In intellectual integrity, one is "bound to consider and judge of it as a matter of reason, and not swallow it, without examination, as a matter of faith."[35] Locke believed that "reason must be our last judge and guide in everything."[36]

Locke's Irish disciple, John Toland, in his book, *Christianity Not Mysterious,* published in 1696, defined the category "above reason" in an equally narrow way. Toland argued that when it is urged that revelation provides us with truths which are above reason, this does not mean truths which are suprarational in any mysterious sense, but simply rational truths which we should not otherwise have known, or events which we ourselves have not been able to observe, and which therefore can be known only on the testimony of others. Toland went a long way toward rationalizing all Christian truth.

This rationalistic interpretation effected a drastic reduction of traditional Christianity to nothing but its inner moral values. Locke, Toland, Arthur Bury, and others of their period felt that the reason for much of the skepticism of the day was a failure to recognize that the essentials of the faith are few. In

[32]*Ibid.,* p. 316.
[33]*Ibid.*
[34]*Ibid.*
[35]*Ibid.*
[36]*Ibid.,* p. 317.

his book, *The Naked Gospel,* Bury argued that nothing is to be regarded as necessary unless it is specifically set forth in the Bible as a condition of salvation.

Matthew Tindal's book, *Christianity as Old as the Creation* (1730), drew still more severe restrictions upon revelation. Tindal argued that true religion consists in a consistent purpose to do whatever good we can, and that we become acceptable to God in this way, and thus fulfill our destiny under God. Tindal boldly rejected as superstition everything in traditional Christianity which is not of a moral nature. He was persuaded that God demands nothing more of man than moral virtue; and he stoutly repudiated the notion that salvation is dependent on the performance of positive duties and ordinances, which in themselves are morally neutral.

The movement of deism represents this rationalistic tendency carried to its logical conclusion. The deists simply went further and turned reason's criticism on the so-called rational evidences themselves, namely, miracle and prophecy. Men like William Whiston, Anthony Collins, and David Hume tore these arguments into shreds. Thomas Woolsten (d. 1733) held that the narratives of the New Testament miracles are absurd and incredible as records of facts, and he supposed that they were originally intended to be understood mystically. Hume argued that a miracle is "a violation of the laws of nature," and that inasmuch as a "firm and unalterable experience" has established these laws, the proof against miracle is as entire as any argument can be.[37]

[37]"Essay on Miracles" in *An Inquiry Concerning Human Understanding* (Chicago: The Open Court Publishing Company, 1927), pp. 114-138. Hume's argument is based on an erroneous definition of miracle. A miracle is not, as Hume put it, "a violation of the laws of nature"; it is rather a violation of what we know about the laws of nature, and this latter, according to Hume's own epistemology, remains always relative. Scientific knowledge can never be absolute.

Thus it was that the pressure of the autonomous reason of the Enlightenment gave birth to the plea for a true, rational Christianity, as opposed to a false, irrational Christianity. Christian rationalism attempted to trim away all the suprarational aspects of the faith—revelation, miracle, prophecy—and to boil it all down to the simple, rational residuum of natural religion.

Several apologists of great stature rose up in reaction to this rationalistic Christianity. Men like Joseph Butler, Henry Dodwell, and William Paley made valiant endeavors to combat the tendency toward an all-out rationalism. But they were rather hard put to defend their cause. Even Butler, the greatest of them, admitted, in the final analysis, that revealed religion's ultimate validation lay in the fact that it rendered natural religion more effective.

In a large way thus Christianity succumbed to the attractive lures of the rational autonomy of Renaissance culture. And it seemed extremely difficult to circumvent this position of rationalism without returning to the old dogmatism of Protestant orthodoxy, reaction against which, in the first place, gave rise to rationalism. *Reason* now became the sole authority in religion, and furthermore, reason in its formalistic character—cold, logical Aristotelian reason. Human discovery took the place of divine revelation; so that not only was faith in Christ as the final revelation of God abandoned, but with it also the idea of God's revelatory activity in history, in any sense. Such exclusive emphasis on divine transcendence and such utter lack of appreciation of the immanental working of God in history, resulted in a strange kind of religion, indeed. Is it any wonder that the result of this process was secularism? Paradoxical though it may sound, the theism of deism fostered atheism, or at any rate, secularism.

Eventually, however, philosophical reason met its Waterloo when it occurred to some of the philosophers of the Enlightenment to turn the critical spotlight of reason upon reason itself. This, too, became a fad, which eventuated in the belief that "to make light of philosophy is to be a true philosopher." The result was that a fearful tidal wave of radical skepticism swept across Western culture, a skepticism of which the figure of David Hume is the classic example.

Rationalism Transcended But Not Subjectivism, in the Theological Renaissance Inaugurated by Schleiermacher in Germany

A theological renaissance finally came, but from Germany, not from England. Friedrich Schleiermacher was a boy of eight years when David Hume died in 1776. Schleiermacher passed through the rationalism of the Enlightenment. He studied at the University of Halle from 1787-90, where he came under the influence of the views of Leibnitz, Wolff, Semler, Plato, Spinoza, and Immanuel Kant. When he graduated, he was a confirmed rationalist.

The spirit of romanticism, however, sprang up right in the midst of this classicism; and romanticism soon began to supplant the spirit of the Enlightenment, especially in Germany. Schleiermacher became hospital chaplain in Berlin in 1796. There he became a member of the most vigorous romantic coterie in Europe, which included such figures as Tieck, Novalis, and Frederick Schlegel. Schleiermacher drank deeply at the fountainhead of this movement. Eventually he reinterpreted Christianity in the light of metaphysical principles drawn from the philosophy of romanticism. A similar reinterpretation of the Christian faith was developed by Samuel Taylor Coleridge in England, and by Horace Bushnell in America.

Schleiermacher passed beyond the rationalism of the Enlightenment when the spirit of romanticism made him aware of the dimension of depth in reason.[38] He became aware of what Blaise Pascal called "reasons of the heart which reason cannot comprehend." And it must be conceded that this new insight of Schleiermacher is correct. Reason, viewed in its wholeness, *does* include emotional as well as formal elements. The philosophers of the eighteenth century were operating with too narrow a view of reason; and we, their children, have only recently been able to liberate ourselves from this one-sided reason, by learning not to be ashamed of our emotions. The structural element of reason is preponderant, for example, in its cognitive and legal functions; but the emotional element is predominant in its aesthetic and communal functions.[39]

Romanticism made Schleiermacher aware of this deeper dimension of reason. He thus transcended rationalism by stressing feeling, or aesthetic awareness as the mode of an immediate apprehension of God, in particular "the feeling of absolute dependence."[40]

Schleiermacher gave himself so resolutely to the task of establishing an empirical method in theology, however, that his system does not wholly escape the dangers of subjectivism. The datum for theology, according to him, is the corporate Christian religious self-consciousness,[41] the vital core of which he believed to be the feeling of absolute dependence upon God.

It is true, of course, that one cannot wholly avoid talking about God if he concerns himself with the feeling of absolute dependence. For somewhere along the

[38]See Friedrich Schleiermacher, *On Religion*, trans. John Oman (London: Kegan Paul, Trench, Trübner and Company, Ltd., 1893).

[39]Cf. Tillich, *Systematic Theology*, I, 89, ff.

[40]See Friedrich Schleiermacher, *The Christian Faith*, trans. H. R. Mackintosh & J. S. Stewart (Edinburgh: T & T Clark, 1928), pp. 12 ff.

[41]*Ibid.*, pp. 76 ff.

line he must consider *the objective referent* involved in such a feeling, namely, *that upon which* one is aware of being absolutely dependent. Nevertheless, making this subjective element of feeling central, rather than *the total religious relation* with God (described in the New Testament as faith), gave Schleiermacher's theology a subjectivistic one-sidedness which causes Emil Brunner, for example, to shout: Pure subjectivism; pure psychologism![42] It is not quite so "pure" as Brunner makes it out to be. Yet there is much truth in Brunner's criticism.

Schleiermacher was not wholly unaware of the fact that the "feeling of absolute dependence" makes a claim on reality, that it leads the subject to something outside himself, that it has an arrow, a reference to objective reality. In his correspondence with Lücke (1820) Schleiermacher wrote: "As I understand it, the religious feeling does not stem from concepts, but rather is *the original expression of a direct existential relationship.*"[43]

Nevertheless, it remains true that Schleiermacher's empirical method did lead him to make the subjective aspect of this religious feeling the major object of theological concern, and thereby he directed Christian thought toward itself rather than toward God.[44]

Further, in Schleiermacher and in liberal Protestantism, of which he is rightly regarded to be the

[42] See Emil Brunner, *Die Mystik Und Das Wort* (Tübingen: J. C. B. Mohr, 1924), p. 174.

[43] Friedrich Schleiermacher, *Sämmtlicke Werke,* Erste Abteilung zur Theologie, Zweiter Band (Berlin: G. Reimer, 1836), p. 586. Trans. and italics R.G.W. In view of this statement, Richard Brandt's criticism that Schleiermacher was not critically aware that the feeling of dependence is the kind of feeling which makes a claim on the world, is somewhat of an exaggeration. See Richard B. Brandt, *The Philosophy of Schleiermacher* (New York: Harper and Brothers, 1941), pp. 292-293.

[44] See H. Richard Niebuhr's balanced judgment of Schleiermacher at this point, *The Meaning of Revelation* (New York: The Macmillan Company, 1941), p. 27.

founder, there was a tendency to absorb revelation in "religious experience" in general. The quality of uniqueness and finality which in New Testament Christianity had been attached to the revelation in Christ came near to being wholly lost sight of.

So, although Schleiermacher escaped the limitations of the rationalism of the Enlightenment, insofar as he recovered the dimension of depth in reason and saw its significance for theology, he did not fully escape the dangers of subjectivism in his theological method. He was less subjectivistic than many of his theological descendants who, says Niebuhr, "used the sin of the father as an occasion for committing sins of their own."[45] For many liberal Protestants who adopted Schleiermacher's method, *religion* became the creative source and sustainer of life. Men came to place their trust and hope in "religion." To it they looked for guidance and spiritual strength, for vision and moral courage. They worshiped religion as the Savior of mankind. The concept of God was removed to the periphera of their thinking. Whether or not there is a God, seemed to be a relatively insignificant question. Perhaps, indeed, all that we need is a socially inspiring idea of God, a poetic personification of our highest social ideals and aspirations.

In some areas of liberal Protestantism, subjectivism won an almost complete victory. The concept of revelation almost wholly disappeared. And we came out with a frank humanism, which had no use for any sort of absolute, but believed absolutely in the glory of human relativism.

Autonomy Avoided but the Doctrinaire View of Revelation Not Wholly Overcome by the Campbellian Movement in America

While the theological renaissance in Germany in-

[45] *Ibid.*, p. 28.

augurated by Schleiermacher tended to weaken the concept of revelation by a distorted emphasis on subjectivism, the indigenous movement in American Christianity, known as the Campbellian movement, was at the same time developing a point of view which endangered the concept of revelation because it failed to deliver itself completely from the traditional objectivistic view of revelation. It is to be said to the credit of this novel nineteenth-century Restoration movement, as it is often called, that although its leaders were strongly affected by the latitudinarianism and liberalism of the day, as Frederick West has ably argued,[46] this inclination toward rational autonomy did not so blind them to the weaknesses and conflicts of reason that they yielded their faith in revelation. They remained aware of the fact that when the human heart is hungry for spiritual bread, it needs something more than the husks of historical relativism. They clung firmly to their faith in the revelation of God in Christ the Lord, mediated through Scripture.

Alexander Campbell, for example, in his debate with Robert Owen, argued that his opponent's error was that of Hume, namely, the belief that "all testimony is to be judged by our *personal experience.*"[47] Campbell contended that if we admit this principle, "we shall be reduced in the measure of our information even below the savage himself."[48] And if we concede Hume's principle, said Campbell, "how comes it that Mr. Owen talks with so much certainty about what will come to pass hereafter! . . . Here the infidel's

[46]West contends, correctly, that Alexander Campbell's "reliance upon reason in appealing to the people and uprooting the authority of theology and the traditional church is much like the cry of reason which the opponents of revealed religion generally make. It is no accident that he was accused of leading his movement into 'Rationalism!'" (Robert Frederick West, *Alexander Campbell and Natural Religion* [New Haven: Yale University Press, 1948], p. 52). Used by permission.

[47]Alexander Campbell, *The Evidences of Christianity, A Debate Between Robert Owen and Alexander Campbell* (St. Louis: Christian Publishing Company, 1906), p. 254.

[48]*Ibid.*

candle goes out, and except he obtains some oil from the lamp of revelation, he must continue in perpetual darkness."[49]

Again, arguing for the validity of Christianity as a religion of revelation, Campbell exclaimed, "Nothing astonishes me more than the impotency of philosophy in all matters and things pertaining to a spiritual system."[50]

Time has proved the wisdom of the evangelical definiteness of this indigenous movement in American Christianity, by which it placed a limitation on rational autonomy. For most of Protestantism has abandoned the autonomy of the liberalism of the Enlightenment and is now questing vigorously for an adequate concept of revelation.

It must be admitted, however, that the original leaders of the Campbellian movement, and many of their followers, were not able wholly to free themselves from the doctrinaire tendency in the reformed tradition, the tradition in which the four great leaders—Barton Stone, Thomas and Alexander Campbell, and Walter Scott—received their primary theological training. This doctrinaire tendency inclined them also to absolutize the letter of Scripture as an external authority and to regard the Bible, in its literal aspect, as the actual content of the revelation of the gospel.

To be sure, there is a vital truth embodied in the resolve of reformed Protestantism to regard the Bible as "the doctrine of heaven,"[51] or as "the Word of God,"[52] or as the book which dispenses "Divine Wisdom,"[53] or as the true system of doctrine,[54] to cite a few descriptions of John Calvin. In a similar vein,

[49]*Ibid.*, p. 256.

[50]*Ibid.*, p. 90.

[51]John Calvin, *Institutes of the Christian Religion,* trans. John Allen, 7th ed. (Philadelphia: Presbyterian Board of Christian Education, 1936), I, 82.

[52]*Ibid.*, pp. 104, 106.

[53]*Ibid.*, p. 93.

[54]*Ibid.*, p. 106.

Thomas Campbell viewed the Bible as a "Divine Standard,"[55] or "Original Standard,"[56] or "the original pattern laid down in the New Testament,"[57] or "a perfect constitution for the worship, discipline and government of the church.[58] There is a basic truth in these judgments about the Bible, for Christianity does center in a revelation of God which has a locus in history. It is anchored to the event of the Incarnation. The original biblical witness to this supreme event does therefore possess a unique normativeness.

Yet the truth of this emphasis on the Bible in reformed Protestantism is easily distorted into an idolatrous biblicism. Revelation through words is easily confused with revealed words. The truth of the gospel, which is apprehended through divine revelation, is quickly transformed and distorted into "divinely revealed truths."[59]

The influence of reformed Protestantism upon Alexander Campbell, combined with that of the rationalism of the Enlightenment, was so powerful that he was unable to free himself from the traditional doctrinaire conception of revelation. He believed that "the term revelation, in its strict acceptation among intelligent Christians, means nothing more or less than *a Divine communication concerning spiritual and eternal things,* a knowledge of which man could never have attained by the exercise of his reason upon material and sensible objects. . . ."[60] That this is essentially the traditional, Roman Catholic conception of revelation is evident when one compares Campbell's statement with Catholic theology, which holds that "Revelation may be defined as *the communication of some truth by God* to a rational creature through

[55]Thomas Campbell, *op. cit.,* pp. 3, 5.

[56]*Ibid.,* p. 4.

[57]*Ibid.,* p. 10; cf. p. 35.

[58]*Ibid.,* p. 16.

[59]*Ibid.,* p. 14.

[60]Alexander Campbell, *The Evidences of Christianity,* p. 146. Italics mine. R.G.W.

means which are beyond the ordinary course of nature."[61]

There are deeply embedded in the original spirit of Calvin's theology and in the original genius of the Campbellian movement clues to enable those in the reformed tradition to transcend and overcome such biblicism, and to use the biblical message as it was originally intended.

Calvin's biblicism was qualified by his doctrine of the Holy Spirit. This qualification is the aspect which arrested the development of doctrinaire biblicism in Calvin's thought. The letter of Scripture, Calvin argued, is dead and of no redemptive value until "it be efficaciously impressed on our hearts by the Spirit. . . ."[62] Scripture can therefore serve to impart a saving knowledge of God only "when the certainty of it shall be founded on the internal persuasion of the Holy Spirit."[63]

The clue in the Campbellian movement to overcoming doctrinaire biblicism was aptly expressed in a watchword which was the favorite of Robert Richardson—the watchword, "We have no creed but Christ." Richardson argued that the Christian faith is not primarily doctrinal, but personal. The truth which Christians cherish is not abstract truth. If God is revealed to us in Christ as the truth, "it is that we may so receive him into the soul, and banish the false idols of sensuality and corruption."[64] The Christian faith is personal; it centers in a personal relation to, and love for, Christ.

In a similar vein, E. V. Zollars argued that to regard belief of doctrines as the content of faith is to fail to recognize the nature of Christ's kingdom. Such

[61]*The Catholic Encyclopedia* (New York: The Gilmary Society, 1913), XIII, 1. Used by permission. Italics mine. R.G.W.

[62]Calvin, *op. cit.*, pp. 107-108.

[63]*Ibid.*, p. 104.

[64]R. Richardson, *Communings in the Sanctuary* (St. Louis: Christian Publishing Co., 1888), p. 102.

doctrinaire faith, he wrote, loses sight of the fact that "Christian faith is trust in a living, divine person, and not beliefs of dogmas, however true they may be."[65]

It is a healthy sign of the prophetic power of the Campbellian movement that many of its leaders, past and present, have grown critically aware of the theological ambiguity of the initial impetus of the movement for the "restoration of the New Testament order," out of which ambiguity has grown a legalistic distortion of the object of the Christian faith. In different ways, these leaders have sought, and are successfully seeking, to purify their movement of this legalistic distortion.

Winfred E. Garrison, for example, contends that in our modern theological climate the basic idea of restoration requires a "reinterpretation to give it continued validity."[66] Stephen J. England and Frederick West repudiate the pattern idea of biblical authority.[67] Edward Scribner Ames similarly rejects the blueprint conception of the Bible and would have all rally round the plea of "loyalty to Christ," as God leads each one to understand this loyalty.[68] Charles Clayton Morrison argues that the whole idea of restorationism is an "illusion," and that it has unduly impeded the growth toward greater unity.[69]

This and similar self-criticism is pointing in a direction which, if followed critically with theological thoroughness, may enable the Campbellian movement finally to deliver itself from the scholastic authori-

[65]E. V. Zollars, *The King of Kings* (Cincinnati: The Standard Publishing Company, 1911), pp. 25-26.

[66]Winfred Ernest Garrison, *An American Religious Movement* (St. Louis: Christian Board of Publication, 1945), p. 149; cf. also p. 155. Used by permission.

[67]Stephen J. England, *The Apostolic Church* (Eugene: Northwest Christian College, 1946), p. 81; West, *op. cit.*, pp. 219-220.

[68]Edward Scribner Ames, *The Disciples of Christ* (Chicago: printed privately, 1943-44), pp. 13-15.

[69]Charles Clayton Morrison, *The Unfinished Reformation* (New York: Harper and Brothers, 1953), p. 155.

tarianism into which it, together with the rest of Protestantism, fell. It can lead in the direction of a concept of revelation which avoids the trap of authoritarianism and which also escapes that rationalistic ordering of human existence which takes the heart out of prophetic religion.

In the contemporary scene, Karl Barth has also attempted to overcome the fallacy of autonomy by spearheading a movement which has developed an interpretation of the place of the Bible in revelation that enables Barth and his followers to make the claim that they stand outside orthodoxy, outside fundamentalism, and beyond modernism. Few of us, however, can tolerate the radicalism of Barth's idea of God as "wholly other." Barth conceives of God as so utterly transcendent that instead of developing a theology which will resolve the conflicts of reason, Barthian theology sounds more like a new brand of heteronomy in disguise; that is, it sounds like a revelation that *shatters* the rational orders of human existence, failing to do justice to the truth of autonomy.

The theological pendulum has thus swung back and forth between rationalistic autonomy and irrationalistic heteronomy. There is obviously truth in both extremes. Unless man is indeed the ultimate center of the spiritual world, a view utterly repulsive to religion, there is truth in heteronomy (being under the rule of the other). And if intellectual integrity is a virtue, there is obviously truth also in the plea of autonomy. The quest for revelation is the quest for a God-centered ordering of human existence which preserves the truth of each, while yet escaping the errors of both.

Dominant Idolatrous Forms to Be Avoided

As we give ourselves to the urgent task of theological reconstruction on the problem of authority, seeking to overcome the errors of the autonomous character of liberal Protestantism and also the equally grave mistakes of the doctrinaire distortion of Protestant orthodoxy, we will do well to keep clearly in mind the predominant idolatrous forms which have proved to be destructive and divisive throughout Christian history. The modern Western era of rational autonomy seems definitely to have exhausted itself. The main current of contemporary Christian thought centers in a strong reaction to rationalistic Christianity. It would seem, therefore, that the real dangers which confront us in our modern period of theological reconstruction are various enticing forms of idolatry.

Christianity has repeatedly fallen into the trap of idolatry by attempting to *identify* the revelation, or the supreme authority in the Christian religion, with a particular historical order of its worship at the altar, or with a particular form of its moral code of behavior, or with a particular body of doctrinal beliefs. The essential and final reality of Christianity has been regarded as the ritual of the altar, or a set of ethical principles, or a theology.

Emil Brunner calls this idolatrous tendency "objectivism," which he defines[70] as a tendency of the human spirit to hold in its own power and to manipulate at will something which in its ultimate nature cannot possibly come under human control. The grace or truth of God cannot be thus placed at man's disposal, because of the absolute dependence of man the creature upon God the Creator.

The fundamental error here is the failure to distinguish between the *medium* and the *content* of revelation. Christians have tended repeatedly to regard the medium of revelation and its excellencies as the actual content itself. Any event may be the medium of

[70]Emil Brunner, *The Divine-Human Encounter,* trans. Amandus W. Loos (Philadelphia: The Westminster Press, 1943), p. 22.

revelation; but the medium is not to be equated with the revelation. It is truly a historical medium only when it directs our vision toward, and leads us to, an experience of that suprahistorical reality which is thus manifesting itself. The finite medium serves to mediate a relation with the Infinite.

It should be humbly and frankly admitted that the major weakness of orthodox Protestantism was a pervasive tendency to equate revelation with doctrine or creed. This tendency represents a vestigial remnant of the medieval, doctrinaire view of revelation. It is undeniable also that one of the weaknesses of liberal Protestantism was its attempt to reduce Christianity to the ethical teachings of Jesus. The entire Christian religion was watered down to the simple humanism of Jesus' moral teachings and example. If orthodox Protestantism tended to distort the inner creative Spirit into a *doctrinal* absolutism, liberal Protestantism tended toward an absolutistic view of the *ethics* of Jesus. It is equally clear also that the major weakness of Roman Catholicism has been, and still is, the identification of Christianity with the *institutional church.* This type of weakness is especially manifest in the Catholic dogma which lays claim to the infallibility of the Pope, in the elaborate system of penance, together with the entire sacramental cultus of the hierarchical church. Catholicism represents a form of Christianity which desires *to hold in its own power* that reality in which lies its security and its life.

The spiritually sensitive Christian mind, however, is aware that the final authority in the Christian religion, that reality which is our "ultimate concern," to borrow Tillich's phrase, lies at a deeper level than the external forms of worship or the ethical code or the doctrinal beliefs, important though all these are. All of these—the altar, the ethic, and the doctrine

—are but outward forms of expression and manifestation. And precisely because they are finite, they succeed in laying hold of the ultimate truth of Christianity only gradually and in part. And when they lose their vital connection with the inner creative Spirit (as has often occurred), Christianity becomes distorted and falls easy prey to the curse of external authoritarianism and objectivism.

When the forms of worship become thus crystallized, the result is a religious exhibitionism, the appeal of which is reduced to the sensuous side of human nature. Christianity becomes an entertaining, sensuously emotional, and even glamorous, exhibition. This is why thousands have rightly become disgusted with the church. They are unable to find the Eternal One in the Mumbo Jumbo of priesthood and ceremony.

When the moral code assumes the central and final position and becomes inflexibly hardened, Christianity is transformed into another kind of Judaism; it becomes religious legalism, with all its inadequacies. The *religious* dimension fades, and Christianity is reduced to a legal, outward morality. The spotlight is turned once again on the external act rather than the inner attitude of the heart, which Jesus brought into focus.

When the doctrines or religious beliefs are made the final authority, the result is an intellectually sterile and often spiritually odious dogmatism. This dogmatism loses the blessed vision which humbles us in an awareness that the God who manifests himself in revelation is infinitely greater than our finite ideas about him. When this vision fades from our eyes, creative and constructive thought lapses into creedalistic thought, and Christianity loses its dynamic spiritual heart. Again and again Christian history has repeated the tragedy of this dogmatic hardening of the revelatory experience.

The religion of the altar, therefore, dramatized God's demand that men accept his righteousness and live by it, and tended to lose sight of the Infinite One behind the finite scenes of the drama. The religion of the code book reduced the divine imperative to legalistic statutes, and was inclined to allow the vision of grace to fade. The religion of the creed indoctrinated the divine reality, and succumbed to the temptation to identify these doctrines with the divine reality itself.[71]

None of these distorted forms of Christianity, however, was able to find the way, as God intends it, which is a way of Spirit that leads to life abundant, to a realization of the ultimate meaning of the world for our day and generation.

Hence the sensitive soul looks through and beyond the altar, the ethic and the doctrine of Christianity, in an effort to grasp and understand the *abiding reality,* the *actual content* of revelation. We seek to know the nature of "life abundant," that eternal life which Jesus promised to the community of his followers.

This does not mean that Christianity should not have its altar, its ethic, and its theology or doctrine. It means simply that none of these *in themselves* constitute the ultimate truth or final revelation of Christianity. No one of these is the revelation. They are simply means of apprehending and appropriating the divine revelation and media through which the revelation becomes manifest. But in themselves alone, they are not the revelation. If we would truly know the nature of revelation, we must search more deeply into the mystery of the Incarnation.

---

[71]Cf. John Wick Bowman, *The Religion of Maturity* (New York: Abingdon-Cokesbury Press, 1948), pp. 261 ff.

CHAPTER FOUR

Revelation as Dynamic Confrontation with the Ultimate

We concluded our survey of the problematical character of the idea of revelation in historical Protestant thought by making three negative generalizations about the content of revelation. There are three things, we said, which the essential content of revelation is not. It is not the church, as an institution; it is not a set of ethical principles; and it is not a set of doctrines about it. What then, positively, is revelation?

This is one of the most urgent and pressing questions confronting the mind of the church in our day. In this chapter, we wish to suggest some basic definitive lines, along which contemporary Christian thought is proceeding in a fruitful way, as it faces the task of theological reconstruction on this problem.

An Event, a Happening, an Occurrence

It is an interesting and somewhat strange theological contradiction that the biblicistic idea of revelation which orthodox Protestantism developed is, in reality, quite unbiblical. The writers of the Bible did not hold a biblicistic concept of revelation. It should prove fruitful, therefore, to begin with, if we clarify the basic aspects of the biblical concept of revelation.

Take the thought of the great Old Testament prophets. Isaiah, for example, understood God primarily as an active participant in the processes of life; and he believed that *God makes himself known in this way.* The God of the prophets was not the static Greek *Logos.* He was dynamic, holy Person. And Isaiah believed that his people were under the condemnation of sin because they gave no attention to *what the Lord does.* As a result, they had no adequate saving knowledge of him or of *what he says in his activity.* Isaiah wrote:

> They have lyre and harp,
> timbrel and fruit and wine at their feasts;
> but *they do not regard the deeds of the* LORD,
> *or see the work of his hands.*
>
> . . . my people go into exile for want of knowledge.[1]

Similarly, Amos contended that *in the various calamities which had befallen Israel God was speaking to them* his word of chastening judgment, and because they had not listened, because they still had not returned to their God, they were to be visited with a terrible destruction.[2] Unrepentant people, they had refused to hear what God was saying to them, in his activity. They had eyes, but did not see; ears but did not hear; hearts which were so insensitive that they failed to understand the word of Jahweh.[3]

The God of the prophets therefore is not a sphinx-like "onlooker." He is active in life. The prophets saw the hand of God in the actions of the nations about them. They not only rehearsed "the mighty acts of the Lord"[4] in his deliverance of Israel from Egypt; they saw his mighty acts of judgment in the war chariots of the Assyrians[5]; they saw in Cyrus,

---

[1]Isaiah 5:12-13; cf. Hosea 4:6; 11:1-3.
[2]Amos 4:6-12.
[3]Cf. Matthew 13:15.
[4]Psalm 106:2.
[5]Amos 6:14.

the Persian war lord, one "anointed" by God[6] to execute his chastening judgments upon the covenant people.

The God of these prophets entered into ordinary daily life as a dynamic determinant. In every crisis he was seeking to make known his will to his people. Historical events were divine words; they possessed revelatory significance. Through them, Jahweh was confronting his people, demanding response, demanding decision. Through historical events, Jahweh was speaking to them his word of judgment and of hope. And the prophets knew from personal experience that such a divine confrontation was a soul-shaking experience.[7]

This *event* of the word of God may be an intensely personal, individual occurrence. Isaiah wrote, for example, "the LORD spoke to me *with his strong hand upon me,* and warned me not to walk in the way of this people."[8] Such an event is an existential happening, for in it Isaiah experienced "the strong hand of the Lord upon him." It was an event which had ecstatic elements in it, if we define ecstasy not merely as psychological enthusiasm, but according to the root meaning of the word, as "standing outside one's self."[9] The prophet found himself in a state of mind which was extraordinary, for in this revelatory event his mind transcended its ordinary situation and condition, and through this event of God's Word, something was disclosed to Isaiah about the relation between the ultimate mystery of being and ourselves.

Part of the total revelatory event is the word, which is to be viewed as one of the media of the

[6]Isaiah 45:1.

[7]Cf. Frederick Schumaker's discerning analysis in *Journal of Bible and Religion,* Vol. XX, No. 4, p. 252.

[8]Isaiah 8:11.

[9]From εκ (meaning "out") and ιστααι (meaning "to place").

revelation. It is the interdependence and interconnection of the word and the deed which makes "the Word of Lord" powerful and concrete.

It is important to grasp clearly the precise relation between word and deed in revelation. Friedrich Gogarten correctly reminds us[10] that this relation is not one of temporal sequence. It is not that the deed happens first and then, at some later time, the word is added to clarify the meaning of the deed. The mode of revelation is rather that the deed occurs *in* and *through* the word. The deed is the dynamic quality of the word, and the word is the structural, intelligible character of the deed. Revelation is the act of *God,* and this means that the power of the revelatory event is Logos power. The event is intrinsically intelligible in nature. The Word of God is an address to the mind of man, but an address of a specific sort, namely, a word of judgment and a promise of hope; it contains a primary and ultimate claim, and a victorious word of promise. As Paul said, "It is the power of God for salvation. . . ."[11]

Numerous passages in the New Testament make it clear that the New Testament writers were also operating theologically with this same dynamic conception of revelation as an event, a happening, an occurrence. When Paul, for example, described his revelatory experience of Christ by saying that God was pleased to reveal his Son to him,[12] he was, to be sure, speaking of a special revelation, which disclosed to him a particular dimension of the divine mystery, namely, Christ the Lord. The basic prophetic meaning

[10]Friedrich Gogarten, *Entmythologisierung und Kirche,* zweite Auflage (Stuttgart: Vorwerk-Verlag, 1953), p. 100.

[11]Romans 1:16.

[12]Galatians 1:16.

of revelation, however, is the same as in the prophetic movement of the Old Testament. By saying that God revealed his Son to him, Paul certainly did not mean that God delivered to him, verbatim, a full-orbed system of Pauline theology. He meant that he too felt "the strong hand of the Lord upon him." His heart and mind were caught in the grip of the revelatory activity of God.

This understanding of the meaning of revelation as a dynamic event is especially clear in the Roman epistle, where Paul wrote that "the wrath of God is *revealed* from heaven,"[13] that is, God's wrathful judgment *appears, takes place, occurs* in the present. That this is the Apostle's meaning is clear from the remainder of the first chapter, where he delineated the fearful judgments of God which have befallen Gentiles who "did not see fit to acknowledge God."

The same meaning of the term "revelation" is evident in the Galatian epistle where Paul wrote: "Now before faith *came,* we were confined under the law, kept under restraint *until faith should be revealed.*"[14] As the eminent New Testament scholar, Rudolf Bultmann, says, in his comments on this passage,

> This expected "revealing" has now become a thing of the present ("Now that faith has *come*"—vs. 25); this does not mean that now a hitherto unknown teaching about faith is being expounded, but that it now has become a possibility, and in those who have faith, a reality—faith has made its appearance, for this is just what " *be revealed*" (ἀποκαλύπτεσθαι) or its noun "revelation" (ἀποκάλυψσις), and also "be manifested" (φανεροῦσθαι, Rom. 3:21), mean when used as

[13]Romans 1:18.

[14]Galatians 3:23.

eschatological terms—appear on the scene, become possibility, or become operative.[15]

Similarly, when Paul commended the church at Corinth for its richness of spiritual gifts and reminded them that they were waiting "for the *revealing* of our Lord Jesus Christ,"[16] he was not referring to some *communication* which Christ would impart, but rather to *his personal appearing at the parousia.* The concrete event or happening of the *parousia is* the revelation. Just as when he wrote of "the day of wrath when God's righteous judgment will be *revealed,*"[17] the revelation *is the actual event of the execution of that eschatological wrath.*

Now this "appearing on the scene" or "becoming operative" or "becoming effective"[18] is to be sure an event occurring to and for man. It does, therefore, enable men to perceive the meaning of the event, for the revelatory power in this event is Logos power. The important point to remember, however, is that it is not merely the perceiving of the meaning of the event, nor the concomitant perceptions of the perceiving subject, but *the total event itself* which is described by the phrase "being revealed."[19]

An Existential Event

These passages make it clear that by the term "revelation" the writers of the Bible meant, first

---

[15]Rudolf Bultmann, *The Theology of the New Testament,* trans. Kendrick Grobel (New York: Charles Scribner's Sons, 1951), I, 275. Used by permission.

[16]1 Corinthians 1:7.

[17]Romans 2:5; cf. 2 Thessalonians 1:7; 2:3, 6, 8; 1 Peter 1:5, 7, 13; 4:13; 5:1; Luke 17:30.

[18]Bultmann's phraseology.

[19]Cf. William Temple, *Nature, Man and God* (London: Macmillan & Company Ltd., 1949), p. 317. Quotations from this book are used by permission of Macmillan & Company Ltd., and St. Martin's Press.

of all, not some objectivistic thing, but an event. But they also make it clear that revelation is not just any and every event, *as such;* although any historical event can be and is the medium of revelation if and when God so wills. Revelation is a particular kind of event; it is an event filled with Logos power, an event, therefore, which generates a vision of life's Ultimate. It is an event which is pregnant with the power of God to engender in the subject the experience of some eternal truth or meaning about human life.[20] Theologians have appropriated from philosophy the term "existential" to describe the dynamic and elucidative character of the revelatory experience. A revelatory event is an existential event.

The term "existence," in the philosophy of existence, is loaded with the idea of personal dynamic and responsible freedom. Things do not "exist," according to Martin Heidegger; they are merely "on hand." Only persons "exist" or are "in-being" or have "being-in-the-world." This kind of existence is on the move, on the make, dynamic. As Friedrich Karl Schumann puts it,[21] the world is something more for man than a mere container for beans and peas. That man is *in* the world means more than the mere fact that he is circumscribed by spatial limits. His existence is *affected by* the world. The relation between man and his world is one of mutual, dynamic determination.

[20]This aspect of the subjective significance of revelation may be correlated with the experience of religious inspiration. The concept of inspiration is a more limited one than that of revelation. The term "inspiration" (*inspirare*—inbreathing) refers to the actual influence whereby the divine Spirit moves the human spirit empoweringly and/or enlighteningly. This divine moving is an aspect of the total event of revelation, the basic character of which we are analyzing in this chapter.

[21]Günther Bornkamm, Rudolf Bultmann, & Friedrich Karl Schumann, *Die christliche Hoffnung und das Problem der Entmythologisierung* (Stuttgart: Evangelisches Verlagswerk, 1954), p. 60.

To say that a revelatory event is an existential event means that it is an event in which something of profound significance happens to the consciousness of the receiving subject, in his "being-in-the-world." There can be no such thing as a wholly factual or objective revelation. This would be a contradiction in terms. There is no revelation until there is revelation to someone, in a concrete, socio-historical situation of concern. Revelation remains uncompleted if no one receives it. It is completed only if it finds fulfillment on the subjective side of the relation.

When God manifests himself to someone in a revelatory event, the whole of one's personality is affected; so that objective and subjective history are intertwined and interrelated. As Paul expressed it, the subject is "apprehended."[22] That is, the subject is grasped or laid hold of by the manifestation of the mystery, with the result that his mind is illuminated concerning some ultimate meaning of life and his heart responds in love. To love God, Paul wrote, is to be known by him.[23] And to know God, through the revelatory experience, is "to be known by God."[24]

It is the personal integrity and validity of the subjective aspect of true revelation which forever distinguishes it from false revelations. It forever excludes what Tillich calls "a non-existential concept of revelation."[25] The false revelation of church dogmas, for example, which are imposed on the individual conscience in an authoritarian way, does not meet the test of this demand of true revelation for subjective perception and integrity. Such authori-

[22]King James Version. Καταλαμβάνω, Philippians 3:12.
[23]1 Corinthians 8:3.
[24]Galatians 4:9.
[25]Tillich, *Systematic Theology*, I, 127.

tarian claims must therefore be rejected, insofar as they lay claim to revelatory value.

Equally important in genuine revelation, however, is its usage of objective, historical facts. Something actually *occurs.* A revelation came to Moses *through the medium of Israel's enslavement in Egypt.* The city of Nineveh became morally dissolute, and Jonah had a revelatory experience. Even the growing of a gourd and its destruction by a worm eating away at its root was of revelatory significance for Jonah. Christians, of course, experience revelation through the medium of that supreme biographical event of the person of Jesus of Nazareth. Always, in genuine revelation, *something actually occurs through which* the ultimate mystery of being grasps someone. This something which occurs is the objective side of the revelatory event, by keeping clearly aware of which one may guard against the false idea of a mystical revelation, which is not mediated through historical facts.

To be sure, we must not fail to appreciate the measure of validity in the revolt of the mystics against medieval Christianity which transformed the medium of revelation into a sacramental object. Against the objectivism of the priestly sacramental system of medieval Christianity the mystics repeatedly raised their voices of protest, demanding more meaningfulness and inwardness in religion.

Thoroughgoing mysticism, however, swings to the other extreme, which is equally erroneous. Under its hands, religion undergoes a process of complete internalization. Radical mysticism affirms that the influence of God on the soul is to be sought and found entirely in the experiencing of the subject. The individual concentrates wholly upon the excitement of his own religious emotions, and takes *these emotions alone* as evidence that the soul is possessed by God. The mystic affirms also that all of this takes place without anything external to the soul being laid hold on, and that it is not necessary that the mind be inspired by great ideas.

Mysticism thus represents an extreme reaction against the objectivism of the priestly sacramental system. It places a thoroughly negative evaluation upon *all* media of revelation and aspires unto a direct (unmediated) union of the soul with God. It wishes to brush aside the whole realm of finitude and enter directly into the Infinite.[26]

Mysticism effects an eradication of authoritarianism, but at too great a price. It abolishes the concrete, historical character of all genuine revelation and makes revelation irrelevant to man's actual historical situation. It wrongly attempts to elevate man above his concrete, historical concerns; and it thereby tends to negate the entire of human existence in space-time.

This tendency of mysticism is most clearly seen in Hindu mysticism, which reduces the entire phenomenal world to illusion.[27] The best example perhaps would be the ontological negation of the empirical self in the Sankya philosophy of India. It is, the Sankya people say, like the reflection of a hibiscus on a crystal ball. The crystal ball is not really colored; it is an illusory reflection. Similarly, the

[26]Cf. Emil Brunner, *Revelation and Reason*, p. 147, also Tillich, *Systematic Theology*, I, 140.

[27]"Maya" is the Hindu term for it.

transcendental, abiding ego does not really undergo birth and death; it is not actually involved in the process of the phenomenal world. The true self is changeless and abiding. That art Thou: Brahman (God) is atman (the soul).[28] The way to salvation and reality is, therefore, to dispel the illusion, which regards the empirical ego as real. The illusion is to be dispelled through direct mystical union with the Ultimate.[29] Such mysticism represents one way in which man refuses to accept the plight of his finitude.

The biblical view of God the Creator of the phenomenal world is obviously irreconcilable with the ontology of Hindu mysticism. In the biblical view, we steer our revelatory vessel clear of the Scylla of authoritarian objectivism, on the one hand, and the Charybdis of mystical subjectivism, on the other. The two sides cannot be separated. If nothing actually occurs, objectively, nothing is really revealed.[30] Yet if there is no subjective receiving, if the event fails to reveal something *to someone*, nothing is revealed. The two sides, subjective and objective, must be held together. Both are indispensable factors in the total event of revelation. A revelatory event has its giving side and also its receiving side.

This is partly what we mean by calling revelation an *existential* event. We mean that it is an event which is concerned with man's *actual situation in existence*, confronted by what concerns him ultimately. The mystery which is revealed is of ultimate concern to us because it is the eternal ground of our being.

[28]*Tat tvam asi.*

[29]Cf. George Foot Moore, *A History of Religions* (New York: Charles Scribner's Sons, 1941), I, 273-274.

[30]Hence, in the final analysis, the mystic can really say nothing; he can only sit in silence and point.

Hence, as Tillich says, "In the history of religion revelatory events always have been described as shaking, transforming, demanding, significant in an ultimate way."[31]

The "I-Thou" Dimension

The dynamic and challenging confrontation with the Ultimate, as interpreted by the concept of revelation, is to be understood also as a relation in the "I-thou" dimension of reality. The concept of revelation belongs really to a personalistic view of the Ultimate. The term "revelation" is irrelevant to the "I-it" dimension of reality, as such. It is a term which describes a relation between persons, between selves. It belongs to the "I-thou" dimension of reality.

One can discover an "it." Science is constantly busy delving into the unknown aspects of the "I-it" dimension. But one could not possibly discover a "thou." The only way in which one can come to know another person is through the willingness of that person to reveal himself or herself to him. Otherwise, this transcendent personal reality will remain forever an unsolved mystery.

If, therefore, God had not willed to make known "the mystery of his will,"[32] there would have been no revelation but only mystery still. This same volitional root of knowledge in the "I-thou" dimension is evident in Jesus' words: "No one knows the Father except . . . one to whom the Son chooses to reveal him."[33]

When we use the term "revelation," then, to clarify and explicate the relation of man to the

[31]Tillich, *Systematic Theology,* I, 110.

[32]Ephesians 1:9.

[33]Matthew 11:27.

Ultimate, we are affirming that the experience about which we are speaking is a particular kind of experience; it is a relation of confrontation. But we are saying also that this experience is something more than confrontation by a nebulous oceanic, all-embracing something, as Karl Jaspers calls the Ultimate.[34] We are affirming that this experience is a dynamic encounter with a personal reality. That is, we are saying that the Ultimate is the kind of reality that can and does will a self-disclosure to man.

Basically, then, our relation to God and our knowledge of God lie in the same dimension as our knowledge of and relationship with our fellow man. They lie in the "I-thou" dimension. The existential event which is revelation involves a personal encounter with the living God. This is something quite different from the God of abstract philosophizing. It is what Martin Buber calls "the primal reality of a life-relationship."[35] Hence the God who is known in revelation is not just another *object* of knowledge. He is "the exclusive Thou of prayer and devotion."[36]

The late Archbishop William Temple was pointing us in the right direction when he wrote of God: "He guides the process; He guides the minds of men; the interaction of the process and the minds which are alike guided by Him is the essence of revelation."[37] Again, Temple wrote: "Its [revelation] essence is intercourse of mind and event, not the communication of doctrine distilled from that intercourse. . . . Knowledge of God can be fully given to man only in a person,

[34]"Umgreifend" is Jaspers' term for it.

[35]Martin Buber, *Two Types of Faith,* trans. Norman P. Goldhawk (New York: The Macmillan Company, 1951), p. 130.

[36]*Ibid.*

[37]Temple, *op. cit.,* p. 312.

never in a doctrine, still less in a formless faith, whatever that might be."[38]

It is an encouraging sign that an increasing number of Christian thinkers are today following along the lines suggested by Temple, that they are liberated from the traditional concept of revelation, in which the truth of God was regarded as identical with some human doctrine about it, and that they are reorienting their thought about revelation conceived as a personalistic event.

---

[38] *Ibid.*, pp. 316, 321.

CHAPTER FIVE

General and Special Revelation

We have described the basic general meaning of the category of revelation, as the biblical writers construed it, and indicated some of its implications for an understanding of the unique or special revelation of God in Christ. It must be remembered, of course, that this is not the only revelation of God. In the awe-inspiring awareness of the supremely valuable redemptive power of the Christian revelation, Christians are frequently led, erroneously, to ignore or to deny the other revelatory acts of God in history and nature.

The Inadequacy of the Medieval Distinction Between Natural Theology and Revealed Theology

In the Middle Ages it was the custom to deal with the problem of the relation between man's knowledge of the ultimate character of human life gained by means of the revelation in Christ, and his knowledge of the ultimate aspect of life gained outside of relation to Christ, in terms of the distinction between "revealed theology" and "natural theology." According to Thomas Aquinas,[1] for example, certain truths about God, man, and the world are within the reach of man's natural powers of knowing. The truth "that God is," for example, can be known by critical analysis and

[1]Anton C. Pegis (ed), *Basic Writings of Saint Thomas Aquinas* (New York: Random House, 1945), 1, 6, 7.

reflection upon the world, as we experience it. No revelation is necessary to enable one to learn this truth. Although, Aquinas admitted,[2] for those who have neither the time nor the ability to philosophize, it is acceptable and proper that they believe such truths, as dogmas of faith. *Essentially,* however, they remain philosophical prolegomena to faith. *Essentially,* they are not articles of faith, but validly established truths of natural theology.

This Thomistic view of the relation between man's "natural powers of knowing" and revelation bears the marks of the dominant influence of Aristotle on Aquinas. The plea for so-called "natural theology" fails to do justice to the Hebraic-Christian emphasis on the God-centered character of all human life and thought. In developing understanding in the realm of natural theology, man stands alone, as it were, apart from any vital relation to God. This wisdom is merely "natural." In "revealed theology," God suddenly becomes active; man is no longer alone with his "natural" thoughts. God is now the giver of a supernatural kind of knowledge.

The basic weakness of this Thomistic view is twofold. First, the idea of a "revealed theology" is fundamentally erroneous. It represents an aspect of the doctrinaire theory of revelation which honest and intelligent thinking has been obliged to abandon. There is revelation *through* words and concepts; but if our definition of revelation as a dynamic event is correct, there are no "revealed words," no "revealed theology," no "revealed doctrine."

Second, the adherents of the Thomistic view failed to recognize the full implications of the fact that what is called "nature" itself represents the activity of God. Indeed, according to the biblical

[2] *Ibid.,* p. 21.

doctrine of creation, God is the ultimate power which originated, sustains, and guides all being. If this is true, the power of God is active not only in man's very being, but in all of his experience, as spirit.

Man's Experience of Value as General Revelation

The "categorical imperative" of conscience represents the moral aspect of the pressure of the Spirit and power of God upon us. The sense of moral obligation which inclines the conscience toward that which is believed to be right is of revelatory significance, for it represents God manifesting himself in human life as that "power that makes for righteousness." Our moral experience represents God *pressing* upon us and revealing himself. The quality or feeling-tone of absoluteness and finality, which is an integral part of our experience of moral value, represents a manifestation of the power of God.

This way of interpreting moral experience represents a religious view of man's sense of moral obligation, as opposed to the naturalistic attempt to explain this moral phenomenon wholly in terms of the force of social pressure. According to the naturalistic view, there is no categorical imperative; there is only a pragmatic, sociological imperative. The sense of moral oughtness, the naturalist contends, can be adequately explained by the social pressure upon the individual conscience, which demands conformity with the mores of the group.

The main weakness of this naturalistic theory of conscience is that it fails to explain the obvious fact that reflective morality often compels an individual to go counter to what is demanded by customary morality, even, sometimes, at the cost of life itself. The religious view of conscience, which holds the individual to sustain also a relation to a suprahuman reality, would therefore seem to be a more reasonable view of the sense of moral oughtness.[3]

Similarly, in the aesthetic dimension of our experience of reality, how are we to explain the tremendous lure of beauty? One thinks of the words of Byron:

> Who hath not proved how feebly words essay
> To fix one spark of beauty's heavenly ray?
> Who doth not feel . . .
> The might, the majesty of loveliness?
>
> *The Bride of Abydos, Canto I, Stanza 6*

Individual judgments of beauty, like individual judgments of the good, vary, to be sure, from culture to culture. But how are we to explain the insatiable drive in the human heart to create the beautiful? Does not this also represent the revelatory activity of God? In every experience of beauty, the sensitive soul becomes aware of the presence and pressure of ultimate power, the power of all being and meaning.

The necessitarian element in the lure and perception of truth represents yet another aspect of the revelatory activity of God. Every true scientist has felt the challenge of God's revelatory activity in this dimension, and has responded with a sense of religious devotion. It is because man's quest for and concern with truth is essentially religious that scientists are correct in their reluctance or refusal to allow totalitarian tyrants to make man's interest in truth wholly subservient to economic and political ends. Such a procedure is indeed the result of a tragic confusion between the ends and means of life. It is a tampering with the sacred; it is an attempt to reduce man's relation to the Ultimate to the function of a means for the production of selfish ends. This constitutes a

[3]Cf. Baillie, *op. cit.*, pp. 325, 326, 346-352, 390; A. Campbell Garnett, *A Realistic Philosophy of Religion* (New York: Willett, Clark & Company, 1942), pp. 51-57, 275-286; Alan Richardson, *The Gospel and Modern Thought* (London: Oxford University Press, 1950), pp. 9-15.

blasphemous reversal of the relation between Creator and creature.

In attempting, then, to understand *all* of man's spiritual experience as a response to the challenge and call of the Ultimate, theologians have abandoned the medieval concept of natural theology and have developed the category of "general revelation," so as to subsume man's experience of value in general under the category of the revelatory working of God.

By the phrase "general revelation" I do not mean to imply the erroneous idea that every thing or historical event *as such* possesses revelatory value. They possess such value and power only when God chooses to use them as media of revelation. I mean rather that God has used numerous such means, *in general,* in contrast to the *special* means of the event of Jesus Christ.

Karl Barth tends to confuse the issue at this point because he fails to distinguish clearly between "natural theology" and "general revelation." He defines natural theology as the doctrine of a bond between man and God which exists apart from God's revelation in Jesus Christ.[4] Our plea, however, is that there *is* such a "bond with God," but that it is misleading to call it natural theology, for it involves the *revelatory* working of God. The question of the degree of validity of the theology which grows out of this bond is another issue. But "natural theology," understood as a work of human reason apart from God's revelatory working, represents a very different way of thinking about man's quest for truth, a way which stems from the ancient Greek anthropocentric

---

[4]"Natürliche Theologie ist die Lehre von einer auch ohne Gottes Offenbarung in Jesus Christus bestehenden Gottes verbundenheit des Menschen; sie entwickelt die auf Grund dieser selbstständigen Gottesverbundenheit mögliche und wirkliche Gotteserkenntnis und deren Konsequenzen für das ganze Verhältnis von Gott, Welt und Mensch" (*Die Kirchliche Dogmatik.* Zürich: Evangelischer Verlag A. G. Zollikon, 1946, II, 1, 189). Quotations from Vol. II and Vol. III of this work are used by permission.

concept of man, which we have rejected. The position taken here is in agreement with the definition given by David Cairns who defines general revelation to mean "that in human experience God, by a continual invasion of His grace, confronts man. Thus there is in all man's existence a relationship to the Infinite Thou, misinterpret it as the natural man may and does."[5]

Such a view of general revelation, correlated with the concept of the special revelation in Christ, would seem to be more consistent with a theistic world-view than the medieval distinction between natural and revealed theology. It is undeniably more God-centered; and it is thereby truer to the biblical point of view. With Temple, we agree that "we can make no truce with any suggestion that the world for the most part goes by itself on its own way while God intervenes now and again with an act of His own."[6]

The Basic Difference Between General and Special Revelation

The major difference between general revelation and the special revelation in Christ would seem to lie in the vividly and profoundly personal character of the revelation of God in Christ, and in its redemptive value, whereas a rose, a sunset, or even a stone or a herd of wild buffalo might be the medium of general revelation. Indeed, as the parables of Jesus make clear, a farmer sowing his seed, a newly discovered buried treasure, a prodigal son who came to himself, a grain of mustard seed, and numerous other events possess revelatory significance.

The reason for this universal revelatory capacity of reality is that all things which are, obviously participate in the power of being. This basic ontological

[5]Cairns, *op. cit.*, p. 198.
[6]Temple, *op. cit.*, p. 304.

character, therefore, supplies them with the capacity to be a medium of the revelation of the ground and power of all being.

Thus a stick or a stone, as well as the Galilean carpenter of Nazareth, possesses the capacity to serve as a medium of revelation. There is an infinite difference, of course, in the limits of the respective capacities, in the kinds of truth which are revealed by these two kinds of media, and in the value of the two revelations.

The ontological contingency of a stone serves as a means whereby, for some, there is generated the awareness of an unconditional element present in man's experience of the world. Hocking reverses this cosmological argument and contends that the judgment of contingency presupposes an 'a priori' intuitive awareness of the really real. He argues that it is only because we already know the reality which is really real that we are able to make the judgment that the world of our day-to-day experience is only quasi-real.[7] The latter judgment presupposes the former knowledge.

While one should not obscure nor minimize the fact that all being and all events possess the capacity to serve as media of revelation, if and when God so wills, yet it is obvious that nonpersonal beings, sticks and stones and deadmen's bones, represent, in the kind of being they possess, a rather limited capacity for reflecting the ultimate ground of all being and meaning. Persons, however, represent a different kind of being. They occupy a more central status in the nature of reality and possess a vastly superior capacity for such revelation.

It is this inherent kinship of personality with the

[7]William Ernest Hocking, *The Meaning of God in Human Experience* (New Haven: Yale University Press, 1924), pp. 31 ff.; cf. Paul Tillich, *The Shaking of the Foundations* (New York: Charles Scribner's Sons, 1948), p. 67.

essential, spiritual nature of the ultimate ground of reality which makes historical revelation—revelation through prophets and through human community—of incomparably greater value in leading to human fulfillment than revelation through nature. Through historical events and sensitive historical personalities the meaning as well as the power of being manifests itself. And it is this essential kinship of personality with ultimate reality which makes possible the transcendent fullness of the revelation in the personality of Christ.

Furthermore, the manifestation of God in the person of Christ is so much more illuminating and transfiguring than God's self-manifestation elsewhere in history that Christians feel it necessary to distinguish this revelatory activity of God from all the rest; hence it is called "special revelation."

Here is a divine disclosure so full of grace and truth that we are inspired to say it is "glory as of the only Son from the Father."[8] A dimension of the life of God is here disclosed which, apart from this revelation, is hidden from our feeble eyes. As Emil Brunner puts it, elsewhere in nature we see God's hands and feet, but not his eternal mercy.[9] In Christ the inner essence of God's limitless grace and matchless love is opened to our view. When men lift up their eyes and see Jesus, they are made to know, somehow, that "God so loved the world that he gave his only Son."[10]

The Demand for a Positive Element in the Relation Between Christianity and Other Religions

If, as we have contended, the meaning of revela-

[8]John 1:14.

[9]Brunner writes that in the revelation of God in nature we find "Gottes Hände und Füsse, aber nicht sein Herz . . . nicht seine vergebende Barmherzigkeit" (*Natur und Gnade* [Tübingen: J. C. B. Mohr, 1935], p. 25).

[10]John 3:16.

tion, in general, is to find oneself in the concrete situation in which life's ultimate mystery makes its impact upon him and confronts him with the challenge to personal, responsible decision, then it would seem strange that Christians have sometimes been guilty of denying any revelatory value whatever to the experiences and insights of great prophetic personalities in other religions.

This negative judgment is frequently made by exponents of theological positivism who see that the only religion which possesses vital transforming power is that which finds its life and substance through a personal involvement in a particular historical religion. It is argued that there is no such thing as universal religion, that all religions are particular, historical communities. And inasmuch as destiny has committed *us* to personal involvement in the Christian community, we are to accept it and find our redemption in and through it, not through any abstract universal religion.[11]

There is here a most difficult problem. It is the problem of how to understand and express the relation which does exist, or which should exist between the particular and the universal. It is certainly true that *thus far* in historic process, dynamic personal fulfillment has been achieved only through the vigorous commitment of faith to relation with the Ultimate through the structural patterns of a particular historic faith.

Some writers[12] are deeply concerned to transcend the sectionalism and sectarian divisiveness of historical particularism, and accordingly plead earnestly for a universal world faith. Yet we must remain aware of the fact that, thus far, the only world religious com-

[11]Cf. the fifth discourse of Schleiermacher's *Addresses on Religion*, where he places high value on positive religions and pours scorn on the idea of a universal natural religion.

[12]See, for example, Floyd H. Ross, *Addressed to Christians: Isolationism vs. World Community* (New York: Harper & Brothers, 1950).

munity which exists is much too nebulous and abstract to serve as a dynamic community for human fulfillment. The criticism of the sectarian character of religious particularism, however, is timely and most inspiring. The revelation in Christ, to be sure, spells judgment upon other religions, as well as upon "Christianity." This does of course place a negative element in the relation between the special revelation in Christ and other religions. Yet if our plea for general revelation possesses validity, there is also a significantly positive element in this relation.

Even John Calvin, in his Commentary on John 1:4, 9 ("In him was life, and the life was the light of men.... The true light that enlightens every man..") conceded a measure of validity to the idea of general revelation. Rejecting the view which restricts the phrase "every man" (vs. 9) only to those who have been renewed by the Spirit of God, Calvin wrote, "I am inclined to adopt the . . . meaning . . . that from this *light* the rays are diffused over all mankind. . . . For we know that men have this peculiar excellence which raises them above other animals, that they are endued with reason and intelligence, and that they carry the distinction between right and wrong engraven on their conscience. There is no man, therefore, whom some perfection of eternal *light* does not reach."[13]

Similarly, Calvin began chapter three of the first book of the *Institutes* by saying, "We lay it down as a position not to be controverted, that the human mind, even by natural instinct, possesses some sense of Deity. For that no man might shelter himself under the pretext of ignorance, God hath given to all some

---

[13]John Calvin, *Commentary on the Gospel According to John,* trans. William Pringle (Edinburgh: The Calvin Translation Society, 1847), p. 38.

apprehension of his existence. . . .'"[14] Calvin developed the idea that a "relic" of man's original endowment remained after the Fall (which he interpreted historically). This "relic" is the basis of our present humanity. Thus, although Calvin said some severe things about man's sinful condition, even he remained aware that man, in his sinful state, still stands in a relation to God which involves moral responsibility.

The belief in general revelation is then not wholly incompatible with an empirical recognition of man's profound ignorance of God, nor with the self-centered opposition of the human will to the will of God. If these rendered the concept of general revelation wholly invalid, there would exist no longer in the image of God in man any basis for a religious explanation of sin's guilt. Indeed, guilt could no longer be said to exist. And the light of Christ would not merely reveal and clarify sin's guilt; it would actually create it. In this case, one should be obliged to say that Paul was mistaken when he argued that the Gentiles' ignorance of God was inexcusable.[15]

The Barthian contention is that the mind of man is so darkened by sin that until illuminated by the special revelation in Christ, one is not able even to recognize God.[16] Such a dismal conception of the pre-Christian man, however, renders the use of the term "sin" ambiguous and problematical. How can man *wilfully rebel* against God (the biblical view of sin,

---

[14]John Calvin, *Institutes of the Christian Religion,* I, 54.

[15]Romans 1:20.

[16]Barth writes that God can be known solely (*ganz allein*) in Jesus Christ. Hence the message of the church, which has to do with the theology of the Word of God, can have nothing to do with natural theology. (Barth, *op. cit.,* pp. 184, 190.) Similarly, he writes that God's will is not "a corrected continuation of our own. It approaches ours as a Wholly Other. There is nothing for our will but a basic re-creation. Not a reformation, but a re-creation and a re-growth" (Karl Barth, *The Word of God and the Word of Man,* trans. Douglas Horton [Pilgrim Press, 1829], p. 24). Used by permission.

which Barth accepts[17]) if he possesses no knowledge of God? In what sense would this be sinning against the light? Barth's extreme view tends to render sin and guilt, in the pre-Christian man, meaningless. Brunner is more nearly correct when he argues that the image-bearing destiny of man, as God's creature, is not only not destroyed by sin; it is the presupposition of sin and lives precisely in man the sinner.[18]

It would seem to be more correct to say that man's ignorance and sinful self-centeredness simply render the fact of general revelation highly problematical, and greatly diminish its value, as a means of human fulfillment.

Even Calvin's position therefore is more nearly in line with the biblical teachings than the extreme view which refuses to recognize any validity whatever in the category of general revelation.

The Paul of Acts declared that God "did not leave himself without witness" among the nations.[19] The natural values of life, he argued, such as food, the rhythm of the seasons, rain, and so forth, are the gifts of God; and as such they engender an awareness of his divine bounty.[20]

In the light of Paul's own writings, as a whole, it must be said that the Apostle painted a rather dismal picture of the sinful state of the pre-Christian man. Yet in the very midst of the most vivid description Paul ever gave of the Gentiles, he argued that the character of our world, as we experience it, can, and for the sensitive soul does, serve as a medium for the manifestation of "eternal power and deity."[21] "What

---

[17]As sinner, Barth writes, man stands in "opposition to God (*Widersprecher gegen Gott, sein Schöpfer*)"; on the basis of "his own act of will, man sins and stands in rebellion against God . . ." (Karl Barth, *Die Kirchliche Dogmatik* [Zürich: Evangelischer Verlag A. G. Zollikon, 1948], III, 2, p. 29). Used by permission.

[18]Brunner, *Natur und Gnade*, p. 10.

[19]Acts 14:17.

[20]Ibid.

[21]Romans 1:20.

can be known about God is plain to them," Paul wrote, "*because God has shown it to them*" in "the things that have been made."[22] Therefore, he concludes, "they are without excuse; for although they knew God they did not honor him as God or give thanks to him, but they became futile in their thinking and their senseless minds were darkened."[23] It is beyond all reasonable doubt that Paul here does not refer to the revelation of Christ, but affirms a degree of validity in the idea of general revelation.

The biblical recognition of the validity of the prophetic activity of Balaam of Mesopotamia and of Melchizedek, the ancient priest-king of Salem, similarly implies a rejection of the attempt to limit revelation exclusively to the special and unique Christian revelation.

Similarly, Amos clearly states that the other Canaanitish peoples, besides Israel and Judah, were in a morally responsible relationship with God. They had violated the moral demands of this revelatory situation by three, yea four transgressions. "Therefore," says the Lord, "I will not revoke the punishment. . . ."[24] Indeed, the God of Amos' prophetic revelation declared that he had the same concern for the Ethiopians as for Israel, and that he providentially guided and delivered the Philistines from Caphtor and the Syrians from Kir just as surely as he brought Israel out of the land of Egypt.[25]

Immanuel Kant was not the first to recognize the religious significance of the moral law within. The Apostle Paul himself contended that the natural awareness of the moral law within conscience shows that what the law requires "is written on their hearts."[26]

[22]Romans 1:19-20.
[23]Romans 1:20-21.
[24]*See* Amos, Chapters 1 and 2.
[25]Amos 9:7.
[26]Romans 2:15.

The author of the Fourth Gospel also confirms our argument for general revelation, beyond all doubt, when he wrote that the life of the eternal *Logos,* the medium of all creation, "was the light of men."[27] This is the light, he said, "that enlightens every man. . . ."[28]

One cannot accept these biblical witnesses as true without conceding that there is validity in the plea for general revelation. The Pauline and Johannine passages cited above imply, beyond all equivocation, that every mature, normal human being stands in a fundamental relationship with the *Logos* of all mental and spiritual life, and that the essence of our humanity lies in an inescapable relation of moral responsibility to God and to our fellow man. This universal *Logos*-confrontation is the ultimate ground of every moral decision. Man is continually in the presence of the *Logos.*

The best and truest Christian attitude toward other religions therefore would seem to include, as one basic aspect, a glad, approving recognition of the works of God, everywhere, and a cheerful willingness to recognize the manifestation of God's creative call to truth and goodness whenever and wherever it is heralded.

Even Richard Niebuhr admits that Christianity must see God at work everywhere; and Niebuhr, like Barth, is highly skeptical toward the use of any apologetical element in his methodology. Niebuhr feels that the Christian community must strive to see the working of God in all events in time, because the Christian God is the Creator "not only of the events through which he discloses himself but also of all other happenings."[29] Yet Niebuhr carefully avoids extending

[27]John 1:4.

[28]John 1:9.

[29]H. Richard Niebuhr, *The Meaning of Revelation* (New York: The Macmillan Company, 1941), p. 86. Used by permission.

this looking upon "all events of time" and finding in them "the working of one mind and will" to the point of placing an apologetical function in his theological method. His existentialism, too, is positivistic in spirit and tone.

We believe, however, that it is a sounder theological method which demands the presence of an apologetical function of reason in the experience of faith, against the positivistic evasion of it, on the one hand, and the more recent bold rejection of it by some kerygmatic theologians, on the other.

The Distortion of Special Revelation by Some of the Kerygmatic Theologians

Some kerygmatic theologians believe that the revelation through Christ is so unique that there is *no common ground whatever* which the Christian shares with those outside the Christian community, by which the unique truth of the gospel could be validated in the eyes of the "outsiders," who have not yet taken up the point of view of faith. The central truth of the gospel, for example, that "Jesus is Lord," has *absolutely no meaning* apart from the community of Christian faith.

These men feel that the numerous syntheses which have resulted, down through the centuries, from efforts of Christian theologians to bring faith and culture together represent a pollution of the divine kerygma, the infallible truth or "hard core" of the gospel, if not indeed a complete surrender of it.

It is argued that the second-century apologists corrupted the Christian *Logos* by identifying it with the Greek *Logos*. Origen corrupted the doctrine of the resurrection of Christ by interpreting it (validating it rationally) by his Neo-Platonic spiritualism. Thomas Aquinas obscured and polluted the idea of the

God of the Christian faith by identifying him with Aristotle's unmoved mover, the abstract God of Philosophy. The deism of the Enlightenment surrendered Christian faith almost entirely, bowing to the demands of autonomous reason, etc.

Theology, it is argued, forfeited its own base when it entered these cultural, philosophical situations. Hence these kerygmatic theologians would have us *not enter the cultural situation at all, as theologians.* It is not theology's business to give "reasonable answers" to the needs and questions of those poor souls caught in life's problematical situations. The Christian missionary is to operate by the method of "radical displacement," to borrow Hocking's phrase.[30] Or as Tillich aptly represents this view, "the message must be thrown at those in the situation—thrown like a stone."[31]

It must be admitted that some cultures have become so hopelessly corrupt that this method of radical displacement is about the only appropriate one to use. And of course, such a method can be very powerful and revolutionary.

The central issue, however, is whether this method fulfills the fundamental mission of the church. Is it not rather the deepest Christian conviction that Christ is Savior *because he meets and fulfills conscious human needs?* What appeal would a Christ possess who said, "Come, and I will give you rest," if the rest offered was wholly irrelevant to man's conscious need?

The Need for an Apologetical Element in Theological Method

The method recommended by these kerygmatic theologians is, in fact, impossible to carry out con-

[30] William Ernest Hocking, *Living Religions and a World Faith* (New York: The Macmillan Company, 1940), pp. 143, ff.

[31] Tillich, *Systematic Theology*, I, 7.

sistently. For even these theologians are obliged to make use of the conceptual tools of their culture in order to interpret and render meaningful the content of the kerygma. One cannot simply quote kerygmatic propositions, verbatim, or affirm the basic historical facts of the gospel, arbitrarily.

His auditors will inevitably inquire concerning the *meaning* of these kerygmatic symbols; and when these theologians begin to address themselves to this inquiry, in reasonable fashion, their method breaks down. If they say *anything at all* that is helpful in explaining the meaning of the kerygma to the sincere, interested inquirer, they have thereby admitted the need for and the validity of apologetical reason.

This need becomes particularly acute at the growing edge of the Christian movement: on the mission field. The very word "God" is meaningless for people of another tongue. The missionary is thus obliged to translate his ideas into terms and concepts which are familiar to his hearers. In China, for example, John's Gospel must be made to say: In the beginning was *Tao,* or *T'ien* or *Shang Ti.* The concept of the Ultimate as *Tao,* or *T'ien,* or *Shang Ti* is very ancient and deeply rooted in Chinese thought. And if the missionary gets to first base in his enterprise, *he simply must appeal to the philosophical framework of reference involved in the concepts of T'ien or Shang Ti.* By doing so, he admits that there is *some common ground,* fragmentary and problematical though it be, between Christianity and other religious philosophies.

Karl Barth has vigorously opposed the introduction of this apologetical concern into theological method. But even he cannot wholly escape it. In a personal discussion in Barth's home in Basel, in the summer of 1954, Barth admitted to the author (in a discussion of Barth's estimate of the point of view of Rudolf Bultmann) that the use of modern philosophy is not only inescapable but helpful in theological explication. Yet he is vigorous in his plea for a "free theology." Had it not been for Martin Buber's philosophy, however, Barth's exposition of the image of God in man[32] would doubtless have been somewhat different.

No careful student of Barth's thought can fail to observe how heavily he has drawn on modern philosophies, in the shaping of his own world-view. Barth has, in fact, drawn upon the philosophies of Kant, Kierkegaard, and Martin Buber, in the formation of his point of view, and he frankly admits that he has done so.

Well, then, the question is: If one must depend upon some particular philosophical grasp of human existence in order to explicate meaningfully and cogently one's theological point of view, must not the theologian be ready to consider critically the merits of this philosophical framework of reference, particularly when he is challenged by a representative of some opposing philosophical outlook? And if he does so, does this not give to reason or apologetics a more positive position in theological method than Barth seems willing to allow?

But even if our kerygmatic theologian should refuse to bend, even if he should stand inflexibly erect, quoting kerygmatic propositions, he really does not escape the conceptual environment of the biblical writers themselves, the character of which constituted a determining factor in the shaping of the biblical message.

[32]See, for example, Barth's contention that the basic meaning of the biblical doctrine of the *imago Dei* lies in the relation of personal community, the "I-thou" relation, which Barth of course grounds in a personalistic explication of the trinitarian distinctions in the godhead. "Because he [God] is not solitary in himself and also does not will to remain apart from external relations, it is therefore not good for man to be alone; he therefore created man in his own image: man and woman" (Barth, *Die Kirchliche Dogmatik,* III, 2., p. 390).

This whole problem of faith and reason is certainly one of the most difficult theological problems of our day. It must suffice here to say that the radically negative view toward cultural situations, which goes hand in hand with the positivism of some of the kerygmatic theologians, cannot be validated empirically. It is simply not the fact that Christians share *no common ground* whatever with other human beings, in the light of which the Christian way may be seen, in some measure, to be reasonable. If Christianity were utterly wholly "unreasonable," it would hardly have advanced to the point where it has become the only meaningful "world community."[33]

Furthermore, if special revelation were utterly discontinuous with reason (which in our terminology is an aspect of general revelation), there would seem to be no safeguard against religious fanaticism. Indeed, there would scarcely be any criteria whereby to distinguish between fanaticism and faith. Also, it is difficult to see how such a revelation would be really relevant to the human situation. If it is relevant, then *in some basic sense*, it must be continuous with reason or the general structure of human existence.

Redemption does not imply a total negation of creation. To affirm that it does is to get caught in the ancient Gnostic heresy once again. The main current of Christian thought has always carefully avoided the extreme negativism of Gnosticism toward the doctrine of creation and maintained that redemption, in correcting, fulfills and completes a distorted creation, not that it creates a wholly new human creation, from the ground up.

Because redemption is not wholly discontinuous with creation, theology is justified in appropriating

[33] Cf. Henry Pitney Van Dusen, *World Christianity* (New York: Abingdon-Cokesbury Press, 1947), p. 32.

and making use of the basic rational tests of the truth-value of religious affirmations. A theological method which holds that these rational tests of truth are utterly irrelevant to the explication and validation of religious truth must be held suspect.

It is true, of course, that the living God, known in the experience of faith, is infinitely more than the God who is nothing more than an abstract concept of philosophical speculation. To equate "God" with a human concept, as some philosophers are accused of doing, is certainly to fail tragically to understand the God of faith. Present-day theologians have therefore rightly emphasized the fact that the God of revelation is not mere object; he is Subject. He is the living God who gives *himself*, out of the fullness of his grace, to the believer. Revelation is an event occurring in the "I-thou" dimension, not in the "I-it" dimension.

It is a distortion of fact, however, to argue that these two dimensions of reality are separated and utterly discontinuous. Indeed, part of the mystery of historical existence lies in the fascinating ways in which the "I-thou" dimension of experience is correlated and intimately interwoven with the "I-it" dimension. For example, A's disclosure of himself, as person, to B is not wholly unrelated to B's awareness of the "it" character of A's being: his physical features and movements. The "it" here is no longer merely an "it"; it is now a medium of revelation. Not only do the structures of the "it" serve as media of revelation; they serve also as criteria for partial validation and confirmation. A husband, for example, can scarcely be expected to go on forever believing that his wife loves him if, in the totality of her social behavior, she offers him no evidences, no tokens whatever of her love. After all, we are not naked spirits; we are spirits with flesh and blood. We are historical human beings, who, as spirits, are profoundly enmeshed in objective history. Subjective history and objective history are not to be understood as isolated from each other. When existentialism fails to remember this, it turns out to be a new form of the radical otherworldliness of mysticism.[34]

The case is similar in the relation of the believer to God. There is here, to be sure, a unique fullness of personal and spiritual content; but this relation is not in a private compartment, isolated from one's involvement in objective, historical creation. The latter serves not only as media of this personal experience of the Ultimate, but also as criteria for the partial validation of it. The believer could scarcely be expected to possess so fanatical a faith as to believe in God's love and grace if, in God's total activity, he acted like the devil, if, that is, there were no rational evidence whatever of God's goodness.

Furthermore, the God of philosophy and the God of faith are not necessarily at antithetical poles. To be sure, God is not merely object; he is absolute Subject. Yet the subject-object relation is not wholly irrelevant to an understanding of the faith-relation. Basically of course one knows his wife not merely as object (the "I-it" dimension), but as loving subject. So, as the Bible says, to know God means to be known by God. To love God means to be loved by God and to respond to this love. Yet *in a sense,* God remains object, for he is *to be loved,* in response. To say that one should love God, and then to affirm, as some theologians have done, that *God is in no sense whatever* object, is to defy the meaning of language and logic.

[34]Kierkegaard hardly faced up squarely to the need for this limited rationalism in the validation and historical fulfillment of the love relation when he poured scorn on the person who can give you "three reasons that there is after all something in this thing of being in love," as if, says Kierkegaard, the love of the beloved itself were not reason enough. (Soren Kierkegaard, *The Sickness Unto Death,* trans. Walter Lowrie [Princeton: Princeton University Press, 1941], pp. 167-169).

God is a unique kind of object, or referent, to be sure. He is the referent which is the ultimate ground of the ordinary subject-object relationships of the world, in the framework of which the being of the *relation* exists. But one cannot even say this without having a concept of God, which inevitably implies that God is, *in some intelligible sense,* an object or a referent.

Furthermore, it is argued that a God who could be known as an object would be a human possession and creation, and that this would be to put man at the center of things, while the God of religion stands at the center and possesses man. The God of philosophy is measured, judged, and validated by the mind of man, while the God of religious faith measures and judges all. Hence, the two are utterly irreconcilable.

But does this objection to rationalistic theism really do justice to the dignity of man? If God created us persons and endowed us with freedom and responsibility, does this not imply that one should move toward intellectual maturity? When I refuse to bow to any external authority, when I refuse to believe anything to be true unless and until I myself can see its truthfulness, am I really rebelling against the rule of God? Am I not rather fulfilling it? To ask one to bow to an authority in a way which involves the nullification of all individual reason, is to confuse tragically between theonomy (being under the rule of God) and heteronomy (being under an authoritarian rule of another). If the authority of God, expressed in the relation of faith, were wholly discontinuous with reason, the highest form of religion would be an irrational or blind authoritarianism. Such a God would scarcely be respecting the dignity which he himself has created nor the freedom which he himself has fashioned. We say, then, that the redemptive experience of God in revelation is not utterly discontinuous with a philosophical understanding of the meaning of this experience and its truth. To say that it is would be intellectual suicide.

It is to be readily admitted, of course, that the rational tests of truth are not the *final* or *absolute* norm of Christian truth, since the rational tests relate only to the actual world, while faith puts one in touch with the ideal, which lies beyond the coherency of the actual. Yet one cannot cling to beliefs which fail wholly to meet the tests of reason and escape fanaticism or obscurantism. A religious irrationalism which demands a faith that is wholly arbitrary and rationally blind has been used repeatedly to perpetrate the Devil's business in history. Such irrationalistic faith forgets that there is a valid intellectual element in the total whole response of faith to the revelatory call of God in Christ. It forgets *too* that the God of the Christian faith is also the Creator and Sustainer of our world.

Since the world is God's world, and since there is an organic unity between the *Logos* of reality and the infinite creative depth of this divine reality—undergirding, informing, and transforming the structural character of the *Logos*—the rational criteria of truth[35] are important and must be used to test the power and relevance of the experience of Christ to man's historical existence, yet in such a way that they do not usurp more authority than rightly belongs to them. These rational tests are secondary to the primacy of revelation; but as such they serve as a reliable check on revelation, by demonstrating its relevance to the actual human situation, and by demonstrating the adequacy of Christianity's social vision of a community of Christlike men.[36]

---

[35]I understand these rational tests of truth to be four in number: (1) the quality of coerciveness, (2) the capacity for coherence with our known order of reality, (3) the test of verification in further experience, and (4) the demand for public verification.

[36]Cf. Nels F. S. Ferré, *Faith and Reason* (New York: Harper and Brothers, 1946), p. 243.

The famous second-century apologist, Justin Martyr, was therefore not far wrong when he argued that "whatever things were rightly said among all men are the property of us Christians."[37] Perhaps, however, Justin himself was not sufficiently aware of the relative character of all human truth, including the understanding of truth by Christians. He was so enamored with the intellectualism of Greek philosophy that he was insufficiently aware of the dynamic depth of the cosmic *Logos,* which forever transcends the structural aspect of reason, and functions as a dynamic counterpoise. The structural aspect of religious truth becomes distorted and crystallized when it is absolutized. It is normative and redemptive only when it embodies meaningfully the ultimate dynamic of Creative Love and gives it concrete expression and fulfillment.

Hocking is perhaps nearer the truth when he suggests the method of "re-conception" as the most constructive way of dealing with the problem of the relation of Christianity to world religions. This method demands of Christians that they take seriously the limitations of their own apprehensions of Christ and allow creative interchange with the thought of living world religions to exercise a therapeutic influence upon them also.[38] Humility will make us aware of the error of pretending "that . . . our finite apprehension needs no improvement."[39] The judgments involved in our grasp of Christian truth contain both certain and uncertain elements. And as Hocking says, "On account

[37]First Apology Ch. XIII.

[38]See Hocking, *Living Religions and a World Faith,* pp. 190 ff.; see also his recent restatement of this method, "Reconception Reconsidered," *The Christian Century,* Vol. LXXII, No. 9, March 2, 1955, pp. 268, 269.

[39]*Ibid.,* p. 197.

of this factor of uncertainty, there is a call from time to time for further induction based on wider groups of fact and on better insight into their nature.''[40] Thus the broadening which is generated by the cross-fertilization of world religions and by their mutual appreciation ''stimulates the deepening which is a search for a better grasp of its own essence.''[41]

We should not make the mistake, then, of equating Christ with our finite Christian apprehensions of him. That Christ is the *final* revelation does not mean that Christian theology has reached its perfect terminus, or that it ever will do so. It means (1) that this revelation will never reach a terminus in history, (2) that no new ''original'' revelation will contradict or surpass the basic motif of *agape* in the revelation of Christ, and (3) that this revelation carries within itself constantly the power of reformation, the power to transcend its own limited historical expression, at any particular time.

The Corrective Function of Special Revelation

From the point of view of the Christian faith, special revelation is related to general revelation also as a corrective, and not merely as a supplement or continuous development.

It is one of the paradoxes of prophetic religion that although special revelation is, *in a measure,* validated by reason or general revelation, yet, because special revelation leads us to a vision of ultimate truth, and is therefore unique and significant in a final way, it cannot be verified in any absolute and complete sense by anything outside itself. To this extent, the plea of the kerygmatic theologians is correct. For by submitting to this kind of verification, its basic claim to

---

[40] *Ibid.*

[41] *Ibid.*, p. 190.

being the final norm would be denied. It is the finality of this norm which makes special revelation also *corrective* in its function.

Reason or general revelation is, after all, problematical, in its value as a norm. Ferré correctly reminds us[42] that the coherency of religion cannot be *wholly* validated rationally simply because, as yet, it is not wholly actual. Jesus' vision of the kingdom, for example, cannot be wholly and unequivocally verified, for it remains still, in large part, a vision.

The coherency of the actual *is* already *what it is,* and can therefore be tested and verified by sound philosophical criteria of judgment. But the ideal of religion is, as yet, so fragmentarily fulfilled that no philosophical reason, but only an act of faith, can proclaim that it is indeed the ultimately real. It can, in a measure, be verified by reason and the world of actuality, but not absolutely and fully.

Theology's vision, generated by revelation, thus stands as a corrective; it helps to keep the philosopher from yielding to the temptation to make this world of actuality central in his perspective and to eliminate the tension from another world, which, as Ferré says, "declares this one to be but a factory under reconversion."[43] Hence religion denies that the coherence of the actual world constitutes our final or absolute test of truth.

If truth is to be limited entirely to the rational knowledge of the philosopher and nothing more, religion will have to be viewed as visionary, in a fantastic and false sense; for religion points beyond the coherency of the actual; its vision is directed primarily to

[42]Nels F. S. Ferré, *Faith and Reason*, pp. 123 ff.
[43]*Ibid.*, p. 136.

the infinite possibilities of the ideal realm which are pressing in upon this actual world, to change and transform it. As Ferré aptly expresses it, "The difference lies between ideal coherence anticipatorily attained and partial coherence as exhibited by rational knowledge."[44]

Theology, then, is forever transcending the coherence of philosophy. For through faith, one stands in vital relationship with the creative depth of reason, with that realm of infinite possibility and ideality which overarches or undergirds the process of reality which we call the world, as it actually is.

It is of the utmost importance that we recognize clearly the problematical, partial, and fragmentary character of general revelation, and the correlative, corrective, redemptive function of special revelation.

One may point out, for example, the weakness of the traditional cosmological and ontological arguments for the existence of God. The weakness of these arguments lies in the vagueness of the conclusion reached, when that conclusion is logically drawn. The radical contingency of things does make us aware of the presence of an unconditional element in reality. Everything cannot be contingent; something must be necessary. Nothing can come from absolute nothingness; for if something came from it, it would prove that the source was not really absolute nothingness, since it obviously contained a positive something, namely, the possibility of that something which it produced. But from an awareness of an unconditional element in reality, we cannot conclude that "God exists." To arrive at this conclusion would call for an enormous jump in the argument. There is thus a limited valid-

[44] *Ibid.*, p. 123.

ity, but also a vagueness about the general revelation of God through the finitude of nature.

This vagueness is evident also in the fact that from general revelation alone we could scarcely have known that God is personal or that his essential nature is *agape.* We have no concern to eliminate the category of general revelation. Yet we must avoid that arbitrariness which, in its interest in abstract universal religious experience, fails adequately to come to grips with the factual distortion of the *imago Dei* by sin.

Some philosophers seem to be insufficiently aware of this problematical character of general revelation and of the corrective function of special revelation in Christ. A. Campbell Garnett, for example, writes that "all a special revelation in history can do is call attention to the witness of the spirit within, which otherwise we are inclined to ignore." Thus, Garnett says, the essential function of special revelation is that of a "stimulus."[45]

The trouble with the pre-Christian man, however, is not that he is merely morally drowsy and fails to pay attention to the Spirit of God working within him; his moral vision is also distorted by a sinful kind of self-centeredness; and his reason is divided within him and disrupted. The revelation of God in Christ to be sure *stimulates* him; but it also *corrects* his wrongness and redeems him from his sinful self-centeredness. Garnett himself seems to admit this when he goes on to say, in a later paragraph in the same article, that in Christ "as in no other, there is a power to break the shackles of spiritual pride and set the sinful spirit free to grow again in grace and in humility."[46]

---

[45]*Journal Bible & Religion,* Vol. XXI, No. 3, p. 159.
[46]*Ibid.,* p. 162.

The particular revelation in Christ also brings a floodlight disclosure of the *agape* character of ultimate reality, which, as an empirical fact, vastly exceeds the disclosure of God as Creative Love anywhere in general revelation. As Garnett himself concedes, in Christ "the Christian has come to see the full meaning of the divine creative love."[47]

There are to be sure partial, piecemeal, and ambiguous disclosures of this *agape* in various contexts of general revelation. Some of it is found in Mo Tih's teaching and preaching of "universal love"; some in Vishnuism in India; some in Socrates among the Greeks; some in Hosea among the Hebrews. But these, when evaluated empirically, must be compared to the revelation in Christ as rivulets to a mighty flood tide. This fact should not be slurred over in the interest in an abstract universal religious experience.

Furthermore, nature, as a medium of revelation, is ambiguous. Her ways are such a perplexing combination of constructive and destructive forces that she keeps us guessing. But when the Son of God appeared and we beheld his glory, "full of grace and truth,"[48] our minds were enlightened by "the light of the knowledge of the glory of God in the face of Jesus Christ."[49]

Thus, while even for one whose life has been caught up by the general revelatory working of God, the "starry heavens above" declare something of the glory of God, and the firmament shows something of his handiwork, this glory is wondrously enhanced for one whose life has been transfigured by the special revelation in Christ. For the Christian, the world is full of the glory of God. Like Francis of Assisi, he now sees that glory everywhere.

[47]*Ibid.*, p. 162.
[48]John 1:14.
[49]2 Corinthians 4:6.

Richard Niebuhr aptly illustrates[50] what happens to us in the special revelation in Christ by comparing it with the experience of trying to master a difficult book. Sometimes the complicated argument of the author baffles us; but we stay with it until we hit upon some revealing passage which suddenly lights up the meaning of the entire book. Revelation is comparable to this experience.

The revealing passage in the massive book of history is, for Christians, the story of the man of Nazareth. From our encounter with this event in the nexus of historical events, there dawns upon our minds a meaning which lights up the purpose or drift of all history. Herein lies part of the corrective function also of special revelation.

---

[50]H. Richard Niebuhr, *The Meaning of Revelation*, p. 93.

CHAPTER SIX

The Final Revelation Through Christ

We call the supreme revelation which constitutes the dynamic center of Christianity a "special" revelation because the experience of it leads us to affirm that it is an event which possesses a unique character. It is not a mere event, nor yet merely an event which includes the subject's existential involvement with that reality which is man's ultimate concern. It is also an existential event of a specific sort, namely, it is the event of a personal encounter with the divine Spirit, through Jesus Christ the Lord.

The New Testament idea of revelation must, therefore, be distinguished from the Old Testament conception. The two ideas are united, to be sure, in regarding revelation to be the divine dynamic working in and through history. Yet at the Old Testament level, revelation has not yet achieved the fullness of the personal encounter with God which it attains through the Christ-event.

Neither is the Christian revelation an utterly mysterious infusion of power rising up to the level of consciousness from the subliminal regions of the *psyche*. Such an impersonal or subpersonal interpretation of grace was suggested by William James.[1]

In contrast to such an impersonal concept of the divine working, Christianity affirms that the revelation in Christ is operative at the level of consciousness,

[1]William James, *The Varieties of Religious Experience* (New York: Longmans, Green and Company, 1917), pp. 483, 515 ff.

the personal level. This revelation represents the power of God becoming effective in the "I-thou" relationship. It is a "divine-human encounter," to borrow the title of one of Brunner's books. As through the New Testament witness we are brought face to face with Christ the Lord, by faith, we find ourselves, too, actually gripped by the eternal power and goodness of God.

"God was in Christ personally," Paul argued, "reconciling the world to Himself."[2] Therefore, Jesus "is justly called the Lord of all. It was in Him that the full nature of God chose to live, and through Him God planned to reconcile in His own Person, as it were, everything on earth and everything in heaven by virtue of the sacrifice of the Cross."[3]

The Original Aspect of the Final Revelation

It is of the essence of the Christian faith that there is a *finality* about this special revelation of God, for in Jesus, the *Logos* of all life became incarnate in human life. Vaguely or clearly, Christians have always known that Christianity is, finally, faith in the person of Christ. The cry "Jesus is Lord" was the primary witness of primitive Christianity. "God has made him both Lord and Christ, this Jesus whom you crucified," said Peter in the pentecostal sermon.[4]

It is the central conviction of Christianity that the eternal God was present and active in the life and person of Jesus as fully as it is possible for God to be present in a truly human life. "The Word became flesh and dwelt among us, full of grace and truth."[5] "God was in Christ personally."[6] He is

[2]2 Corinthians 5:19. J. B. Phillips trans., *Letters to Young Churches* (New York: The Macmillan Company, 1948). Quotations from this volume are used by permission.

[3]Colossians 1:19-20, Phillips trans.

[4]Acts 2:36.

[5]John 1:14.

[6]2 Corinthians 5:19, Phillips trans.

therefore a Christian who, when confronted by Jesus Christ, finds himself in a morally responsible relationship with life's final mystery. He stands face to face with the Eternal One and responds affirmatively in the decision of faith. The awesome silence of eternity has been broken. God and man meet in one.

This experiential way of conceiving Jesus as the final revelation of God is to be seen in sharp contrast to the doctrinaire view which regarded Jesus as the revelation of God merely because he taught us some divinely revealed truths about God. This scholastic view held New Testament *doctrine* to be the *content* of the revelation. According to this notion of revelation, the continuous working of the Spirit becomes unnecessary. The Spirit exhausted its revelatory function when it handed down to us mortals a final deposit of supernatural dogmas to be believed. Those who hold this doctrinaire theory of revelation are obliged, when consistent, to affirm that Jesus is the final revelation of God merely *because he communicated to us new truths about God*. He taught us to believe, for example, that the proposition "that God is gracious" is a true proposition. But as Buber points out, "One can 'believe that God is' and live at His back; the man who trusts Him lives in His face.'"[7]

The dynamic view of revelation which we have advocated leads us to recognize Jesus as the final revelation of God because he is himself the very incarnation of God, because God makes *himself* known to us, personally, in Christ, in all the warmth and power of his graciousness, so that we can trust him, and "live in His face." The teachings of Jesus, like his inspiring example and his death on the cross, are only a part of the total dynamic event.

There is a wide difference between these two conceptions of revelation, and in the kind and quality of

[7]Buber, *op. cit.*, p. 40.

religious relationship which they promote and foster.[8]

As we look more closely at the character of this event of the personality of Jesus, we are led to see that the unique thing about this revelatory event, that which makes it "final," is that a redemptive fullness of the Spirit of the infinite indwelt the person of Jesus. As a result, Jesus possessed the power to negate himself, as a finite historical being, without losing himself, for the Spirit of the Infinite is the Spirit of sacrificial love. The medium of the final revelation must therefore possess the capacity for total surrender (love) and for total sacrifice of his finite historical self. Only such a one could rightly be designated "the Christ, the Son of the Living God." Only such a one can become completely "transparent to the mystery he reveals."[9] Only such a one can serve as a medium through which Eternal Love can manifest itself, in a unique and final way, in history.

It is because Jesus became "completely transparent" to the ultimate mystery which he reveals that Paul could say: "even though we once regarded Christ from a human point of view, we regard him thus no longer."[10] Jesus' acceptance of the cross, during his ministry and at its close, was the supreme test of his perfect unity with the Father. It was the supreme test of his perfect transparency, as a finite, historical being. Only as the *crucified* Christ does he fully disclose grace and truth. Only as he sacrificed his flesh is he Spirit or Creative Love. As the Apostle Paul pointed out, Christ is the true Son of God precisely because he did not selfishly grasp at equality with God, but emptied himself, gave himself up, that is, gave up his finite self, even unto death.[11]

[8]For a brief analysis and exposition of this difference, see Ralph G. Wilburn, *Christianity vs. Legalism* (Los Angeles: Associated Publishers, 1949).

[9]Tillich, *Systematic Theology*, I, 133.

[10]2 Corinthians 5:16.

[11]Philippians 2:6-8.

This same revealing transparency is manifest in the fourth Gospel portrait of Christ who says, "He who believes in me, believes not in *me* but in him who sent me."[12] Again, "The words that I say unto you *I do not speak on my own authority;* but the Father who dwells in me does his works."[13]

Tillich is therefore correct when he argues[14] that that which makes it possible for Jesus to be the final revelation is the unique combination in him of two characteristics: (1) his maintenance of unity with God, and (2) his sacrifice of everything he could have gained for himself from this unity. For the key to an understanding of this paradoxical character of the incarnation is the dynamic of creative love. If the love of Christ was a perfect sacrificial love for others, then we would seem here to have reached a limit; we are already confronted by the Infinite, in the finite. The late William Temple correctly wrote that "there cannot be more love than absolute self-giving to all."[15]

If creative love is the content of this final revelation, then Jesus' complete self-denial and self-sacrifice become the manifestation of a perfect unity with the Father, whose inner essence is *agape* or creative love. The more perfectly Jesus renounces his self-centeredness, as a finite, historical self, the more perfectly he proves that he is united to the universal ground of all being, and the more perfectly does he, through such self-sacrifice, reveal life's ultimate mystery and meaning. Had he failed in this perfect self-renunciation, just to this extent the revelation through him would have remained ambiguous and opaque; just to this extent he would have manifested not the infinite

[12]John 12:44.

[13]John 14:10.

[14]Tillich, *Systematic Theology,* I, 135.

[15]William Temple, *The Universality of Christ* (New York: George H. Doran Company, 1922), p. 64.

Spirit of God, but only his own finite historical self. Hence the perfection of Jesus' self-consciousness lies in the fact that at every moment it was determined by his God-consciousness. His will was consistently to do the will of the Father; and this is the secret to his being the final revelation of God.

This perfect sacrificial love of Christ defines this revelation also as theonomous; that is, it is that which keeps the authority of this revelation from being authoritarian in nature. It guards against the attempt to impose Jesus, *as a finite, historical self, on other finite beings.* This is the fallacy of the glorification of the "theology of Jesus" which was popular in liberal circles in the nineteenth century. This theological point of view was oriented solely to the "historical Jesus." It wished no longer any theology *about* Jesus, but only the theology *of* Jesus. Hence Pauline Christology was distasteful to these liberals. This liberal view failed to remember, however, that it is not the *finite* aspect of Christ's being that should be absolutized; it is the infinite, the inner spirit of Creative Love. Faith is not interested in any wholly objective "Jesus of history," but only in the Jesus "whom God made our wisdom, our righteousness and sanctification and redemption."[16]

It has been said that this explication of the significance of Jesus Christ is docetic in nature. The charge is false, however. The ancient heresy of docetism was the heresy of denying the genuineness of Jesus' humanity. On the contrary, we affirm that Jesus was genuinely human, so human, indeed, that his life was caught in the meshes of historical relativism, as are all genuinely historical beings. Yet God was present in a unique and redemptive way, in the life of Jesus. This is what faith means when it professes Jesus to

[16] 1 Corinthians 1:30.

be the Christ, the Son of God. It sees *through* the limited human medium, the Eternal One. Or one may say that the eternal God draws us into the orbit of the redemptive power of his love and grace *through* the instrumentality of the historical Jesus.

It would, therefore, be an error to allow our Christology to be distorted into a mere Jesusology. For the *historical Jesus* is the medium of the final revelation precisely because he sacrificed himself completely to *Jesus as the Christ*.

The Continuous Aspect of the Final Revelation

It is at once apparent that if we should conclude our analysis of the meaning of revelation with this *original* revelation in Jesus, we should regard it as a vigorous life and movement of the now dead past, and could therefore safely commit it to the archives of history or leave it buried in the tomb of Joseph of Arimathea. How erroneous such a view would be, every Christian knows full well.

There are in reality *two* foci about which the final revelation of God in Christ turns: (1) the incarnation of the creative love of the Ultimate in Jesus, and (2) the continuous revelatory and redemptive activity of the living Lord of the church's experience.

Christianity is not merely a thing of the past. The church worships not a dead Jesus, but a living Christ. Christianity therefore is also *a revelatory and redemptive working in the present life of humanity.* For "the last Adam," wrote Paul, "became a life-giving Spirit."[17] Without this supreme and all-commanding, present reality, Christianity would indeed have little relevance to the concrete issues of daily living here and now; and it would possess inadequate power for the transfiguration of human life into the image of Christ.

[17] 1 Corinthians 15:45.

This is what Paul meant when he rebuked the Corinthian Christians for denying the resurrection from the dead.[18] The heart of the Christian message, he wrote, is the belief that Christ rose from the dead. If, however, there is no resurrection, and Christ did *not* triumph over death and is not now a *living abiding reality,* then, said Paul, all our talk of growing into vital union with the Lord[19] is nonsense. It is a legend, a fabulous tale; and so far as the issues and problems of our present daily life are concerned, Christian faith would have little meaning and relevance. Each would be obliged to find his way as best he can, alone. Christianity would be but a memory of a dead past, a bare reference to a remote figure of antiquity.

No, this is not Christianity! Christianity is a present creative dynamic that makes for righteousness; it is a revelatory illumination which makes for a knowledge of truth here and now, in the vital process of ongoing human life. The resurrection means that Christ is not merely the Jesus of history, but also the living Lord of the church's ongoing experience.

When Paul said, "We are ambassadors for Christ, God making his appeal through us,"[20] he implied that to believe in the resurrection of Christ is to believe that *Christ continues to speak* through the word of the gospel proclamation. Indeed, Christ *is* the creative Spirit, by virtue of union with whom the church lives and grows into increasing measures of Christlikeness. Paul wrote: "Now the Lord is the Spirit, and where the Spirit of the Lord is, there is freedom. And we all, with unveiled face, beholding the glory of the Lord, are being changed into his likeness from one degree of glory to another; *for this comes from* the Lord who is the Spirit."[21]

---

[18]1 Corinthians 15:12 ff.

[19]Romans 6:5-11; Colossians 3:1-3; Galatians 2:20.

[20]2 Corinthians 5:20.

[21]2 Corinthians 3:17-18.

Furthermore, the resurrection means not simply that Jesus somehow managed to survive, escaping death. It means that *by the power of God* he has been exalted as Lord. He was "designated Son of God *in power*," said Paul, "by his resurrection from the dead."[22] The author of the Ephesian epistle spoke of the "immeasurable greatness" of the divine power "in us who believe," the "great might" by which he raised Christ from the dead and exalted him as Lord over all.[23] The life of the historical Jesus has been raised to a cosmic status. Christ incarnate has received a cosmic dimension, that is, a locus in the actual living of historic process.

We must say therefore that the supreme event of the gospel revelation of God *continues to take place.* By the power of God it is not allowed to become simply a fact of the past; it continually takes place anew, in the present. Jesus is the Christ thus only if and when *he becomes the Christ to someone.*

The New Testament is full of witnesses to this continuous aspect of the final revelation, which expresses and releases the transforming power and illuminating light of the living Christ, who works in our midst and in our hearts. Paul wrote that the gospel is "the power of God" working mightily through faith.[24] "The fact is," wrote the author of the Ephesian epistle, "that what we are we owe to the Hand of God upon us."[25] The church, he said, is the place "in which God Himself lives by His Spirit."[26] And he prayed for his readers that "God may give you a spirit of wisdom and of revelation in the knowledge of him, having the eyes of your heart enlightened, that you may know. . . ."[27] In another passage of the

[22]Romans 1:4.
[23]Ephesians 1:19-23.
[24]Romans 1:16.
[25]Ephesians 2:10, Phillips trans.
[26]Ephesians 2:22, Phillips trans.
[27]Ephesians 1:17-18.

same epistle, he prayed "that out of the glorious richness of His resources He will enable you to know the strength of the Spirit's inner re-inforcement—that Christ may actually live in your hearts by faith. And I pray that you, firmly fixed in love yourselves, may be able to grasp (with all Christians) how wide and deep and long and high is the love of Christ—and to know that love for yourselves. May you be filled through all your being with God Himself!"[28] And John added, "if we love each other, God does actually live within us, and His love grows in us towards perfection. And . . . the guarantee of our living in Him and His living in us is the share of His own Spirit which he gives us."[29]

These scriptures introduce us to the continuous dimension of the final revelation. God's revelation of himself through Christ is continuous, in the ongoing process of history. The glory of the once-for-allness of the original aspect of final revelation through Jesus must not blind our eyes to the splendor and validity of the continuous aspect of revelation.

The Johannine Christ promised: "He who has my commandments and keeps them, he it is who loves me; and he who loves me will be loved by my Father, and I will love him *and manifest myself to him.* . . . If a man loves me, he will keep my word, and my Father will love him, and we will come to him *and make our home with him.*"[30]

Again, the Johannine Christ said, "I have yet many things to say to you, but you cannot bear them now. When the Spirit of truth comes, he will guide you into all the truth. . . ."[31] That is, as Jesus had been with them for a short time, as a revealer, so the Spirit would be with them always, continuing this work

[28]Ephesians 3:16-19, Phillips trans.
[29]1 John 4:12-13, Phillips trans.
[30]John 14:21-23.
[31]John 16:12-13.

of revelation. Accordingly, it was to be the Spirit's function not merely to interpret the truth of Christ, but also to preserve for Christian truth, throughout the ages, its prophetic revelatory character.[32]

It is of the utmost importance, as we develop an adequate concept of revelation, that we keep clear before our minds these two dimensions of the problem, the original and the continuous aspects of the final revelation. They must be clearly distinguished, though they cannot be separated. They are organically interrelated aspects of the total event of the revelation of God in Christ.

The original and continuous aspects of the revelation are the same, to be sure, insofar as both are to be categorized as genuine revelation, in the dynamic, personal sense in which we have defined the term. Yet there is a significant difference between them. The original revelation took place in a nexus of factors which never occurred before; while continuous revelation is based upon original revelation, including its original reception.

To be specific, Peter received an *original* revelation at Caesarea Philippi when he perceived Jesus as the Christ. We today, however, are first introduced to the Jesus of Peter's (and the other apostles') faith and experience. We have no possible way of getting at the Jesus of a reputedly objective history, directly. We can know this historical figure *only as he is portrayed through the eyes of faith* by those who bore testimony of him in our Gospels. These writings were primarily not historical biographies. They were interpretations of Jesus as Messiah, as *Logos,* as Redeemer. They were creations of faith, and should be so understood.

[32]Cf. Ernest Findlay Scott, *The New Testament Idea of Revelation* (New York: Charles Scribner's Sons, 1935), p. 233.

It therefore follows that the reception of Jesus as Lord and Christ by the first witnesses, together with the witness they bore, by which they pointed others to Christ and interpreted the meaning of their experience of Jesus as a confrontation with God, is *an organic part* of that original revelatory activity of God in history, through which continuous revelation must remain forever mediated, in a vital and determinative way.

To be drawn into the nexus of the final revelation today, we are dependent upon the witness of the recipients of the original revelation, the testimony of whose faith points us to Jesus, as the Christ. But only when, through the correlation of our own personal history with that of the early church, we, too, find ourselves actually confronted by Christ the Lord, who stands above us and in our midst, in judgment and in mercy, only then, through such living faith, do we become Christians of the New Testament order.

There is an illuminating passage in which Luther described this personal involvement of faith. Speaking of the Sophistae, Luther wrote:

> They believe in Christ with a [merely] historical faith, like a Turk; but [genuine] faith makes you and Christ almost one person, so that you are not separated from Christ, but are bound up with him and in a way are, by faith, one flesh with him, much like the bond which unites man and woman.[33]

Richard Niebuhr has correctly emphasized the need for a correlation of our own personal history with that of the Hebraic-Christian community, in an adequately Christian understanding of the outer history or the objective facts of the gospel. One may, of course, attempt to study the historical events on

[33] "Ipsi historica fide credunt in Christum ut Turca, Sed fides facit ex te et Christo quasi unam personam, ut non segregeris a Christo, imo inherescas . . . convicti per fidem in unam 'carnem, os' multo artiore vinculo quam masculus et femina" (*D. Martin Luthers Werke*, bearbeitet von O. Bremer, K. Drescher, A. Freitag, J. Luther [Weimar: Hermann Böhlaus Nachfolger, 1911], XL, I, 285-286).

which continuous revelation rests from an objective, scientific point of view. "So regarded," says Niebuhr, "they have no greater value than other events."[34] How then can revelation mean history? Only because "the history to which we point when we speak of revelation is not the succession of events which an uninterested spectator can see from the outside but our own history."[35]

We believe that Niebuhr is right in placing the locus of revelation in the inner history of selves. This means that revelation is concerned fundamentally with the meaning of facts, with history *as that which happens to me.*[36] The original aspect of the revelatory event remains, in a sense, changeless and fixed, since the objective historic event of Jesus remains forever the constant factor in all periods of the church's history. Yet there is constant variability in the meanings which are involved on the subjective side of the faith relation. There is constant transformation in the receiving activity of continuous revelation. Try as they may, no traditionalism, creedalism, or biblicism can escape this variability and relativity of the subjective side of continuous revelation.

There is, to be sure, a sameness and identity about the primary reception of the original revelation and the contemporary reception of continuous revelation, insofar as both represent the dynamic impact of the

[34] H. Richard Niebuhr, *The Meaning of Revelation*, p. 55.

[35] Ibid., p. 59.

[36] Gogarten feels that we must abandon the old concept of history, in which the basic meaning of history was found in *objective events* or bare facts of the past. The science of history, so understood, was conceived as the reconstruction of past history, on the basis of traditional records. The new concept of history, generated by the Heideggerian philosophy, views the world as no static, fixed object, set over against the knowing subject, who contemplates it in a sphinxlike detachment. Rather, says Heidegger, the world is that reality *in which* and *out of which* man lives. The relation between "the world" or "history," and the knowing, experiencing subject is much more interdependent and interrelated than the Cartesian philosophy of the subject-object relation would lead one to expect. The conflict between these two basic concepts of history is the major cause of the contemporary tensions in German theology regarding Rudolf Bultmann's theological point of view. See Gogarten, *op. cit.*, pp. 53 ff.

redemptive act of God in Christ. It is this identical confrontation which unites twentieth-century Christians with primitive Christians in an intimate and inseparable bond of unity.

Schleiermacher aptly expressed the dynamic quality of this common element in all Christian faith when he described preaching as a form of testimony which somehow arouses in others the desire to have the same experience. So that "the impression which all later believers received in this way from the influence of Christ . . . was just the same impression which His contemporaries received from Him directly."[37]

It is precisely at this point, however, where continuous revelation has again and again become distorted. The tragedy of Christian history is that the revelatory Spirit frequently departs, and we are left with formal scholastic biblicism, of which medieval scholasticism and scholastic Protestantism are impressive examples. Christians have repeatedly attempted to deify the letter of the Bible, as if one could capsule the Spirit of the Living God in the literal letter of Scripture.

Man's basic idolatrous tendency allows the revelation to become distorted. Instead of using the original proclamation of the gospel for *what it actually is*, namely, a witness of faith to the supreme fact of the person of Christ, we distort its significance and turn it into a set of infallible dogmas, and thereby get caught in scholasticism.

Scholastic Christianity is a Christianity which regards the *content* of revelation to be an authoritatively given body of doctrines which are to be simply and directly, that is, in a way external to one's own inward religious experience, taken over from the con-

---

[37]Schleiermacher, *The Christian Faith*, p. 69.

fessions of other men. This medieval distortion of continuous revelation prevails so long as people appropriate, in this inwardly meaningless way, other men's expressions of the redeemed life, and hold the belief that *by so doing* they become exactly like those other men, i.e., good Christians. Scholastic biblicism is that theory of revelation by which people believe that they themselves are good Christians because they have accepted the Bible, in this purely formal way.

The expressions of faith in the New Testament, however, were creative and constructive expressions of the early disciples' *actual experience* of God in Christ. Hence by trying, in this peculiar scholastic way, to be like New Testament Christians, one turns out to be very unlike them, and this at the fundamental point of prophetic religion: the actual experience of God in Christ.

It is one of the great tragedies of Christian history that this scholastic blockage has repeatedly stifled God's working in history and prevented the birth and development of that vital, redemptive relationship with the Eternal One which alone can redeem human life. When the continuous dimension of God's revelation in Christ is obliterated by scholastic dogmatism or by autonomous reason, original revelation for us loses much, perhaps most, of its redemptive significance and power.

If our plea for continuous revelation in the ongoingness of the historic church is valid, the scholastic use of the biblical teachings is erroneous. For it reduces the Bible to authoritative doctrine or information about a past revelation and thereby loses sight of the revelatory power of the Word, in the ongoing Christian community.

We hold that Wilhelm Herrmann was correct when he insisted that we can be helped by others' testimony of faith, and indeed by the entire religious tradition in Christianity, only if, through them, we ourselves can be led to perceive that which can serve as a genuine revelation of God *in our own lives.*[38] And, said Herrmann, if Jesus is to be *our* Redeemer, then the redemptive power of his Person must be a fact, of which not only others inform us, but which we ourselves experience.[39]

True revelation, then, is *what God does,* when working through Christ and the Scripture and the Christian community, he lifts an individual into actual communion with himself. As Herrmann elsewhere put it,

> For the Christian, indeed for the religious man in general who searches only for God, it is self-evident that God is ever the content of revelation. All revelation is the self-revelation of God. We can call any kind of communication revelation only when we have found God in it. But we find and have God when he incontestably touches and seizes us so that we are compelled to submit wholly to him. We cannot find him in any other way, for God is the all-powerful One. We have not yet found the all-powerful God, however, if we shy away from our dependence upon him in our secret thoughts, in that which gives us joy and anxiety. We experience the revelation of the Almighty in that moment when we yield ourselves to his power and deep joy. God reveals himself to us in that he compels us to trust him wholly.[40]

Revelation, then, whether original or continuous, has revelatory power only for those who enter into the revelatory correlation personally and experientially.

---

[38] D. W. Herrmann, *Ethik* (Tübingen: J. C. B. Mohr, 1913), p. 107.

[39] *Ibid.*, p. 120.

[40] D. W. Herrmann, *Der Begriff der Offenbarung* (Giessen: Verlag von Alfred Töpelmann [vormals J. Ricker], 1908), p. 10. Trans. R.G.W.

CHAPTER SEVEN

Media of the Final Revelation: Scripture and the Church

The interpretation of final revelation as a dynamic confrontation with life's ultimate mystery, through Jesus Christ, obviously calls for a reinterpretation of the part which the Bible plays in God's revelatory activity. To give ourselves to this task of reinterpretation is to proceed along theological lines which Jesus and Paul laid down. Both Jesus and Paul accepted the authority of the Scriptures, yet each gave himself to the task of biblical criticism. They vigorously repudiated the literal-legalistic view of the authority of Scripture which was popular in their day, and demanded a critical reinterpretation of the nature of biblical authority. Our task, at this point, is highly similar to that of Jesus and Paul.

We believe that the conception of revelation which we have been elaborating can enable us to rescue the Bible from the deadening, formal clutches of scholastic bibliolatry, into the whirlpool of which it was sucked by scholastic Protestantism, and make it come alive with light and power from on high.

The Scripture as a Medium of the Final Revelation

It would be a serious error for one to draw the conclusion that since the content of revelation is no objective thing, but rather a continuous happening in the ongoing process of life, the ancient writings of the New Testament should therefore be regarded as having no normative significance whatever in our experience of revelation today.

This conclusion was, in fact, drawn by some eighteenth- and nineteenth-century biblical scholars, whose discovery of the historical character of the Bible led them, in all honesty, to abandon the scholastic notion of biblical authority. Laboring under the rationalistic spell of the Enlightenment, these men were led to develop a precariously unhistorical conception of "religious experience" as our only norm. It was argued, for example, that since the Bible is a human product, it should not be regarded as a base "which enables us to distinguish what is Christian from what is not Christian."[1] The Bible is, to be sure, an interesting and inspiring book, but "there is no more finality here than in the admittedly illuminating work of Thomas Aquinas or of Calvin and Luther. Such peaks must not blind us to the fact of continuity, to the fact that we today are not only the bearers but the makers of tradition."[2]

Some liberals were thus led to cut themselves loose from an anchorage to the historic Jesus, as the Incarnate One. They recognized only one method of biblical study to be valid, namely, the historico-critical method; and to be true to this method they felt that they must eliminate any concern for a study of the Bible as revelation, as religious authority. Accordingly, the view was developed that the Bible is *merely* a literary deposit of the life of the early church. It is to be viewed *solely* as a written record of other men's experiences. It is a historically interesting, but normatively unimportant literary offshoot of the ongoing Christian community. The life of the church

---

[1]Eugene Garrett Bewkes, et. al., *Experience, Reason and Faith* (New York: Harper and Brothers, 1940), p. 637. Used by permission.
[2]*Ibid.*, p. 638.

moved on. Our only interest in the Bible today, therefore, is to regard it as an object of historic curiosity, worthy of the time and effort to delve into its pages for those who have a peculiarly dominant inclination toward historical study and research.

This "scientific" view of the Bible, which became quite prominent in the liberal Protestantism of the eighteenth and nineteenth centuries, is also a distorted one. To be sure, the Bible is a historic record. In establishing this fact securely in our thinking, the historical method is to be highly commended. And the Bible is a record which is to be studied carefully and critically like any other book, as all historico-critical exegetes have rightly argued.[3] There is a basic truth in the emphasis of the historico-critical school of biblical science which must not be denied. This school of biblical study has conclusively demonstrated the historically conditioned form of the messages of the Bible. It has proved that the form of these messages was determined by the language and mythological concepts of the intellectual milieu of biblical times. It has done this by a careful, critical comparison of the form of biblical concepts with those of the Hebraic and Hellenistic world views. It is no longer a point of debate among thoughtful students of the Bible as to whether or not the form of the biblical message was conditioned by the relative force of history. Biblical criticism has brought this fact to light and proved it beyond any reasonable doubt.

Yet if the Christian belief in revelation is true, the Bible is for Christians more than a *mere* historic document. There is a content in its form which pos-

[3]For example, Alexander Campbell, *The Christian System*, p. 3; Ernest Cadman Colwell, *The Study of the Bible* (Chicago: The University of Chicago Press, 1937), pp. 122-123; and Erich Dinkler, *Bibelautorität und Bibelkritik* (Tübingen: J. C. B. Mohr-Paul Siebeck, 1950), p. 30.

sesses a normative religious value. It is indispensable as a medium of the Christian experience of revelation. It is not only the record of revelation; it is also the bearer of revelation. For the original revelation, which constitutes the giving side, or the medium for continuous revelation includes not only the supreme event of the life, death, and resurrection of Christ, but also the reception of the meaning of this event, in faith, by the primitive Christians. Indeed, there is no way in which one can get at the former except through the latter. The Jesus of history is accessible *only through* the faith of the primitive Christian community, through the biblical witness of their faith.

It is an unwarranted oversimplification, however, to express this normative aspect of the Bible in revelation by bluntly calling the Bible "the Word of God." The Bible nowhere so describes itself.

Brunner is, in the main, correct when he contends that "in theory there is no particular need to bring the Word of God and the written word into a specially close connection. . . ."[4] Similarly, Tillich argues that to call the Bible the Word of God is to generate unavoidable confusion, for it results in "the dictation theory of inspiration, dishonesty in dealing with the biblical text, a 'monophysitic' dogma of the infallibility of a book, etc. . . ."[5]

It must be borne in mind that although we do hear the Word of God for our lives today *through* the Bible, these two are not identical. Revelation is not identical with the Bible as a historical book, as we have clearly shown. Although the two are closely related, they must be carefully distinguished from each other.

---

[4]Brunner, *Revelation and Reason,* p. 125.

[5]Tillich, *Systematic Theology,* I, 158; cf. Dinkler, *op. cit.,* p. 31.

It should be possible to avoid the use of expressions which do not describe correctly the place and function of the Bible in God's self-revelation, and to find and use expressions, both in devotional and theological language, which convey accurately and correctly the true meaning of the Bible, as a medium of continuous revelation, so as not to distort the meaning of revelation and weaken or destroy its power.

The author finds himself in agreement with Clarence T. Craig, when the latter argues[6] that the word "authority" should be retained to designate "the indispensable place of the Bible in relation to the Christian faith," despite the fact that most of the accepted definitions of the word "authority" are poor descriptions of the unique position which the Bible holds. This is due to the fact that the kind of authority with which we are dealing in biblical revelation is unique. It is essentially different from all other kinds of authority which we find in human society. Unlike all other authority, the authority in revelation is supported by no earthly power. One can reject this authority without becoming involved in any visible punishment. As Peter Brunner reminds us,[7] the gospel is empowered solely by the invisible Lordship of Christ. It is an authority which redeems all who believe in him and which judges, even now, all who are confronted by him, but who harden their hearts in unbelief. The authority of this message must be characterized as eschatological.

It is important also not to confuse the form of the gospel with the form of a philosophical treatise. The gospel is not a set of general philosophical beliefs,

[6]From *Biblical Authority for Today*, edited by Alan Richardson and Wolfgang Schweitzer (Philadelphia: The Westminster Press, 1951), p. 32.

[7]*Evangelisch-Lutherische Kirchenzeitung*, ed. Richard Eckstein, Berlin, 9 Jahrgang, Nr. 9, May 1, 1955, p. 135.

common to all mankind. It is rather a story; and one can find this story only in the Bible. As Craig puts it,

> There is no substitute for the accounts of this event which come from those who witnessed it with eyes of faith. When faith responds to the testimony of the Bible that its witness is true, then the Bible has for that person a position for which the word "authority" is not too strong a term. There is a compulsion which comes from faith to faith.[8]

Precisely *how* "faith responds to the testimony of the Bible that its witness is true," exactly *how* faith is generated in the heart through the hearing of the gospel story, cannot be described in a simple formula. There is here an ineradicable element of mystery, in the personal dimension of the experience of revelation. The "reason" of general revelation obviously plays a significant role; yet the spiritual depth of the experience of faith goes vastly beyond mere reason.

At the actual moment when faith arises in the human heart, we come upon the limits of biblical criticism. Dinkler reminds us that there is no *method* which, as such, leads one to an understanding of the Bible *with the eyes of faith.*[9] Biblical criticism does, of course, provide a method for determining *what* is presented to be believed, but not for determining *that* it shall be believed. Furthermore, historical criticism can neither eliminate nor diminish the affirmation of faith, but of course neither can it increase it. At best, it can only lead faith back to its fundamental, historical roots.[10]

In the biblical writings themselves and in those of traditional Protestantism, this mysterious ex-

[8]Richardson and Schweitzer, *op. cit.*, p. 32.

[9]"Es gibt . . . keine Methode, die als solche zu einem gläubigen Verständis der Bibel führt" (Dinkler, *op. cit.*, p. 32).

[10]*Ibid.*, p. 23.

perience in which faith is generated in one's heart is described as the working of the Holy Spirit.

Richard Niebuhr adopts Kierkegaardian language to describe it when he writes, "There is no continuous movement from an objective inquiry into the life of Jesus to a knowledge of him as the Christ who is our Lord. Only a decision of the self, a leap of faith, a *metanoia* or revolution of the mind can lead from observation to participation and from observed to lived history."[11]

The gospel must be preached; the supreme facts[12] upon which it forever rests must be proclaimed. As Brunner reminds us,[13] the original witness of those who first received the revelation in Christ was in the second person: "You are the Christ, the Son of the Living God."[14] The secondary form of this apostolic witness of necessity assumed the form of the third person: "God has made him both Lord and Christ, this Jesus whom you crucified."[15] The apostles wished others to share their experience of Christ; hence they bore their testimony *concerning him.* "Every day in the temple and at home they did not cease teaching and preaching Jesus as the Christ."[16]

However, for their hearers to share in the actual experience of the meaning of the Christ-event, for them to participate in the redemptive encounter with Christ and know him as Lord, personally, *Christ himself* must enter into personal rapport with them. The apostles could succeed in their mission of preaching only if God, in his eternal quest for the human heart, used their testimony of faith as a medium

[11]H. Richard Niebuhr, *The Meaning of Revelation*, p. 83.
[12]Cf. 1 Corinthians 15:1 ff.
[13]Brunner, *Revelation and Reason*, pp. 120-121.
[14]Matthew 16:16.
[15]Acts 2:36.
[16]Acts 5:42.

whereby to bring others also into the personal relation with himself which is faith.

Today, of course, we are confronted by the apostolic witness in written form, in the New Testament. But obviously there can be no revelation through the preaching, teaching, or reading of the Bible today unless God continues to act, and, through these means as through the early apostolic preaching, *actually* discloses himself. Otherwise the story of the gospel would belong exclusively to outer or objective history. It becomes inner history only when God confronts us, in and through it, actually and personally. One listens today to Christian testimony, biblical or contemporary, but only through the inspiration of the Spirit can he make the supreme commitment of faith and personally say: "Jesus is Lord." The biblical witness becomes of genuine, revelatory value only when God acts, through it, to shine in our hearts also "to give the light of the knowledge of the glory of God in the face of Christ."[17] As Dinkler aptly puts it, the authority of the Word of God in the Bible is perceived "only when it lays hold of us as readers and hearers, compelling us to a decision, when it is a power that overcomes us in our present existence, a power which presses in upon us, questioning us and seizing our very souls."[18]

In this dynamic view of continuous revelation, the Bible, then, must not be confused with the ultimate ground or cause of our faith. The ultimate cause of our Christian faith is God acting in Christ, or what the sixteenth-century Reformers chose to call the "*testimonium spiritus sancti internum.*" It is not man, even an apostle, who possesses the power to bestow the blessed assurance of faith, "that Christ is Lord."

[17]2 Corinthians 4:6.

[18]Dinkler, *op. cit.*, p. 32. Trans. R.G.W.

Only God himself possesses this power; but he exercises it by confronting one and inspiring him to open his heart to receive the apostolic witness as true.

That faith is thus engendered primarily by the working of God's Spirit is beyond all doubt what Paul meant when he wrote that "no one can say 'Jesus is Lord' except by the Holy Spirit."[19]

This revelatory working of God through the Bible, however, is the kind of authoritative reality which avoids the errors both of rationalistic autonomy and authoritarianism. It is not an external authority or a coercive influence which ignores the vital importance of man's responsible freedom. Jesus[20] and Paul[21] were both keenly aware of the fact that the working of God is often blocked and frustrated by man's freedom. Nor yet is revelation and faith a cold-headed, rationalistic affair, as the men of the Enlightenment mistakenly thought, in which certain intellectual propositions are submitted for our philosophical consideration and Socratic evaluation. This kind of autonomy is a violation of the theocentric heart of the gospel.

The theonomy of faith escapes both of these errors for it rehabilitates man's broken and divided freedom, without violating its integrity. The power of Christ serves to challenge and inspire man's freedom; and thereby it liberates and redeems.

Basically, therefore we must say that it is not a book, but Christ the Lord who creates faith in the human heart. But evidently he wills to do so through the use of historical means, among which stands the New Testament message. For the life of the Spirit does not exist, and cannot be generated and sustained,

[19]1 Corinthians 12:3.
[20]Matthew 23:37.
[21]Romans 10:21.

for historical beings at any rate, apart from its external historical embodiment in a religious community with its visible, institutional rites and its sacred writings.

We must never confuse the historic *means* of the experience of faith, however, with its suprahistorical *cause.* It is erroneous to cite Scripture as the reason for, or basic cause of, faith. Brunner rightly argues[22] that one does not come to have faith in Christ *merely because an apostle tells him* that Jesus is the Son of God. He believes in Jesus Christ, rather because *God himself* has convinced him that Jesus is the Christ, "just as He has convinced the Apostle."[23] The witness of the apostle is, therefore, but an instrument, a means whereby God's revelation comes to us. Hence one does not believe in Christ because he believes the word of the witness. He really believes the witness at the same moment that he responds, in faith, to Christ as Lord. In one act, faith in Christ and belief in the truth of the apostolic witness are generated, under the influence of the one Spirit who guides us into all truth.

Since the ultimate cause of faith is the working of God's Spirit, it would be more correct to say that one believes the Bible because he believes in Christ, than to say that he believes in Christ because of the testimony of Scripture. To attempt to make the Bible itself the ultimate ground of our faith, as some have done, is to distort Christian truth and transform it into a legalistic, doctrinaire affair, and faith into a mere intellectual act, which, even so, would be lacking in rationality.

Such a legalistic corruption of the authority of the Bible results from a failure to understand the

---

[22]Brunner, *Revelation and Reason,* p. 169.
[23]*Ibid.*

significance of the personalistic character of the faith-relation. One of the fundamental ambiguities which plagued orthodox Protestantism lies in its understanding of the faith-relation. Two concepts of this relation have been struggling for mastery of the Protestant mind. One of these is the view which regards faith as belief in the divine truths written in the Bible. This concept interprets faith as a doctrinaire affair, and accordingly ends up with a rationalistic and legalistic understanding of the religious relationship. The other concept, which we hold to be more sound, is one in which faith is regarded as a relation between persons; it is the relation of one's personal affirmative response to the call and claim of Christ.

The former conception of faith, the doctrinaire view, does not know that there is no "law," no external letter which can make alive.[24] It has not yet learned that the Word of God is not a dead letter, but God addressing us in Christ. It has not seen what Paul saw with penetrating clarity, namely, that "the written code kills, but the Spirit gives life."[25] The "Word of God" is not an objective book, but a communication, a call which comes to us in an *event,* in the *act* of God, in and through Christ. As Dinkler aptly expresses it, the revelation of God is *in the Scriptures* only because it happened *before the Scriptures.*[26]

Furthermore, it would seem to be quite legitimate to judge any writing, any human witness, by the norm of the Word of God in Christ. We do not measure God's Word in Christ by the canon of Scripture. Rather, we judge as to the canonicity of any allegedly apostolic writing by whether or not it treats of Christ and possesses mediatorial power to instrument and

[24] Galatians 3:21.
[25] 2 Corinthians 3:6.
[26] Dinkler, *op. cit.,* p. 31.

augment the experience of God in Christ. Inasmuch as the church of the third and fourth centuries exercised this prerogative of judging as to what should and what should not be regarded as canonical, there is presumably no valid reason why the church of the twentieth century may not do likewise, especially since we today possess a critical knowledge of the Christian sources which was unknown to the third and fourth centuries. To absolutize now and for all time to come the judgments of the mind of the church of the third and fourth centuries would surely be an unjustifiably arbitrary way to proceed, theologically.

This is not to say that the canon of Scripture is unimportant. The apostolic writings will always be among the church's most treasured possessions. Yet the emergence of a tragic misunderstanding of revelation accompanied the process of the canonization of the Christian Scriptures, in the third and fourth centuries; for the *content* of revelation now came to be regarded as *the Bible,* which the bishop, as the church official, expounded and interpreted. Henceforth, not only were revelations in other religions boldly repudiated, but also all revelations in the Christian religion, except the Bible. The canonization of Scripture brought the early period of the Spirit-controlled church to a close. The bishop (and eventually the Pope) henceforth took the place of the Holy Spirit in the Christian community.

The pathway which the episcopal church thus followed proved tragic, for it led the followers of Christ once again back into the servitude of an external authority and thereby dwarfed their spiritual growth.

In contrast to this kind of episcopalianism, the faith which is evoked by the revelation of God in Christ continually delivers us not only from such external episcopal authority, but also from a childish kind of acceptance of and submission to the writings of Scripture itself. As Paul put it, it liberates us from the restraint under which we were kept by being "confined under the law."[27] It brings us to maturity in Christ. To borrow Brunner's terms, it enables us to transcend both "the mystic's freedom from the Bible, and also the Fundamentalist's bondage to the Biblical text."[28] It establishes a freedom which rests on man's absolute dependence on God; and it secures a dependence on God which creates and fulfills genuine spiritual freedom, the freedom of righteousness and Christlikeness of character.[29]

Say, then, that the Bible is an integral part of continuous revelation, not as a mere source book for the study of objective history, nor as a legalistic blueprint for the church today, nor yet as a systematic book of infallibly true dogmas, but as a normative inspiration and guiding, provocative witness.

The New Testament is the original proclamation, or witness, by which the early disciples point us to and interpret the significance of the supreme revelation of God in Christ, in the language and thought-forms of the age in which they lived. The *form* of this apostolic witness was inevitably determined by the forces of historical relativism. Hence the truth of the Christian faith, its inner substance, is by no means dependent upon the scientific correctness of the early Christians' concept of history, for example, in which their faith lived and through which it found meaningful expression, for their day and age. But the truth of the Christian faith does depend on the fact *that it is grounded in this history,* which thus assumed a particular form of expression in the primitive Christian view of history. It does depend on the truth of the

[27]Galatians 3:23.
[28]Brunner, *Revelation and Reason,* p. 182.
[29]Cf. Romans 6:12-14; Galatians 5:13-24.

belief that the revelatory and redemptive power of God was present in this historical event. As Dinkler puts it, our faith is thus liberated from any necessary bondage to *a particular philosophical view of* history, but not from its dependence upon the historical event.[30] The Christian faith is rooted in this historical event.

The Christian faith is rooted in this event in a particular way. For there is revelatory power in the message of the New Testament witness. The kerygma of the New Testament is to be understood as the cry of a herald (Κήρυξ). The herald sounds forth the call not in his own name, but by the authority of the one whose herald he is. The kerygma of Jesus' proclamation of the kingdom of God thus was already a vital part of the incoming of this kingdom.

This dynamic character of the kerygma of Jesus' preaching is especially clear at the beginning of his ministry when, in the synagogue at Nazareth, Jesus stood up and read the passage from Isaiah:

> The Spirit of the Lord is upon me,
> because he has anointed me to preach good news to the poor.
> He has sent me to proclaim release to the captives
> and recovering of sight to the blind,
> to set at liberty those who are oppressed,
> to proclaim the acceptable year of the Lord.[31]

Luke says that Jesus closed the book, gave it back to the attendant, and when all eyes in the synagogue were fixed on him, Jesus said: "Today this scripture has been fulfilled in your hearing."[32]

The meaning of the kerygma of Jesus here is quite clear: the kerygma is already an *event*. That which Jesus proclaimed *became a reality in and through his proclamation of it.* In this sense, the

[30]Dinkler, *op. cit.*, p. 23.
[31]Luke 4:18-19. See Isaiah 61:1-2.
[32]Luke 4:20-21.

word of Jesus is the Word of God; and he who hears him hears God.

Similarly, the kerygma of the apostles shared in the dynamic of the kingdom so that Jesus could say to them: "He who hears you hears me, and he who rejects you rejects me, and he who rejects me rejects him who sent me."[33]

The kerygma of the New Testament must not be viewed as *a mere report* of some wholly objective or merely factual happening; for a reporter is not yet a real herald. Gogarten is correct in arguing[34] that the kerygma is not mere information about something which the word of the kerygma itself does not actually contain or about something which does not occur immediately *in* and *through* this kerygmatic word. On the contrary, the mode of revelation is that the revelatory and redemptive event occurs *in* and *through* this word. The revelatory event is grasped through the hearing of the word[35]; or better perhaps, it grasps the hearer of the word.

It is this dynamic quality in the word of the gospel which obliges us to distinguish the character of this "word" from the ordinary meaning of the term "word," in which it signifies mere information about this or that, or some proposition about this or that. The word of the gospel is something more; it is "the power of God for salvation. . . ."[36]

There is, therefore, no book like the Bible. More than any other writings, those of the New Testament serve as a means whereby God lays his saving hand upon us, and a means whereby there is generated in our hearts the picture of Christ, our inspired and inspiring norm. Through the New Testament thus we too are drawn into the life-giving, historical correla-

[33]Luke 10:16.
[34]Gogarten, *op. cit.*, p. 69.
[35]Romans 10:17.
[36]Romans 1:16.

tion of the events of the redemptive community and experience the transforming power of the Christ who lives and reigns, through his Spirit, in his body, the church. It is the unique connection of the biblical writings with the history of this redeemed and redemptive community and with the dynamic of continuous revelation which gives it its normative significance and authority. Above all, it is its unique connection with the life of Jesus Christ which guarantees for it forever a primary place in the life and thought of the church and in the revelatory working of God.

In conclusion, we may summarize some of the more popular ways in which this revelation has been weakened or distorted in the history of the church. In the order of the church's historical development, some of the more significant of these pitfalls have been:

(1) the absolutizing of the canon of Scripture into an infallible, external authority;

(2) the subordination of the word of revelation in the Bible to the official interpretation of the episcopal, and eventually hierarchical-papal church; in the Roman Catholic church, despite its formal recognition of the authority of the Bible, it is actually church dogma which holds the supreme place of authority; this is particularly evident in the dogma of papal infallibility;

(3) the freezing and hardening of biblical revelation in the creeds of Protestant orthodoxy, in the seventeenth century;

(4) the weakening, and at times forthright abandonment of the authority of biblical revelation by the glorification of philosophical reason as the supreme norm, by the men of Renaissance humanism and the eighteenth-century Enlightenment;

(5) the robbing of Christianity of its character as a religion of authority by some of the scholars of the

historico-critical school of biblical scholarship, in the eighteenth and nineteenth centuries; the reactionary character of this emphasis on the historical character of the biblical writings is, of course, quite understandable, but its curious silence in reference to the deeper, personal aspect of Christian experience is hardly excusable.

There are elements of truth in all of these theological points of view. Yet all of them represent certain distortions; and each, in its own way, has served to weaken or destroy the primary norm of the Christian religion: the biblical word of God's revelation in Jesus Christ our Lord.

There *is* a primacy and authority in the witness of the apostolic writings; but the dynamic character of this authority was weakened and distorted when the Scripture was transformed into a canon, which became an infallible, external authority.

There *is* an authority which characterizes the voice and confessional statements of the church; but it is the relative authority of corporate, Christian experience, the context within which the word of God's revelation in Christ always occurs. It is not the authority of infallible dogmas, whether it be a papal dogma or a Protestant creed.

There *is* an authority in the light of reason, inasmuch as the response of faith to the divine confrontation is not wholly blind and irrational; but this authority is also relative, not absolute. Furthermore, reason is a problematical authority, for it is distorted by man's sinfulness. It is corrupted also by another distortion whenever the formal aspect of reason is absolutized and overemphasized, to the neglect of the dimension of depth, for this leads to an erroneous concept of Ultimate Reality as static, a concept by which one is blinded to the deeper kind of authority in the experience of faith. Perhaps the most tragic aspect of eighteenth- and nineteenth-century rationalism, however, lies in the fact that it allowed itself to be snared by the law of autonomy. Autonomous reason breaks the authority of revelation (theonomy) in a tragically serious way.

There *is* a scientific authority in the historico-critical school of biblical scholarship. This science *has demonstrated conclusively* that the Bible is a genuinely historical book. This truth became distorted, however, when the erroneous conclusion was drawn that the Bible could therefore be *nothing but* a historical book. This *nothing but* also tended to rob Christianity of its basic character as a religion of revelation.

By keeping our Christian faith and life oriented toward God's act of revelation in Jesus Christ, we can perhaps look forward to a future in which the church will be able to avoid some of these tragic pitfalls into which she has fallen in the past, pitfalls in which the real power or authority of the revelation of God in the Bible was broken and nullified. If we have the humility and wisdom to learn what history can teach us, the church may be able to look forward to a future fulfillment more glorious than any she has enjoyed in the past, a future in which the redemptive power and meaning of God's saving Word may find a more effective release and fulfillment in man's historical existence.

The Church as a Medium of Revelation

To say that the word of the biblical witness is a medium of revelation implies that the religious grouping called "the church" is also a medium of revelation, for apart from the church there would have been no biblical writings in the first place, no one to decide what writings were to be considered "canonical" or "apostolic," no group sufficiently interested in the biblical message to preserve it for future generations, no linguistic scholars competent to translate it, and no theologians able to interpret its meaning, keeping its message relevant to the process of ongoing life.

The Christian community is therefore, in a sense, even more fundamental to the revelatory working of God than Scripture, since Scripture, in all its manifold expressions, is a product of the life of the church, and furthermore, since only a relatively few people become Christians through a direct reading of the Bible. The majority will admit that the primary medium through which they were brought to the revelation of God in Christ was the witness borne by the living members of the church, the *viva vox ecclesiae*.

It is to be remembered, of course, that the Christian community is organically rooted in the Hebraic community, which community is also integrally related to the revelatory working of God. Not only so, but the rise and development of the church were similarly dependent on the preparatory phases of God's revelatory working among the Greeks.

These religious communities were fundamental, as works of preparation and promise, to the original revelation of God in Christ. That this is true will be clear if we reflect for a moment on the fact that, apart from this preparatory work of God, looking forward to the appearance of Christ,[37] the revelation in Christ could not have been meaningfully received and assimilated. The concepts and symbols, in terms of which the impact of Jesus' personality and influence was interpreted by the primitive Christians, were drawn from Judaism and Hellenism. These were the only familiar frameworks of reference which they knew.

[37] Cf. Galatians 4:4.

To interpret the phenomenon of Jesus' personality as "Messias" was profoundly meaningful to the Hebraic mind; and to explicate this same phenomenon as a supreme incarnation of the *Logos* was most illuminating to the Greek mind. The entire eschatological hope of Judaism must be construed as part of the preparative, revelatory activity of God, and as well, the widely prevalent longing for salvation among the Greeks, to which the numerous mystery religions of the Graeco-Roman world bear eloquent witness. Indeed, the remarkable success of the early Christian mission could scarcely have been possible apart from this work of providential preparation.

It becomes evident, then, that groups, as well as individuals, can and do serve as media of revelation. God reveals himself to groups through individuals and also to individuals through groups. Usually, the individual is grasped by the revelatory activity of God through a group.

The living Christian fellowship must therefore be placed among the media of continuous revelation. The church represents not only the *communio sanctorum;* it is also the *mater fidelium,* for she carries within herself the power of the living Christ to engender faith. God reveals himself not only *to* the church, but also *through* the church.

The revelatory function of the Christian fellowship is basically fourfold. God reveals himself through the church, first of all, through the preached word, and second, through teaching. The church is composed of followers of Jesus, but followers who are commissioned to preach and teach the saving word of the gospel.[38] God is pleased, Paul wrote, "through the folly of what we preach to save those who believe."[39] Paul

[38]Matthew 28:19-20.

[39]1 Corinthians 1:21.

believed that Christ sent him "to preach the gospel," for in this preached "word of the cross" lies "the power of God."[40]

It is obvious that not all preaching or teaching carries revelatory power. Preaching does not carry such power merely because it is based on some biblical text. Even making the sermon entirely one of biblical exposition is no guarantee that it will possess revelatory power. The popular expression "preaching is an elusive art" is one way of calling attention to the dimension of mystery in the revelatory character of Christian preaching.

Sometimes the Spirit moves people mightily through preaching; at other times the sermon seems to be as "dry as dust." Sometimes the sermon is overintellectualistic, in the sense that the preacher fails to remember that the thought-content of his sermon is not, *as such,* the Word of God. The preacher may be delving into profound philosophical speculation (a luxury which is quite proper in its place), but this is not necessarily a medium of revelation. He may be vigorously elaborating the orthodox dogmas of "the faith of the fathers" (history, too, is a legitimate study, in its proper place), but the dogmas of orthodoxy are, in themselves, not revelation. He may be elaborating the teaching the Scripture, but Scripture, *qua Scripture,* is not revelation, as we have clearly shown.

Revelatory preaching is that preaching in which and through which *God* succeeds in *finding* the listener and becomes *his* God, in the relation of faith. It is that kind of preaching in which the preacher remains aware of the personal character of Christian truth and allows Christ to speak and act. It is the kind of preaching in which the preacher shares the conviction of Paul:

---

[40]1 Corinthians 1:17-18.

"We are ambassadors for Christ, God making his appeal through us. We beseech you on behalf of Christ, be reconciled to God."[41]

Revelatory preaching points away from itself and toward Christ. It is addressed *to* man, but *toward* Christ. When the preacher gets to thinking that he is preaching a wonderful sermon, his preaching is thereby likely to lose much of its revelatory power. Revelatory power is present when self is forgotten and the thought of Christ is predominant, when the motive behind the sermon is to help create the relation of faith with Christ, the sovereign Lord of all life.

Like the witness of the New Testament, this kind of preaching performs a pointing function. It points away from and beyond self, to Christ. It has a preparatory function similar to that of John the Baptist.[42] It serves as a human instrument, placed at the disposal of God, who seeks to bring the hearer into personal relationship with himself. Whenever preaching serves this end, it possesses genuine revelatory significance and power.

The revelatory significance of this hortatory proclamation must not be confused with dogmas spoken by ecclesiastical authorities, *ex cathedra,* and decreed *themselves to be* the revelation of God. This Roman Catholic concept, which holds dogmatic proclamations to be the content of revelation, is, as we have seen, an objectivistic distortion of revelation. It is an attempt to imprison the sovereign Lord of life in human pronouncements. It is to substitute an idol for the living Lord.

There is, to be sure, authority in the preached word, but it is the authority of revelatory power; it is not the authority of infallible dogmas. It is an author-

[41]2 Corinthians 5:20.

[42]John 3:30.

ity which stimulates the imagination and kindles the fires of the spirit. It is the authority of the indirect pull of the love and mercy of God.

There is nothing infallible about the analogies, concepts, and thought-forms of the sermon; these belong to the relativities of history. Just as there is no infallibility in the text and concepts of Scripture; these, too, belong to the relativities of history. Yet this does not keep the Bible from being a supreme and unique authority, in mediating the Christian experience of God. Neither does the fallibility of the minds of the church keep Christian preaching from possessing prophetic power and authority.

Our tangible religious authorities in Christianity express themselves with redemptive power in a way which is quite compatible with their historically relative character. They are *true* to the extent that the meaning and power of the Ultimate find redemptive expression and clarification in them. They are *true* to the extent that they grasp and fulfill the meaning of the Christ-event, which is creative love or community.

The second mode of expression of the revelatory function of the Christian fellowship is teaching. The major difference between this aspect of revelation and preaching is that the preaching function is proclamatory, as well as interpretative, while the teaching function is mainly one of interpretation. Through teaching, the new being created by revelation is nurtured and supported, and its power to transfigure and redeem the historic patterns of life is released and fulfilled. Through teaching, the meaning and significance of the new life in Christ are explicated and made clear. Through teaching, the revelation becomes relevant to concrete life situations.

The church should therefore take the theological aspect of her task with the utmost seriousness; though sad to say, she often fails to do so. For to the extent that her preaching and teaching fail to transcend the theological vagueness of pietistic sentimentalism, she weakens or nullifies her power to serve the ends of God's revelatory working.

Many Christian groups, particularly in the United States, have not yet been able to overcome the prejudice against theology which was generated by the pietistic reaction to medieval and Protestant scholastic theology. Many naïvely still identify "theology" with the scholastic type of theology. When they hear the term "theologian," they picture to themselves a thirteenth-century religious thinker like Albertus Magnus, who felt it to be the theologian's business to inquire about every speculative thing under the sun: Do the lost continue to sin in hell? Do they will any good at all? Is a smoky atmosphere a congenial element for demons? What are the age and stature of those who rise from the dead? Etc.

This is about as good a representation of theology as medieval alchemy is of the science of chemistry. But it in no sense justifies the continuation of the widespread prejudice against theology. It would be equally unintelligent to perpetuate a prejudice against chemistry as a science.

Rightly conceived, theology is simply a sincere and profound intellectual attempt to understand the meaning and content of our Christian faith. This is the theological aspect of the church's task. The aim of theology is to understand the *meaning* of our basic Christian affirmations, to show *why* we hold them to be the truth about our human lives, and to show *how* this religious faith is relevant to concrete individual and social situations today. Theology deals with the *what,* the *why,* and the *how* of our faith. It asks: What is its meaning? Why is it true? How is it relevant to human life? It deals with the content, the reason, and the significance of our faith.

The two major dangers confronting the church in her preaching and teaching, against which the church must be forever on her guard, are (1) sentimental pietism, and (2) doctrinaire dogmatism. By the former, the church lapses into theological vagueness and obscurantism; by the latter, her religious life crystallizes and hardens into formalistic intellectualism and dogmatism; by both, the church forfeits her capacity to serve the redemptive ends of the revelatory working of God.

The fulfillment of revelation demands both intellect and emotion, both reason and dynamics, for the Ultimate is both *Logos* and creative force. By holding these two aspects in mutual balance and creative interrelationship, the church can escape the dangers of religious fanaticism on the one hand and, on the other, the deadening fixation of creedalism and formalism, which forgets that "the kingdom of God does not consist in talk but in power."[43] Thereby the Creative Love which lies at the heart of the reality of revelation can find expression and fulfillment through the traditional forms which are still able to serve meaningfully; and it will also be left free to alter and transform these traditional structures, and to seek out new ones, which will more adequately fulfill the values of creative love.

A third mode of expression of the revelatory power of the church is to be found in the sacraments and the cultus of worship. Every sincere Christian worshiper has experienced the cleansing, the inspiration, the renewal of spirit, which God's revelation

[43] 1 Corinthians 4:20.

brings, in a supreme way, in the fellowship of worship. Here, Christ makes his presence known and felt with healing power in a way that is beyond the capacity of words to mediate. To borrow Scott's description of Paul's thought, "when men are assembled in the name of Christ they are sensitive to powers which would not otherwise touch them."[44]

In the experience of worship, we become aware of the inadequacy of mere words to appropriate and express the power of the Word of God; hence we resort to the use of the symbolism of worship; we experience the power of revelation in the sacramental action of the church. Here, too, the living Christ is present and active in a most powerful way.

Thus not only human words and speech, but other media can bear revelatory power. God reveals himself to us through the channels of sense, in the bread and wine of the Lord's table, and in the spiritual renewal of baptism.

This mode of expression of revelatory power, however, must not be confused with its erroneous interpretation in the theory of the Catholic mass and the holy water of baptism. Revelatory power is not magic and superstition. It is moral and spiritual power. The power of the Eucharist, for example, cannot be separated from its function as a corporate act of remembrance of Jesus. It is part of the main function of the Spirit to glorify Jesus Christ in Christian thinking and imagination.[45] Hence, in the church's corporate act of remembrance, Christ makes himself known as the Spiritual Presence with healing, uplifting, unifying power. Here again we see that the continuous revelation of the Spirit is dependent upon the original revelation of the Incarnation.

---

[44]Scott, *op. cit.*, p. 240.

[45]Cf. John 16:14.

Finally, God makes himself known, in eloquent power, in the Christlike behavior of devoted followers of Jesus. Inasmuch as the vital content of the final revelation centers in the dynamic of creative love, it seems most appropriate that God should choose the living community of the redeemed to serve as a medium of revelation. The New Testament makes it clear that, from the outset, participation in the Spirit of the Christian revelation is of the nature of a shared experience. The outpouring of the Spirit on Pentecost was a group experience, not the experience of isolated individuals.[46]

Henceforth men and women became followers of the Way by responding affirmatively to the challenge of the *agape*-type of life which indwelt the Christian fellowship. Through this inspiring fellowship they felt the impact of the meaning and power of Eternal Love. They listened to the witness of Christian preachers, to be sure; but perhaps even more attractive (if we may make such comparisons) was the way of life which obtained in the Christian group, the way of Christlikeness in social relations.

This living incarnation of the Spirit of Christ by members of the Christian fellowship possesses, beyond all doubt, more revelatory power than any other medium of continuous revelation. A distinguished leader of Japanese society, for example, recently sent his daughter to one of our Christian universities in America to learn whether Christianity is *in fact* what Christian missionaries say that it is. "If it is," said the father, "we would like to become Christians."

Apart from the figure of Jesus, there is no aspect of revelatory power comparable to that manifested in and through the Christian fellowship, whose members actually incarnate the Spirit of Christ in their hearts

[46]See Acts, Ch. 2.

and lives. The spirit of such a community is inspiring and sustaining. It stimulates a moving vision of the kingdom. It challenges the self-centered person to repentance. It fosters and develops the fruit of the Spirit: love, joy, peace, patience, kindness, goodness, faithfulness, gentleness, self-control.[47] It is the redemptive "salt of the earth"; it is the life-giving "light of the world," a light by which others are inspired to "give glory"[48] to the Eternal One who is the ultimate ground of all being, meaning, and value, whom to know is to love in humble obedience, and whom to love is life eternal.

---

[47] Galatians 5:22-23.
[48] Matthew 5:13-16.

PART THREE

Protestantism and The Contemporary Challenge of Christian Unity

CHAPTER EIGHT

Historical Concepts of the Ministry and Their Significance for the Cause of Ecumenical Christianity

We have devoted Part Two of this volume to the problem of revelation. Tht problem of unity is also inseparably bound up with the problem of revelation and authority. For it is only through a closer and clearer bond with the dynamic center of prophetic Christianity that significant and fruitful unity can be achieved. The horizontal dimension of unity is inseparable from the vertical dimension. Our relation to one another in the church is based upon our primary relation to God in the revelatory disclosure through Jesus Christ. The prophetic Spirit which stems from this revelation is thus the creative fountainhead of genuine Christian unity. It is to the contemporary challenge of Christian unity, in the ecumenical movement, that we turn our attention in the third part of this work.

The prophetic spirit of undenominational Protestantism is, in our day, beginning to attain a fulfillment in which it is bearing hopeful fruit toward a solution of the age-old problem of Christian unity. Every careful student of Christian history will agree that the ecumenical movement, in all of its scope and vigor, is one of the most amazing phenomena in the entire history of the church.

Such an accurate writer as Henry Pitney Van Dusen makes bold to affirm that for eighteen hundred years the Christian ideal of unity was only saluted by leading Christian thinkers; the ruling tendency was centrifugal. During the past one hundred fifty years, however, the dominant tendency has been centripetal.[1] The former thesis is somewhat overdrawn. In view of the achievement of unity in the great Middle Ages, theologically, ecclesiastically, and culturally, however valid be the protest against the principle of church authority upon which this unity was based, one can hardly describe this period as one in which the "dominant trend" was centrifugal. Nevertheless, there is much truth in Van Dusen's argument. And, of course, when one considers the invigorating democratic quality of the contemporary ecumenical unity of the church groups throughout Christendom, it is indeed true that never before has history witnessed such a bond between people who espouse the Christian faith and are dedicated to Christian ideals, and between various ecclesiastical bodies in Christendom.

Something of its novelty, theologically, may be seen in a remark of Samuel M. Zwemer. At the Lausanne Conference on Faith and Order in August, 1927, Adolph Deissmann, chairman of the Commission of the Church's Message to the World, submitted a draft which, with minor modifications, was adopted unanimously by the Conference. The statement is an excellent summation of the modern Protestant understanding of the faith. At the close of the vote, Zwemer turned to William Adams Brown, and "in a voice of deep feeling," according to Brown, said: "To think that I should have lived to see the day when Professor Deissmann and I could join in a statement of this

[1] Van Dusen, *op. cit.*, p. 80.

kind!'"[2] To anyone who is familiar with the divergent theological positions of Deissmann and Zwemer, something of the novel significance of the current ecumenical trend will be obvious.

The fact that this movement for unity has its roots in Protestant Christianity, the seemingly most divided wing of Christendom, is eloquent witness to the prophetic power of the Protestant spirit. And the heartening formation and development of ecumenical forms of expression and realization are further confirmation of a major thesis of this volume, namely, that the Protestant understands Christianity as a truth or spirit which is something more than any of its historical forms of expression, a reality which seeks ever anew more adequate forms of fulfillment.

Precisely what institutional forms the church of the future will assume, through the transforming power of the ecumenical impulse, no one of course knows. Our vision is still rather dim at this point. The problem has been debated thus far in terms of federation or organic union. One of the main blockages in the pathway which leads toward greater organic union is the theological position of the high churches regarding the nature and status of the ministry. To understand the full significance and scope of this problem, one must view it in its historic setting. In this chapter, therefore, we shall develop a realistic understanding of the ministry, by viewing it in its historical development.

The "Catholic" or Hierarchical View of the Ministry

The concept of the ministry which has enjoyed the longest history (but not necessarily therefore the

[2]William Adams Brown, *Toward a United Church: Three Decades of Ecumenical Christianity* (New York: Charles Scribner's Sons, 1946), p. 103. Used by permission.

better or truer view) is what is usually referred to as the "Catholic" view. It would be more accurate to call it the hierarchical view, for in many respects it is not as truly catholic or universal as the Protestant view. For the sake of expediency, however, we may continue to call the hierarchical view the "Catholic" view, since Romanism has given the term "Catholic" a content which goes far beyond the root meaning of the word.

The Absolutizing of a Structural Element

One's concept of the ministry is inevitably determined by his concept of the nature of the church. What then is the Catholic concept of the church? It is a view in which the *essential nature* of the church is regarded as something institutional, and which therefore holds the ministry to be a hierarchical office. The ministry constitutes an authoritative caste. Indeed, it is the apostolic ministry which *makes* the true church, in the final analysis. The hierarchical view holds the ministry to be a fixed and authoritative order or governing body; the ministry is a sacred caste of "rulers" in the church. The distinction between clergy and laity is not relative and functional, but organic and ultimate. It lies in the essential constitution of the church. By right of divine authority, the clergy rule and the laity are ruled.

Kenneth E. Kirk expressed this indispensability of the ministry in the essential structure of the church, when he wrote, "The Church is dependent on the ministry: *Ubi episcopus ibi ecclesia catholica.* . . . Church and ministry are wholly intertwined. Each owes its being, not in any way to the other, but directly to its divine Originator; yet apart from each other they are meaningless and nonexistent. The Catholic Church cannot be found except as gathered round the apostolic ministry; the apostolic ministry cannot exist except in the bosom of the Catholic Church."[3]

Similarly, F. W. Green, Canon of Norwich Cathedral, expresses his conviction that the true church is blessed with a "definite and permanent order and structure." Canon Green feels that "there is much danger in a false interpretation of the promise that the Holy Spirit is to lead the Church into all truth: as if under His guidance the Church were to expect to see itself transformed into a quite different shape in each new age and lose all real continuity with its past. . . . Therefore there are of necessity certain things in the Church which remain always the same, even while the Spirit of life is continually throwing fresh light upon them."[4] Canon Green then proceeds to list the familiar four points of the Lambeth Quadrilateral: canon, creed, sacraments, and the apostolic ministry.

In a similar vein, the ancient Cyprian vigorously opposed the martyrs' claim to possess the Spirit and, with it, the authority to absolve sins. Cyprian responded to the martyrs' claim with the counterclaim that the authority of Christ is vested solely in the apostolic episcopate. The concept of episcopal authority was the weapon with which Cyprian did successful battle against all spiritualists and individualists.

The popes of Rome have similarly always remained suspicious of the doctrine of the Holy Spirit. They have been keenly aware that if the Spirit were permitted to operate freely, the mystics, the Brethren of the Common Life, and the predestinarians would overthrow the hierarchical establishment of the church. And it is a matter of common knowledge that many a mystic paid with his life for his belief in a

[3]Kenneth E. Kirk (ed.), *The Apostolic Ministry* (London: Hodder and Stoughton, 1947), pp. 29-30. Used by permission.

[4]*Ibid.*, p. 549.

personal union with the Spirit; for consciously or unconsciously he was threatening to undo the *status quo* of Roman hierarchicalism.

The root principle of the Catholic view is, therefore, clear. It holds that the ministry, through which flows the succession of apostolic authority, is essential to the being of the church. Dr. Bright puts it succinctly by saying that "the church began in the Clergy."[5]

Now first of all, we proceed to establish two things about this Catholic view of the ministry: (1) that the meanings of this hierarchical view were in fact determined by the relativities of history, as are *all* of our theological beliefs; and (2) that the notion of apostolic succession underwent a long, complex process of development. Let us develop these theses briefly.

Ancient Historic Roots

The historic roots of the hierarchical view are discernible very early, as early as Clement of Rome (c. A.D. 96), and Ignatius of Antioch (c. A.D. 110). Ignatius contended that it was not lawful without a bishop to baptize or to celebrate a love feast.[6] He even urged the Magnesians to do *absolutely nothing* without the bishop. Nothing at all should appear commendable to anyone, apart from the bishop's approval. Ignatius believed that "he who does anything without the knowledge of the bishop does [in reality] serve the devil."[7]

In the third century, Cyprian, the bishop of Carthage, wrote that "the church is founded on the bishops, and every act of the church is controlled by these same rulers."[8]

---

[5] *Ibid.*, p. 30.

[6] *Ad Smyrnaeans*, Ch. viii.

[7] *Ibid.*, *Ante-Nicene Fathers*, American Edition (Grand Rapids: William B. Eerdman's, 1950), I, 90. Used by permission.

[8] Epistle XXVI, sec. 1, *Ibid.*, V, 305.

The sovereignty of the Almighty was now conceived as being tied inseparably to and bound up with the action of the episcopate. To do business with God, religiously, one must negotiate with his appointed representatives, the bishops. One cannot have the correct piety except he belong to the bishop-controlled church and obey her rules. Cyprian wrote:

> They are the church who are a people united to the priest. . . . Whence you ought to know that the Bishop is in the Church, and the Church is in the Bishop; and if any man is not with the Bishop, that he is not in the Church.[9]

The crux of this Catholic view of the ministry is summed up in the popular phrase, "apostolic succession." The phrase, however, is ambiguous. Its meaning has been construed in several ways. In general, of course, it means that the ministry stands in a specific episcopal traditional line, whereby it receives *something* from the apostolate of the primitive church, which is not directly accessible to the ordinary layman. Putting it a bit crudely, one might say that the episcopal tradition is a special pipeline of the means and the ministry of grace. The laity has access to this healing flow of grace and truth only by tapping this pipeline. In general, thus, the phrase connotes a hierarchical distinction between the clergy and the laity.

Specifically, however, the notion of the apostolicity of the episcopate has undergone a manifold historical development. During the subapostolic period, the episcopate came to be regarded as invested with apostolic quality and authority, though precisely *how* bishops came by this authority was not made clear by Clement or Ignatius. Ignatius believed that the bishop was *a direct representative* of Christ in each local community. He also promoted the novel idea of the

---

[9]Epistle LXVIII, sec. 8, *Ibid.*, pp. 374-375.

monarchical episcopacy in the local congregation, and fathered the distinction between the function of the bishop and that of the presbyters, evidently due to the pragmatic value of these concepts, for the sake of order and efficiency in the local church.

In the main, however, down to the middle of the second century apostolic authority turned about the figure of the ancient *presbyter*. It was felt that, because he had had a very close connection with the original proclamation of the apostles, he was in a uniquely authoritative position to vouch for the true tradition. Till the middle of the second century, thus, the genuineness of the Christian revelation was certified by the ancient presbyter.

Significant Transition in Irenaeus

The writings of Irenaeus reveal a significant shift of authority from the shoulders of the ancient presbyter to the bishop, who is now thought of as being able to guarantee the true canonical writings and the "rule of faith," even though he be a young man, *because he is an official member of the episcopate.* In fact, Irenaeus himself vacillates between these two methods of authenticating the gospel tradition.

A kind of exchange of functions now took place. The bishop, who formerly governed, became now the supreme guardian of the true faith; while, as the church grew in size, the presbyter, under the bishop, assumed the task of leadership in worship.

It was in connection with this second-century transition in the function of the episcopate that there came into being, for the first time, an explicit theory of apostolic episcopal succession. The first clear statement of this theory appears in the writing of Irenaeus. According to Irenaeus, the bishop's official succession is derived from his own deceased predecessor in the same See, and back through this immediate predecessor to his predecessor; and so on, back to the original apostolic founder of that particular church. Irenaeus wrote: "We are in a position to reckon up those who were by the Apostles instituted bishops in the Churches and to demonstrate the succession of these men to our own times."[10]

This Irenaean method of interpreting apostolic continuity, of course, makes no provision for the idea which was developed at a later time, namely, continuity through a sacramental succession *from bishops of other churches,* by means of the laying on of hands.

It is to be noted also that the function of apostolic succession was construed by Irenaeus, and also by Tertullian, mainly as furnishing the church with the guarantee of the purity of apostolic teaching. The Montanist and Gnostic crises made the need for an authoritative interpretation of the apostolic writings acute. This greatly augmented the doctrinaire aspect of episcopal authority. There seemed to be no way to meet the Gnostic and Montanist claims of a secret tradition of a more authentic brand of the faith, handed down by an esoteric succession of private teachers, save by *absolutizing the public tradition* through the official teachers, the succession of bishops.[11] The birth and development of this doctrinaire episcopal absolutism constitute one of the most significant revolutions in the history of Christian thought.[12]

Function of Episcopacy Altered by Church Growth

As the churches of the large metropolitan areas increased in numbers, the jurisdictional function of the

---

[10]*Ad. Her.* III, Ch. iii, sec. 1, *Ante-Nicene Fathers,* I, 415.

[11]See Irenaeus, *Demonstration of Apostolic Preaching,* 2; also Tertullian, *Prescription Against Heretics,* chap. XXXII.

[12]Cf. Alexander V. G. Allen, *Christian Institutions* (New York: Charles Scribner's Sons, 1897), p. 99.

episcopate became increasingly heavy and complicated. Down to the days of Hippolytus, in the latter part of the second century, the main function of the bishop was the ministration of the Word and the sacraments, in the local congregation. As Hippolytus puts it in the prayer which he lays down for use at the ordination of the bishop, request is made that God pour forth his "royal Spirit" upon the people's choice for the bishop, enabling him "to serve as thy high priest without blame, ministering night and day, to propitiate thy countenance without ceasing and to offer thee the gifts of thy holy church. And by the Spirit of high-priesthood to have authority to remit sins. . . ."[13]

The prayer at the ordination of the presbyter, according to Hippolytus, asks that God will grant to him "the Spirit of grace and counsel of a presbyter, that he may sustain and govern thy people with a pure heart. . . ."[14] The presbyter's task, then, was that of "governing" the congregation. It is significant also that the presbyters stood with the bishop and laid their hands also on the oblation, while the bishop said the eucharistic prayer.[15]

T. W. Manson argues[16] from these passages that we are to see in the Hippolytean bishop "a specialized presbyter." The bishop is a representative of the presbyters and now himself performs functions which were formerly exercized by all the presbyters, on a rotation basis. When, therefore, at a later date, the major task of the presbyters became the ministry of the Word and the sacraments, this was not a wholly new development; it meant simply that the presby-

---

[13]Burton Scott Easton, trans., *The Apostolic Tradition of Hippolytus* (Cambridge: The University Press, 1934), p. 34. Used by permission.

[14]*Ibid.*, p. 37.

[15]*Ibid.*, p. 35.

[16]From *The Church's Ministry*, by T. W. Manson, Copyright, 1948, by W. L. Jenkins, The Westminster Press, p. 74. Used by permission.

ters were resuming functions which they had exercised in an earlier period of the church's history.

By the middle of the third century the growth of the church in the metropolitan areas rendered the Hippolytean pattern of congregational episcopacy highly problematical. The bishop could not serve as *minister* or *priest* to a congregation of forty or fifty thousand, which is the estimated size of the church in Rome at that time. But it was decided *not* to break up the metropolitan church into several independent groups, each with its own bishop. By this decision, the bishop, by the necessities of the situation, became the governor of the church. He was obliged, finally, to intrust the ministry of the Word and the sacraments to his presbyters. That is, the functions of the bishop and the presbyters once again changed hands.

The *Chorepiscopoi,* first mentioned in the thirteenth of the Canons of Ancyra (314), emerged in this period. These were something like modern suffragan bishops, with limited powers. They exercised supervision over the church in rural districts. Their presence indicates the steady development of the authority of the metropolitan bishop, in this instance, his authority over the rural areas of church life.

Cyprian's Novel Addition to the Concept

In the middle of the third century Cyprian injected another novel element into the notion of apostolic succession. He radically enlarged the idea by adding to the episcopal office also the function of a priest, vested with the authority of Christ to remit sins, and entrusted with the task of offering up sacrifice to atone for the sins of the people. And to have something to offer, Cyprian transformed the meaning of the Eucharist. Formerly, it had been thought of as a sacrifice of praise, an ἐυχαριστία. Cyprian made it a sacrifice in a *literal* sense, a literal, albeit nonbloody, *repetition* of Calvary. The episcopal office thereby took on the elements of sacrifice and priesthood, in the ancient, pre-Christian, Jewish sense of the terms.

Thereby also the meaning of grace, mediated by the episcopacy, underwent a significant change in the third century. Grace was no longer thought of as God's loving favor, but as some *holy thing*, something quasi-physical, by imbibing which one became substantially infused with the quality of immortality; and it was a sacramental grace which was now in the control of the bishop-priest.

Rationalizing the Concept by the Petrine Theory

The authoritative aspect of the episcopate was also theoretically strengthened in Cyprian's day, and shortly before, by the development of the Petrine theory of episcopal authority. The Roman bishop, Calixtus (d. 222), seems to have been the first one to use the Matthean passage on the authority of the keys[17] to support the Petrine character of his office. This was, of course, not yet a papal claim, but only the claim of apostolic power to forgive and retain sins. Hippolytus (217-235), the first antipope; the Roman bishop Zephyrinus (198-217); and the latter's successor, Bishop Calixtus (217-222)—all three adopted the idea that Peter was the first Roman bishop. Hippolytus referred to Victor as "the thirteenth bishop of Rome from Peter."[18]

Cyprian, bishop of Carthage (248-258), also carried forward this argument for the Petrine authority of the episcopate. But he fought vigorously against the tendency at Rome to delimit this peculiar authority

---

[17]Matthew 16:19.

[18]According to Eusebius, *Ecc. Hist.*, V, xxviii, 3, *The Nicene and Post-Nicene Fathers*, trans. Phillip Schaff and Henry Wace (New York: The Christian Literature Company, 1890), I, 246.

to the Roman bishop. Cyprian took the *Tu es Petrus* passage as the charter, not for the Roman papacy, but for *the entire episcopate* of the church. He felt that *each bishop* possessed that full authority which our Lord conferred upon Peter, and that Peter was therefore a prototype and fountainhead of *all* bishops.

Cyprian's opponent, the Roman bishop Stephen, was the first one to appeal to the Petrine passage as a basis for claiming the supreme authority of the Roman chair, which would give its bishop primacy over all other bishops. Stephen seems to have felt that such an arrangement was necessary for the sake of peace and order in the church. Thanks to Cyprian's vigor, Stephen encountered considerable difficulty in exercising this claim effectually.

The Expansion of Papal Power

Damasus (Roman bishop, 366-384) fared somewhat better than Stephen, for he was able to secure from the Emperor Gratian a rescript (378) which gave legal status to the claim of the Roman bishop to supremacy. This put some teeth into the claim. The rescript ordered all offending metropolitans to come to Rome for trial—or else "to appear without delay before those whom the Roman bishop names as judges." The rescript also gave the Roman bishop the right of intervention in cases where bishops were suspected of "partiality or prejudice." And it released the Roman bishop from the embarrassment of being tried by his fellow bishops, and held him responsible to the Emperor alone.

So the story of episcopal development goes. Its political power was greatly increased by Leo the Great (440-461). In a series of sermons which Leo preached periodically to some two hundred of his metropolitanates, celebrating the anniversary of his consecration as "Pope," he contended that the work and merits of the blessed Peter continue to live in the deeds and decrees of the Roman bishop, that the superior apostolic authority of Peter prevails in the Roman See, and that the Pope's exhortations should therefore be regarded as the very voice of the blessed Peter.[19] Leo contended "that it is reasonable and just" to regard "the holy Roman church, through St. Peter, the prince of the apostles," as "the head of all the churches of the whole world."[20] He wrote that Peter, who has the care over all the shepherds and the sheep committed to him, should be seen in "my humble person," for Peter's "dignity is not lacking in me, his heir, although I am unworthy."[21]

Hilary, archbishop of Arles, vigorously contested Leo's high pontifical claims over the metropolitans. In due time, however, he was overpowered by Leo, who secured from the Emperor Valentinian III the celebrated rescript of July 8, 445. The rescript declared that it would henceforth be unlawful for the bishop of Gaul or for any other bishops to do *anything* without the authority of *"the venerable Pope,"* and that papal decrees, past and future, were to be regarded as the law for everyone.[22]

The actual extension of this high papal claim of the Roman pontiff over the secular as well as the spiritual princes reached its high-water mark during the reign of Innocent III (1198-1216). Innocent was the first pope to claim that Peter's successor was not only the "vicar of Christ," but in very truth the "vicar of God." In a letter to Acerbius and to other clergy in Tuscany, Pope Innocent compared the re-

[19]See B. J. Kidd, *The Roman Primacy* (London: Society for Promoting Christian Knowledge, 1936), p. 118.

[20]Oliver J. Thatcher and Edgar H. McNeal, *A Source Book for Medieval History* (New York: Charles Scribner's Sons, 1905), p. 86. Used by permission.

[21]*Ibid.*

[22]See Kidd, *op. cit.,* p. 127.

lation between the papacy and the secular power with the sun and the moon. Just as the Creator has set these two luminaries in the firmanent, "so He set two great dignities in the firmament of the universal church . . . the greater to rule the day, that is, the souls, and the lesser to rule the night, that is, bodies."[23] And as the light of the moon is derived from the sun and is inferior to it, "so the royal power gets the splendor of its dignity from papal authority. . . ."[24]

The Bull *Unam Sanctum*, published by Pope Boniface VIII, on November 18, 1302, similarly declares:

> There is only one, holy Catholic and Apostolic Church. And we believe and hold that outside of her there is no salvation. . . . if the temporal power deviate from the true path, it is judged by the spiritual power; but if a minor spiritual power deviate from the true path, it is judged by its superior; if the supreme power (the Papacy) deviate, it can be judged not by man but by God alone. . . . every human creature is subject to the Roman Pontiff,—this we declare, state, define and pronounce to be altogether necessary to salvation.[25]

The Final Dogma of Papal Infallibility

The theological aspect of this papal concept of church authority reached its apex in 1870, when the Vatican Council of Pius IX made a dogma of the notion of papal infallibility. This Council declared that by the appointment of Christ, "The Roman Church possesses a superiority of ordinary power over all other churches," that all persons "of whatever rite and dignity" are bound to submit to Rome in matters of faith and morals, and in matters of discipline and church government, and that "this is the teaching of Catholic truth, from which no one can deviate without loss of faith and of salvation."[26]

---

[23]Thatcher and McNeal, *op. cit.*, p. 208.

[24]*Ibid.*

[25]"Poro subesse Romano Pontifici omni humanae creaturae declaramus, dicimus, difinimus et pronuntiamus omino de necessitate salutis" (Denzinger, *op. cit.*, p. 218). Trans. R.G.W.

[26]Denzinger, *op. cit.*, pp. 491 ff. Trans. R.G.W.

The Decrees of this Council conclude with the affirmation that its framers "teach and define that it is a dogma divinely revealed: that the Roman Pontiff, when he speaks, *ex cathedra* by virtue of his supreme apostolic authority . . . is possessed of that infallibility with which the divine Redeemer willed that his Church should be endowed in defining doctrines of faith or of morals; and that therefore such definitions of the Roman Pontiff are irreformable of themselves, and not from the consent of the Church."[27]

This, it would seem, marks the nth degree in the development of absolutistic, episcopal authority. The voice of the Pope is now *the very voice of God.* Thus, finally, what we really get in the concept of apostolic succession is not so much a representative of Christ, but, as Luther perceived so keenly, a veritable *replacement* of Christ.

This brief historical survey has shown clearly two things: (1) the undeniable fact that the hierarchical and papal concepts of the order of the ministry were *in fact* shaped by the forces of historical relativism; and (2) that their meanings underwent a long and complex process of development, being shaped by these same forces.

In view of these indisputable conclusions, it would seem to be painfully obvious that the "Catholic" concept of the church, which attributes an absolutistic character to the apostolic ministry, is beset with a deep contradiction. How is it possible for a ministry which, *as a matter of fact,* has been determined by *historically relative* forces, to be absolutely true, in any one of its historically diversified forms? Does not such conditioning by historical relativism forever shatter the claim for ministerial absolutism?

---

[27] *Ibid.,* p. 508. Trans. R.G.W.

Similarly, how is it possible for any particular concept of the apostolic ministry or apostolic succession to be *absolutely* true, when *all* of these concepts have been shaped and fashioned by the *relative* forces of history?

The Protestant or Evangelical Concept of the Ministry

Our survey of the development of the episcopate should enable us to realize that the Protestant or non-episcopal view of the ministry rests on fundamentally different premises.

Martin Luther may be taken as a representative figure for our exposition, for it was the profound personalism of Luther's conception of faith that broke the back of the papacy, removed the hierarchical mediation of the priesthood, and re-established the individual's personal relation with Christ the Lord, thereby enabling the believer to be "lord over all and subject to none," as Luther expressed it.[28]

Luther's View of the Nature of the Church

If, for the hierarchical view, the idea of apostolic episcopal order is the normative principle which constitutes the church, for Luther, the church is a fellowship of believers, constituted in and by the dynamic of the Word of God. Luther claimed that the life and substance of the church are in the Word of God. This Word of God is Jesus Christ who exercises his authority through the word of Scripture and through the preached word.

Luther believed that the Word is the sole vehicle of the grace of God, that by it the kingdom of God is established in the hearts of men, and that therefore it is the one and only true mark of the church. Luther

[28]See "On Christian Liberty."

felt that the Word of God cannot be without God's people, and that God's people cannot be without the Word.

This central emphasis on the Word of God makes the Protestant conception of the essential nature of the church basically different from the episcopal concept of the church. As Luther stated it in his reply to Augustine von Alfeld, "According to Scripture . . . the Church is called the assembly of all believers in Christ upon earth, just as we pray in the creed: 'I believe in the Holy Ghost, a communion of saints.' The community or assembly consists of all those who live in true faith, hope and love; so that the essence, life and nature of the church is not a *bodily* assembly, but an assembly of *hearts* in one faith."[29]

In Luther's view, the church is something internal, spiritual, and nonphysical. It is the realm where *Christ* rules in the hearts of men. It is the realm of *faith.* If Cyprian said, "where the *bishop* is, there is the church," Luther said, "wherever *Christ* is and wherever *He* exercises His Lordship effectively, *there* is the church." The living heart of the church is not the power of the bishop, but the authority of Christ, realized in the experience of faith. For Luther, the church is only a servant, not a master. The church is a means, never an end.

In the main, Protestantism has followed Luther in affirming that the Christian lives out of a confrontation by God, acting in Jesus Christ, and in the final analysis *only* out of this personal encounter. Hence, if the Protestant is asked, "What is your norm?" he replies: "Jesus Christ the Lord, *this and nothing else!*" and he adds, by way of clarification, that whoever sets over against the Lordship of Christ *any other norm,* thereby mitigating or qualifying the supremacy

[29]From "On the Papacy" in *Works of Luther,* I, 349.

of Christ, is an idolator. Protestants believe that Roman Catholicism has been guilty of just such idolatry.

If the church is truly a spiritual fellowship of faith and love, it exists wherever Christ, in the free sovereignty of his Lordship, evokes the response of faith. It cannot therefore, said Luther, be tied down to Rome or to any other place. Christ the Lord is not under human control and manipulation. Luther contended that the church is not bound "to Rome or any other place, but it is where there is faith in the heart, be a man at Rome, or here, or elsewhere. It is a nauseating lie, and Christ is made a liar when it is said that the Church is in Rome, or bound to Rome —or even that the *head* and the *authority* are there by divine right."[30]

Said Luther, from the essentially spiritual character of the church, "it follows that . . . the true church may not and cannot have a head upon the earth, and that no one on earth, neither bishop nor Pope, can rule over it; only Christ in heaven is the head, and He ruleth alone."[31]

Luther clarified this thesis by saying, "How can a man rule over anything which he does not know or understand? And who can know whether a man truly believes or not? Aye, if the power of the Pope extended to this point, then he could take away a Christian's faith, or direct its progress, or increase it, or change it, according to his pleasure, just as Christ can do."[32]

Luther was quite aware that the church requires outward and visible forms; but with prophetic enthusiasm, he attacked the view that the church is constituted by permanent and definite forms, the view

[30] *Ibid.*, p. 350.
[31] *Ibid.*, p. 357.
[32] *Ibid.*

which says that the church's life is unrealizable except through certain specific forms.

Luther believed that the church is a *human response* to the call and authority of Christ, and that therefore the *orders* of church organization are purely human and relative. *There is no absolutely correct order,* episcopal or otherwise. Christ is our only absolute. Nothing must be allowed to idolatrize Christ, no order, no system, no human arrangement. Furthermore, since priests, deacons, bishops, and popes do not possess the power to make Christians, they therefore do *not* belong to the *essential nature* of the church.

To be sure, the church must find its realization in historical time. It cannot exist therefore without some forms of order and external structure; but these do not belong to the essence of the church's life.

This was the prophetic insight which liberated the conscience of the Augustinian monk of Wittenberg from slavish submission to the *magisterium* of the Roman hierarchy.

Other reformers, like Zwingli and Melanchthon, came more fully under the sway of the humanism of the Renaissance than Luther; they therefore perceived even more clearly than Luther that the institutions of the papacy had actually been derived from and developed by the relative situations of history. Protestantism was thereby set free from the papal rule of Rome and was (and still is) able to quest for new and better forms of expression for the life of the church.

Protestantism's Functional Concept of the Ministry

What now is the character and function of the order of the ministry, according to this Protestant view of the church? The character of the ministry is defined in keeping with the great doctrine of the priesthood of all believers, a doctrine which eliminates any hierarchical distinction between clergy and laity.

This insight effected an exhilarating liberation of the Christian conscience from the tyranny of the medieval sacrament of orders. When Luther established a direct relation of the believing soul to Christ, he at once abolished the entire sacrament of priestly mediation and authority. All believers were now thought of as priests equally. As we pointed out in our opening chapter, this classical Protestant doctrine of the priesthood of all believers means essentially three things: (1) a termination of clerical domination of the Christian conscience; all are now laymen alike, or rather priests alike, equally worthy to appear before God, to pray for and to teach one another mutually; (2) an affirmation of the Christian obligation to serve one another in Christlike love; this service of mutual love is the positive content of the priesthood of our faith; (3) a functional differentiation of the ministry; differences remain in the tasks of Christian service, but they are now regarded as functional in character, not hierarchical; the peculiar function of the clergy is now the ministry of the Word.

The Relative Character of Ordination

The Protestant minister is set apart from the congregation *only insofar as* he is charged by and accepts the congregational decision that he give himself to the ministry of the Word, a task which not every member of the church can fulfill effectively, since special theological training is required to proclaim the Word effectively.

In the Protestant view, therefore, there are only two *essential* things in the *making* of a minister: (a) the call of Christ, and (b) the benediction of his Spirit. It is Christ who *makes* ministers. As Manson aptly expresses it, "The Christ who is for us the only and ever-present King and Head of the Church, is the

Maker of ministries. And he needs no vicar to act for him."[33] Ordination is simply a recognition by the congregation of the genuineness of one's ministerial call and of his ability to serve in this capacity. Ordination means that the church accepts and formally acknowledges Christ's gift.

If this is the status of the ministerial order, it would seem to be a purely relative matter whether one is ordained by a bishop, a presbyter, or by the congregation itself. If one's calling to the ministry comes essentially and ultimately from Christ and not from men, no ecclesiastical assembly can make one's calling any more valid than it already is. It may make it more valuable. The kind of ecclesiastical ordination which one receives may affect one's opportunities for service; but it cannot augment or mitigate the genuineness of the call of Christ to service, which he has heard and to which he has responded affirmatively.

The process of ordination, therefore, is simply a pragmatic arrangement for the sake of order and effectiveness. It is in no sense hierarchical, for *every member of the congregation* possesses *equal ecclesiastical right* to serve as a minister.

Furthermore, *all* the ministries of the church are functions of the body of Christ. They represent simply the body of Christ functioning through its various organs. It is therefore the entire body which is apostolic, not merely a privileged class in it. Even an apostle is yet an organ of the church. Similarly, a minister is an organ of the church; and his apostolicity stems from his derivation from, and organic union with, the church, the apostolic body of Christ.

There are, therefore, no sacerdotal favorites in the church of God. No special class or group pos-

[33]Manson, *op. cit.*, p. 103.

sesses any monopoly on grace. There is a homogeneity about the working of the Lordship of Christ throughout the whole body. Each functioning member or ministry stands on equal footing with the others, spiritually. "One is your Father," said our Lord, "and you are all brethren." It is then the organic connection of the ministry with the body of Christ from which it derives its status. It does not bypass the body; it does not possess a special, hierarchical, more direct access to Christ himself, *apart from* the body. It is simply an integral part of the body of Christ, this and nothing more.

Is This Ecumenical Dilemma Soluble?

Is there a way for us to transcend the theological cleavage precipitated by these two major historic concepts of the ministry? Or is it simply a choice between these two concepts? If the latter, the prospects for greater ecumenicity would seem to be rather dim.

Need for Humility and Appreciation

Perhaps a way out can be found if we all clothe ourselves in the first of the Christian virtues and refuse to judge our Christian brethren. If we all allow our hearts to be chastened with humility, we will be able to admit the limitations of *all* historical understanding of the gospel, including our own, and manifest a willingness to learn from each other's traditions, as the recent Lund report puts it, "by cultivating an appreciation of their values, not rejecting what may be profitable because it belongs to another tradition."[34]

It is encouraging to note that the order of worship in many Protestant groups has been greatly

[34] *Faith and Order Report,* 1952, p. 23.

enriched and improved by the influence of the liturgical churches. Indeed, the whole of Protestantism is, at present, experiencing a liturgical revival.

All Protestants are learning things. Many thinkers among the free churches have come to recognize the value of the episcopal function; but they contend that this function *can* be fulfilled through offices other than that of the bishop. Presbyterians are recognizing a kind of episcopal function in the presbytery which confers ministerial standing. Congregational churches are also coming to see positive values in some forms of episcopacy.[35] State secretaries among the Disciples of Christ are gradually assuming the responsibilities of a practical kind of episcopacy. Most of the free churches are seriously attempting to regain the character of true catholicity.

On the other hand, the People's Church in Germany has learned, through the bitter experience of the Nazi period, that there are positive values in the free churches which they had overlooked to their tragedy and loss. From firsthand acquaintance, the author can say that the People's Church in Germany today has more respect for and appreciation of the free churches than ever before.

Similarly, numerous Anglicans, like Bishop Stephen J. Neill and A. E. J. Rawlinson, have been listening, with appreciated humility, to the witness of the free churches, and have become willing to recognize the value *and the validity* of the working of Christ's Spirit in the nonepiscopal ministries.

It is encouraging also to learn that our Roman Catholic brethren are learning things from their Protestant brethren. In the early years of our century,

[35]Cf. Daniel Day Williams, *What Present-Day Theologians Are Thinking*, p. 144.

the Catholics were still bitter and hostile in their attitude toward Protestants. This hostile attitude is particularly sharp and clear in the works on Luther written by the Dominican Denifle (1903-06) and the Jesuit Grisar (1911-12). Since that time, a reaction has set in, among Roman Catholic theologians, against this extreme attitude toward the Protestant Reformation.

Sebastian Merkle, for example, a contemporary church historian at Würzburg, Germany, and Franz Xavier Kiefl, Cathedral Dean at Regensburg, have begun to recognize Luther as a deeply religious man, and to view the Reformation as a historical necessity, in view of the conditions prevailing in the church in the sixteenth century. They are saying that the Reformation was indeed a justified reaction to these conditions.[36]

Similarly, Arnold Rademacher of Bonn and Johann Hessen, Professor of Philosophy at Cologne, have written much about the Lutheran doctrine of *sola fide, sola gratia.* They contend that Catholicism in Germany has suffered many religious distortions as a result of the extremes taken in the Counter Reformation.

Of equal interest to Protestants is the Liturgical Reform Movement that has influenced the whole of Catholicism in recent years. This movement emphasizes the importance of, and need for, personal participation and personal faith, in the liturgy of the Mass. This means, as the recent Lund report states, that "churches which emphasize particular forms of con-

[36]See the interesting account of this shift of emphasis in Roman Catholicism by Heinrich Hermelink, *Katholizismus und Protestantismus: im Gespräch um die Una Sancta* (Stuttgart: Ehrenfried Klotz Verlag, 1949), pp. 16 ff.

tinuity as essential are finding the need to integrate more clearly in their thinking the two elements of Faith and Order."[37]

Similarly, the Anglo-Catholic, Dom Gregory Dix, in his book, *The Shape of the Liturgy*, attempts to revise the liturgy of Anglicanism, emphasizing the need for a greater grasp of the essential meaning of worship.

One thinks also of the Lay Movement for Catholic Action and of the Biblical Movement, which is particularly vigorous in Roman Catholicism in Germany. The Biblical Movement is centered in the reform efforts, by use of the Bible, which are aimed at a fructification of the entire life of the Church in Catholicism. Pastor Bärtle, director of the Roman Catholic biblical campaign in Stuttgart, Germany, is thus aiming to use the Bible in daily worship and devotion, in order to put new life into the old bones of orthodox Catholicism.

One may say that these movements represent Protestantizing tendencies in contemporary Roman Catholicism. The Movement for Liturgical Reform is easily correlated with the personalistic aspect of the Protestant view of faith, over against a blind submission to mechanical externalism. The Lay Movement for Catholic Action approaches the great Protestant doctrine of the priesthood of all believers. The Biblical Movement approaches the central emphasis of Protestantism on biblical authority. And the recognition of the validity of the principle of church reform approaches the basic principle of Protestantism, which demands that all institutions and human ar-

[37]*Faith and Order Report*, 1952, p. 15.

rangements be continually brought under the judgment of the transcendent light of the gospel.

It is the basic belief of ecumenical Christianity that we all have much to learn from one another; and it is its fundamental hope that in the process of creative giving and receiving, *all* of us will be able to transcend our present status, theologically and ecclesiastically, and find a larger oneness in the catholic church of our Lord—if only in humility we are willing to be transformed in the process, and do not cling, in sinful self-centeredness, to outmoded and inadequate forms for the advancing church of God; if, that is, we can rid our hearts of the denominational attitude which ceases any longer to examine and reform itself under the transcendent light of the Word of God's continuous revelation in Christ.

The Protestant Recovery of Catholicity

In the Protestant type of churches, one of the most hopeful signs is that, after a couple of centuries of a denominationalism which threatened to disintegrate the body of Christ and which woefully obscured the vision of the wholeness of the body, Protestant theology is today, at long last, beginning to recover the principle of catholicity. The problem of expressing the catholicity of the faith is the problem of making a particular grouping of Christians, in a concrete historical situation, a significant expression and fulfillment of the church universal. This, I take it, is the true meaning of the word "catholicity." In this sense, the Protestant churches are steadily striving to recover, to assert, and to fulfill their "catholicism."

Precisely how to express this catholicity, however, is still an acute theological problem. T. W. Manson offers a fruitful approach in his book, *The Church's Ministry*. He approaches the problem with an analysis of the nature of the church, as the body of Christ. Our understanding of the ministry, he says, must be derived from this organismic character of the church.

Hence, Manson writes that when Bishop Kirk argued that Christ endowed his church with two great gifts, the means of grace and the ministry of grace, his complaint is not that Kirk's doctrine is too high, but that it is not yet high enough. For Christ did more than give gifts to his church; he gave it his own real presence, which is "the supreme 'means of grace' and the supreme 'ministry of grace.' "[38] All other means and ministries of grace, says Manson, are derived from and dependent on this.

Manson argues that to accept the church as the body of Christ implies that we must abandon the idea of the absolutism of ministerial orders. The belief in the centrality and continual presence of Christ in his church, by implication, eliminates the notion of a special hierarchical class. Christ needs no vicar; he himself makes and orders the different ministries in the church.[39]

Furthermore, the ministry is a work, not an office; it is a service, not a position. Jesus said: "Whoever would be great among you must be your servant . . .," and Manson adds, "just as the ministry of the Messiah is the manifestation of the Kingdom of God, so the ministry of the disciple is the manifestation of the greatness he seeks. In the Kingdom of God service is not a stepping-stone to nobility: it *is* nobility, the only kind of nobility that is recognized."[40] This

[38]Manson, *op. cit.*, p. 23.
[39]*Ibid.*, p. 103.
[40]*Ibid.*, p. 29

is Manson's answer to the distinction between the *essential* and *dependent* ministry, of which Kenneth Kirk and his colleagues make much in their large volume, *The Apostolic Ministry.*

To take the idea of the church as the body of Christ seriously means, says Manson, that Catholics, when confronted by "the inescapable fact of the existence of genuine Christians not belonging to the Roman fold" must not shut their eyes to this fact by talking airily about "the soul of the Church." Neither must Calvinists resort to talking about the invisible church, "the whole number of the elect." Nor can we make much sense of the distinction between the local church "which is a concrete manifestation of a sort of Platonic idea of the church." That the church is the body of Christ means, says Manson, that it is an empirical reality, or entity, not a mere idea. And *as such* it somehow embraces all of its different parts in one organic unity. "It even embraces those who would indignantly repudiate the idea that they are united in the Body with certain others that they could name."[41]

The fundamental task, therefore, of the ecumenically concerned is to realize more profoundly and to articulate more clearly and effectively that unity of Spirit which already exists among us and makes us all part of the body of Christ. There *is* a unity which exists and which binds us all together in the one body of Christ, in spite of our divisions, yes, in spite of our spirit of sectarianism and exclusiveness. In a profound sense, Christians are already *one, if only they would recognize it, confess it,* and learn to cherish one another as brothers.

[41] *Ibid.*, pp. 93-94.

Daniel T. Jenkins, a British Congregationalist, has written a stimulating book on the nature of catholicity from the point of view of contemporary reformed theology. He argues that "the Gospel of God is Jesus Christ. Where Christ is, His Church is. *Ubi Christus ibi ecclesia.* 'Jesus is Lord,' marks the foundation of the Church."[42] The inquiry into the nature of catholicity, therefore, is the same as the inquiry into the nature of the church. It is simply the question: Is Jesus Christ in the church? True catholicity inheres "in Jesus Christ, God's Word, and nowhere else."[43]

Jenkins charges the Roman church with a failure to attain true catholicity, because she has failed to understand the relation in which the church stands to Christ. True catholicity consists in the presence of Christ "as He is known through the Apostolic testimony in the Word and the Sacraments and the bringing of the form of the church under the judgment of Jesus Christ that His Lordship might be manifest in it."[44]

The fullness of the church's catholicity would thus mean: loyalty to the ever-present, acting, judging, and redeeming Word of Jesus Christ. And those forms which give significant expression and community life in the social body to the reality of this Word are genuinely catholic.

Protestantism's Unique Contribution to the Understanding of the Church

Protestantism's unique contribution to the understanding of the nature of the church, however, has yet to make itself felt in its full force among the "Catholic" churches. At the heart of the Protestant

---

[42]Daniel T. Jenkins, *The Nature of Catholicity* (London: Faber and Faber Limited, 1942), pp. 19-20. Used by permission.

[43]*Ibid.*, p. 36.

[44]*Ibid.*, p. 58.

type of the faith stands a dialectical principle characterizing the relation of the human to the divine. This principle calls for the affirmation and negation of every particular temporal fulfillment of eternal values. It means that we must view all historical structures, through which the Spirit of Eternal Love seeks to express and realize itself, in terms of judgment as well as fulfillment, in terms of negative as well as positive worth. It calls for liberation from all idolatrous absolutisms.[45]

When this supreme dialectical principle of prophetic religion shall have found effective lodgment also in the "Catholic" churches, the doctrinal and ecclesiastical absolutisms which have blocked the path to unity shall melt like the mist before the rising sun, and the glad day of organic unity will become an immanent possibility.

Then we shall all see clearly that because God is accessible only through concrete historical forms and orders, does not mean that these forms and orders are divine *in themselves*. Then the mind of the church will be liberated from the historic illusion that it has a "definite and permanent order and structure."[46] No longer shall we be guilty of absolutizing the relative forms of expression of the inner life of the church's Spirit. We shall recognize, to be sure, that both Roman and non-Roman Catholics are correct in affirming that God speaks *through* the church; but we shall avoid, with prophetic enthusiasm, the tragic error which makes the voice of the church *identical* with the Word of God.

Then we shall see that the prophetic heart of Christianity lies in the personal relation of the in-

[45]See *supra*, pp. 18 ff.

[46]Kirk, *op. cit.*, p. 549.

dividual and the community to Christ, that no ministerial order possesses the power to create faith in the heart, and that these orders can only establish favorable conditions for the birth and growth of faith. But the ministry cannot and does not usurp the power and authority of Christ, the Lord. As Karl Barth rightly says, "God remains the Lord of His own house."

Then we shall see that the testimony of the apostles is authoritative not merely because the apostles uttered it, or because bishops after them uttered it, but because and insofar as the apostles and the ministry forgot themselves, indeed pointed away from themselves, as witnesses to Jesus Christ.

Then we shall see that grace is not an impersonal thing, which can be manipulated by the sacerdotal order of an apostolic ministry, and which works *ex opera operato.* It is God's forgiving favor, apprehended personally in the experience of faith.

The business of the ministry therefore is not to exalt *itself,* but to glorify *Christ;* not to rule, but to serve. Tho only Lordship in the church is that of Jesus Christ. His is the only *essential* ministry. All other ministries—deacons, evangelists, bishops, teachers, pastors, synods—are equally derived from and dependent on the primary ministry of Christ; they are therefore all functional, not hierarchical in character.

The Relevance of Repentance for All of Us

It is to be hoped that our divided churches are beginning to learn the lesson of humility and repentance. We all now accept one another *as churches,* in some sense, to be sure. Thus far, we have already come—but, let us confess it, only haltingly. The ministerial aristocracy of our denominational exclusiveness is still blocking the path to greater unity and catholicity. We still have not yet reached the point of a genuine and theologically unqualified, mutual recognition of one another's ministries, particularly in the right to administer the sacraments.

The Church of England cannot seem to make up its mind about its stand on the ministry. Verbally, it has renounced the Roman position, which holds that the ministry is apostolic in the sense that the voice of the episcopate is infallibly that of Christ himself, and that therefore the apostolic ministry, so conceived, is *the abiding essence* of the church. Some feel[47] that the Church of England's attachment to the idea of the apostolic ministry is not so much a matter of theological principle, but rather the result of a deeply entrenched conservatism and perhaps also represents the Church of England's sense of oneness with traditional Catholicism, a bond which has always enabled it to distinguish itself from the free churches.

But if the sin of the Church of England, in this regard, is a reluctant conservatism, the sin of our other Protestant bodies has been sectarianism and denominational exclusiveness. This has been, and still is, a dreadful blight on the church. The cause of ecumenicity and catholicity is still terribly impeded because many, perhaps most, church groups are still too much at ease in Zion. They are denominationally complacent. They are too content with merely enjoying their own brotherhood life and too zealous merely to perpetuate their own traditions, creeds, and operational ways. It seems only too true also that our seminaries, in an unjustifiably large measure, have succumbed to this denominational trap and are not as responsible as they might and should be, in training men for the work of the truly catholic body of Christ.

[47]For example, Jenkins, *op. cit.*, pp. 150-151.

All of us must bring our ministerial orders under the prophetic judgment of the Word of God, and become genuinely and humbly willing to allow our present ministerial structures to be cleansed of isolationist and sectarian elements and transformed into instruments worthy of the truly catholic body of our common Lord.

CHAPTER NINE

Theological Problems Calling for More Adequate Ecumenical Solution

In this final chapter we wish to set forth and discuss briefly some of the basic theological problems upon a more adequate solution of which further ecumenical development depends.

The Problem of Developing and Establishing Securely an Evangelical Christianity Which Avoids the Errors of Dogmatism and also the Mistakes of Relativism

We are confronted with a challenge to find and establish securely an evangelical liberalism which saves us both from the frozen stalemate of dogmatism and from the flood tide of relativism which washes us away from the blessedness of securing our moorings to the shores of the Eternal.

As we have seen, the prophetic spirit of the sixteenth-century Reformation loosened the faith from an idolatrous attachment to papal authority. But the difficult task of shaping an adequate conception of religious unity and carrying it through to creative fulfillment, combined with the handicap of centuries in which the Christian community was conditioned by scholastic dogmatism, proved to be too much. The sixteenth-century reformers were not wholly successful in securing the Protestant principle of reform and in establishing a constructive theological method. The result was a creedal absolutism, which, combined with

Catholic absolutism, threatened the complete disintegration of the Christian enterprise. The Thirty Years' War, which ended with the Peace of Westphalia in 1648, stands as a tragic witness to this failure to attain a solution to the problem of Christian unity.

The prophetic spirit, however, was not wholly extinguished. The widespread seventeenth-century Protestant movements of Pietism and Latitudinarianism, however inadequate as theological solutions to the problem of unity, were nevertheless significant expressions of a profound awareness that the scholastic method of Protestant orthodoxy was inadequate to lead to the fullness of Christian fellowship.

The eighteenth century, and to some extent also the nineteenth, saw large segments of Christianity frankly abandon the dogmatism of orthodox Protestantism, thanks partly to the awareness of the deadening effect of scholastic theology, and partly to the attractive lures of rationalistic humanism. Out of this impact of the Enlightenment upon Christianity, liberal Protestantism was born. It attempted once again to establish the antidogmatic principle, securing liberty and bringing the faith to a more meaningful fulfillment, in terms of the thought-forms of contemporary culture. As we have seen, however, Liberalism succeeded in a somewhat distorted way, for it allowed itself to get caught in the autonomy of modern culture. Christianity was thereby diluted spiritually and lost much of its prophetic power.

An indigenous movement emerged in the framework of Americal Christianity, however, which shared in a large way the liberal reaction to the creedalism of the Protestant denominations, but which did see (though with insufficient clarity) the need for combining the liberal faith with Christianity's prophetic spirit and power, thereby escaping the snares of an autonomous culture. Its instigators called it the "current reformation."

We make mention of this Campbellian movement at this point particularly, because of the numerous unity movements in Christendom in the past few hundred years, the plea of this movement for a Christ-centered, noncreedal basis of Christian unity is unique, and because its theological outlook proved to be truly prophetic.

One of the outstanding leaders of this unity movement, Alexander Campbell, for example, went a long way with the liberalism and rationalism of his day; but in his heart he carried with him always the prophetic spirit of a Christ-centered faith. And however adequate or inadequate his biblicism proved to be, as a solution to the problem of unity, many of the major elements of the contemporary ecumenical attempt to solve this problem were actually in the original vision of the Campbellian movement: (1) freedom from any authoritative use of the creeds, (2) directing the Christian spirit to the only source and power of creative Christian unity, the revelatory act of God in Christ, (3) the normative significance of the Bible in effecting the redemptive fulfillment of the power of Christ, through faith, (4) respect for the liberty and integrity of each individual, as he seeks to understand Christian truth, (5) the refusal to hold a judgmental attitude toward Christians of other theological persuasions, all being recognized to possess equal right to sit together at the table of the Lord. All these ecumenical principles, often blurred and distorted to be sure, were embedded in the original impulse of the unity movement led by the Campbells and their associates.

Like all historical religious movements, the Campbellian movement has frequently fallen from the grandeur of its initial vision. The Disciples of Christ, however, may find some comfort in the fact that a similar tragedy has befallen every other prophetic movement in Christian history.

Thomas and Alexander Campbell evidently used the traditional Protestant plea that the Bible is "our only rule of faith and practice"[1] to convey their resolve to liberate the individual conscience from any and all authoritative use of human interpretations of the Bible and to direct absolute religious devotion once again to the Lordship of Christ, the Christ pre-eminently of Scripture.

It is one of the paradoxes of history, however, that out of this biblicism has grown a biblical absolutism which in some areas of the Campbellian movement today is dishearteningly tyrannical, uncharitable, and sectarian. The movement which began as a noble impulse to transcend denominationalism has, in some areas, become a rigid denomination, which acts as if it thought that this denomination is the whole body of Christ.

This is unfortunately true of a large number of the schismatic segment which has perpetuated its identity by denominationalizing the name "Church of

[1]This norm is typically Protestant. The "Formula of Concord" (Lutheran) begins with the words: "We believe, confess, and teach that the only rule and norm, according to which all dogmas and all doctors ought to be esteemed and judged, is no other whatever than the prophetic and apostolic writings both of the Old and of the New Testament. . . ." (Phillip Schaff, *Creeds of Christendom* [New York: Harper & Brothers, 1905], III, 93-94). Article VI of "The Thirty-Nine Articles of the Church of England" (1571) reads: "Holy Scripture conteyneth all thinges necessarie to saluation: so that whatsoeuer is not read therein, nor may be proued therby, is not to be required of anye man, that it shoulde be belieued as an article of the fayth, or be thought requisite (as) necessarie to saluation" (*Ibid.*, p. 489). Question 2 of "The Westminster Shorter Catechism" reads: "What rule hath God given to direct us how we may glorify and enjoy him?" Then follows the answer: "The Word of God, which is contained in the Scriptures of the Old and New Testaments, is the only rule to direct us how we may glorify and enjoy him" (*Ibid.*, p. 676). Used by permission.

Christ." To this very day, there are other areas of this movement, and of numerous others also, which are similarly suffering from the same blight of theological and ecclesiastical isolationism and sectarianism.

Yet the original vision of the Campbellian movement had in it something sound and true. Many of the major elements of the ecumenical vision are actually embedded in it. As William Adams Brown suggests, in the unwillingness of Thomas Campbell and others of similar mind "to be satisfied with any half-way stage to unity, we have the direct antecedent of the faith and order movement."[2]

The Campbellian movement of course represents but one of many significant ecumenical roots. We mention it here particularly, because unlike the other denominations, it is an indigenous movement in American Christianity and because we feel that the combination of liberalism with Christianity's prophetic spirit and power, which it worked out, represented the theological *gestalt* of the World Council of Churches more than a century before the latter became a reality. Its unique combination of liberalism and Christocentrism has been picked up by the ecumenical movement and is being carried out with a more critical awareness of the issues involved and on a grander scale.

The ecumenical movement has power and holds promise, however, because it has a large number of roots throughout the whole of Christendom. As Brown says, "It is the convergence at a single point of many different streams of influence, each of which has made its contribution to the final outcome."[3]

The ecumenical movement represents an encouraging fruition of the true genius of prophetic Prot-

[2]Brown, *op. cit.*, p. 20.
[3]*Ibid.*, p. 13.

estantism, for through the unique combination of the two principles of liberalism and Christocentrism, the spirit of denominational divisiveness and exclusiveness is gradually being broken down. A new kind of recognition of and concern for one another has grown up in our divided churches and is spreading among their memberships. Must we not say that the Holy Spirit, the creative Spirit of Eternal Love, is finally beginning to overcome the sinful barriers to fellowship which we "Christians" have erected?

It is not too much to say that ecumenical Christianity is a Christianity which has learned some lessons from history. It holds great promise because, on the one hand, it is resolved not to get caught in dogmatic or ecclesiastic absolutism—the fate of Protestant orthodoxy. Thus in May, 1938, when a representative body chosen by the churches met at Utrecht, Holland, and drafted a constitution for the World Council of Churches, they defined the authority of the World Council explicitly by stating that the World Council "shall not legislate for the churches," but that "it shall offer counsel and provide opportunity of united action in matters of common interest."

Ecumenical Christianity would seem thus to represent an attempt to establish *a dynamic kind of oneness* which avoids the pitfall of traditional Protestant and Catholic authoritarianism.

One of the major concerns, therefore, of the ecumenical movement has long been one of the strongholds of Liberalism. It is the resolve to maintain continual vigilance in the matter of religious liberty. It is a form of Christianity which refuses to forget that Socrates and Jesus, John Hus and Michael Servetus were killed by orthodox worshipers of the *status quo*. This concern for liberty is voiced, for example, by Karl

Barth when he says that "church government will not be the concern of the 'synodical congregation' " (under which concept he subsumes the idea of an ecumenical church); "Church government," he says, "must remain in the hands of Him who is Lord of all His many congregations."[4] Similarly, W. A. Visser 't Hooft insists that the World Council is in no sense to be a "super-church."[5]

The delegates at the World Council in 1948 were all equally concerned to secure religious liberty. To the explicit statement in the constitution that the council "shall not legislate for the churches" was added an explanatory memorandum which says that the Assembly and Central Committee "will have no constitutional authority whatever over its constituent churches" and that the Council exists "to serve the churches, not to control them."[6] Ecumenical Christianity is thus firmly resolved to safeguard and to guarantee the values of religious liberty. It aims thereby to preserve the truth which is present in the plea for autonomy.

On the other hand, the ecumenical movement represents a Christianity which has become aware of the lack of prophetic power in radical liberal Christianity, due to its involvement in the modern spirit of a distorted kind of autonomy. This awareness also is reflected in the common and central Christocentric faith of the body which drafted the constitution of the World Council. The body of delegates from churches of various countries designated itself as "a fellowship of the churches which accept our Lord Jesus Christ as God and Savior." When the World Coun-

---

[4] *Man's Disorder and God's Design; The Amsterdam Assembly Series* (New York: Harper and Brothers, 1948), I, 74.

[5] *Ibid.*, pp. 182 ff.

[6] *Ibid.*, p. 181.

cil of Churches was formed at Amsterdam in 1948, it was decided that this Christocentric faith, so stated, would remain the basic requirement for membership in the World Council.

This emphatic Christocentrism indicates that the ecumenical movement represents a theological point of view that lies beyond the rationalistic humanism of radical liberal Christianity. The ecumenical quest for unity is one which is being pursued by a generation of theologians and Christian leaders who are aware that the kind of unity which radical Liberalism advocated is somewhat lacking in depth. Because of the diversity of theologies within the Christian community, many liberals felt that the only bond of unity which was feasible is our united faith in freedom and in human values in general.

Some liberals have objected to defining "Jesus Christ as God and Savior" as a basis of unity, arguing that this phrase represents a divisive theological interpretation of the significance of Jesus. Have those who raised this objection, however, adequately recognized that to retain any kind of reference to Jesus in the ground of Christian unity is "theological"? Any religiously significant reference to the figure of Jesus is of necessity freighted with theological meaning.

The kind of unity promoted by radical liberalism, however, proved to be lacking in evangelical depth. Often also, it lacked the quality of imperativeness. It was somewhat weak theologically. It did not possess an adequate vision of that supreme and all-commanding reality, dedication to which alone can bring the fulfillment of significant Christian unity. The basis of its plea for unity rested too much in man, not enough in God's unitive working through Jesus Christ. Or as Professor Edmund Schlink of the University of

Heidelberg puts it, in his lectures: the unity of Liberalism was not yet a unity in evangelical faith.

Furthermore, one cannot ignore the fact that in the New Testament there is recognition of such a thing as a *misuse* of the name of Christ. Nor should one ignore the New Testament teaching with regard to the different functions which the various members of the body of Christ exercise "for the building up of the body of Christ, until we all attain to the unity of the faith and of the knowledge of the Son of God, to mature manhood, to the measure of the stature of the fullness of Christ."[7] Christian unity is a oneness in evangelical faith, a oneness in an experiential knowledge of Christ.

The fact that the ecumenical quest for unity makes the redemptive act of God in Jesus Christ central is evidence that ecumenical theology is outgrowing the limitations of the old Liberalism and is recovering the creative springs of prophetic religion. While recognizing the inevitability of diversity in theological interpretation, it is nevertheless finding that there is in the midst of such diversity what Williams has called "a controlling and directing substance of faith,"[8] or what is often referred to as a "hard core" of faith; and that this abiding identity of the faith unites us, theologically diversified though we are.

The fact that the missionary impulse has been one of the main sources of the ecumenical movement is further evidence of its prophetic character. Kenneth Latourette reminds us that if the ecumenical movement ceased to hold obedience to the Great Commission as its major objective, it would become sterile.[9]

---

[7]Ephesians 4:12-13.

[8]Williams, *What Present-Day Theologians Are Thinking*, p. 15.

[9]Kenneth Latourette, *The Emergence of a World Community* (New Haven: Yale University Press, 1949), p. 55.

It would seem, therefore, that the ecumenical movement represents an attempt to mediate between authoritarianism or creedal absolutism, and the humanistic self-sufficiency of radical liberalism by finding a liberal, evangelical perspective which lies beyond each.

It is abrogating traditional theological absolutism and developing a catholicity of outlook which is to be contrasted sharply with "Roman" catholicism. The catholicism of the ecumenical movement avoids the authoritarian domination of the human spirit.

Yet at the same time, in orienting itself to the Lordship of Christ, it is developing an evangelical definiteness which places it beyond that brand of liberalism which lost this meaningful connection with Christian history. But ecumenical theology is also resolved to preserve the liberal emphasis on contemporaneity. By orienting itself to the divine call and challenge in Christ, ecumenical Christianity has established a principle which can enable us to overcome the liberal distortion of the truth of autonomy.

Ecumenical Christianity, we believe, is beginning to establish a new evangelical liberalism which avoids the dogmatism of orthodox Protestantism and the equally grave mistakes of liberal relativism.

The Problem of Securing the Principle of Comprehension and Giving It Institutional Extension

Ecumenical Christianity is developing, in a fruitful way, a unity which possesses an evangelical character and personal depth, yet which also *comprehends* difference in points of view. Ecumenical unity stands thus in marked contrast to the old orthodox concept of unity in terms of doctrinal congruency. The success of the ecumenical movement will depend upon the clarity and adequacy with which this inner principle of comprehension is grasped and in the *consistency and thoroughness* with which Christian individuals and groups carry it out.

The principle of comprehension, which in fact has been determinative of Christian community in relations between individuals through the centuries, represents a way of holding together profound religious conviction and great humility of spirit. It leads one to recognize the need for deep conviction, for Christianity is a religious faith, a dynamic commitment to the Lordship of Christ, which calls for convictions worth living and dying for. Yet it also keeps one keenly aware of the fact that all our human attempts to grasp, understand, and live the truth of the gospel fall short, caught inescapably, as they are, in the fallibility and finitude of all things human. Hence to hold to this principle is to clothe oneself in moral and intellectual humility. It is to refuse to be ensnared in the sin of self-centeredness. It is to recognize that because our human apprehensions of Christian truth are a limited response to the call of God in Christ, we must forever press forward to new visions of truth and to higher levels of holiness. Our human response to the call of God must become increasingly adequate and true.

To hold the principle of comprehension means to recognize the twofold character of Christian truth, the distinction, namely, between the inner fullness of the Word of God in Christ, on the one hand, and the relative outer forms of man's response to the Word, on the other. To determine one's religious attitudes by the basic principle of comprehension demands a flexibility of spirit which recognizes that variability in man's response to the Word is inevitable, and that such variability is valid, when it represents simply the inevitable historical relativism of all human thought and not willful caprice.

One might illustrate the principle of comprehension by the ancient, oriental story of the four blind men and the elephant. Each felt of the elephant, but only for a moment. Each thus received a partially true but one-sided impression of what the elephant was like. Failing to recognize the partial character of his experience of the elephant, each was moved, on the basis of his own limited experience, to deny the other three's description of an elephant. They claimed, respectively, that the elephant was like a large leaf of cabbage (the ear), a post (the leg), a convex wall (the side), and a rope (the tail). Each was correct, of course, but mistaken in failing to recognize that there were other aspects of the truth about the elephant besides those of his own limited experience. The full truth of the elephant would comprehend these and other different limited experiences of the elephant.

Similarly, the principle of comprehension calls for a recognition of the fragmentary character of man's response to God's redemptive call in Christ. It condemns as sinful the absolutizing of any particular confessional expression of this truth. It knows in its heart that the abiding essence of Christianity lies beyond any creed, or any set of beliefs. Indeed, it measures and evaluates all confessions, *including its own,* in the light of the inner fullness of Christ. It insists that Christian beliefs, institutions, and practices must forever be judged, corrected, and purified by the divine fullness of the inner truth of God's revelation in Christ. This thoroughly Protestant orientation to the transcendent Word is the heart and soul of ecumenical Christianity.

At this point one recognizes the influence of the liberal insistence on the primacy of experience over doctrine. Liberalism has helped make it possible for us to realize that we are actually one, in our experience of the Lordship of Christ, even if our finite attempts to grasp and express the full meaning of this experience are diversified and sometimes even contradictory.

Beneath the diversified outward forms of expression lies the "hard core" of the Christian perspective, in general. The ideological elements involved in the meaningful articulation of the Christian experience, at any time in history, are, of course, eaten away by the "acids of modernity," but the fundamental Christian perspective on human existence remains, a perspective determined by man's affirmative response to the call of God in Jesus Christ. No theology can ever give a perfect expression of this basic perspective; yet it is the source of Christianity's abiding power. Williams aptly reminds us that we may get so concerned about our theological diversity that "we forget all the diversity would be meaningless unless behind it there is a controlling and directing substance of faith which has an enduring integrity."[10]

Shailer Mathews' statement of the principle of comprehension, namely, "that everyone is a Christian who calls himself a Christian," is a bit too relativistic perhaps, for it veers from the dynamic center, which is Christ. More adequate is Alexander Campbell's wording of this principle in the famous Lunenberg letter. In reply to the question, "Who is a Christian?" Campbell wrote, "Every one that believes in his heart that Jesus of Nazareth is the Messiah, the

[10]Williams, *What Present-Day Theologians Are Thinking*, pp. 14-15; cf. also Alan Richardson, *Christian Apologetics* (New York: Harper and Brothers, 1947), p. 83. Used by permission.

Son of God; repents of his sins, and obeys him in all things according to his measure of knowledge of his will.''[11] This last phrase "according to his measure of knowledge of his will" is an admirable expression of the principle of comprehension. It says that the duty of every Christian is to walk in the light of Christ *as God gives him to see this light.* There is no other way in which one can walk, in integrity of heart. Nor is there any other way in which one should expect his brother to walk.

The Swiss Reformer, Huldreich Zwingli, was using the principle of comprehension when, in spite of his disagreement with Luther on the interpretation of the words of the institution of the Lord's Supper, he reached out the hand of fellowship at the famous Marburg Conference. Luther's natural stubbornness, his political prejudice against the Swiss, and his religious conservatism caused him to violate it and to draw away in a spirit of exclusiveness.

In the fourteenth chapter of Romans, the Apostle Paul gave a moving plea for the principle of comprehension, urging the liberal-minded to be humble and charitable toward the brother of scruples, and reminding the brother of scruples that he should certainly abide by his conscience, but that he has no right to judge his brother, merely because his conscience did not include the same scruples. The ecumenical concept of a unity which comprehends difference leads one to condemn the judgmental attitude as sinfully divisive of the body of Christ.

The ecumenical movement represents genuine novelty, however, because *for the first time in Christian history* it is attempting to secure the operation

[11]*The Millennial Harbinger,* I (New Series, 1837), p. 411.

of the principle of comprehension in ecclesiastical as well as in individual relations. It is an attempt to carry out the principle of the fourteenth chapter of Romans on an institutional scale. As Herrmann Sasse says,[12] "the creation of the World Council of Churches means that for the first time the churches accept the consequences flowing from the classical doctrine, taught by practically all churches in the Council, according to which the church of Christ includes all those who confess his name, even if their confession is incomplete or mixed with error."

As Visser 't Hooft has aptly said, "If it is recognized that Christ is at work in other churches, it is the duty of each church in the fellowship to listen to the witness of these churches, to open itself to the truth of God which it may learn from them, and to be ready to let its own faith and life be enriched or corrected by this fraternal contact."[13] Such *creative fraternal fellowship* constitutes the heart of the principle of comprehension.

What it will mean to *carry through* on this principle, in terms of ecclesiastical forms and practices, is inseparable from the question of just what ecclesiastical forms are to characterize the unity we are striving to achieve. If organic church union be the goal, the principle of comprehension would be applied by a procedure which recognized a measure of validity, for example, in each of the three major, traditional types of church government: presbyterial, episcopal, and congregational. The functional significance of each, of course, would require reinterpretation, in the light of its new supplementary relation to the others, within the new ecclesiastical unity of the church as a whole.

[12]*Man's Disorder and God's Design*, I, 192.
[13]*Ibid.*, I, 192.

This kind of experiment is actually taking place in our day. The Church of South India is the best example of it, combining as it does in one new complex ecclesiastical form the three major Protestant groups: Anglican and Methodist, Presbyterian and Reformed, and Congregationalist. Similar attempts are made by the United Church of Canada, and by the Church of Christ in Japan. Such experiments are eloquent witnesses to the depth of the church's longing for unity.

Yet, even if such ecclesiastical merging is inherently sound, some feel that it cannot, at the present juncture, be regarded as the next step toward unity; first, because none of these unions has drawn into it all the Christians of the particular country involved, not even all Protestants; and second, because the essence of this way to unity lies in the formation of a rearranged version of traditional forms of church life, and this method has repeatedly failed to supply the answer to the problem of unity.[14]

It would seem to be both timely and urgent, however, for ministers throughout Christendom to establish the principle of comprehension securely and permanently in the matter of attitudes. Denominational pride and complacency have, through the years, become so deeply ingrained that this education of attitudes will admittedly not be easy to accomplish. But ministers who neglect this task will certainly be failing to serve the cause of prophetic Christianity in this hour of urgent need. Because of the incompleteness and relativity which characterize all human response to the Word, we are duty bound, in humility, to do all that we can to establish the principle of mutual recognition and to work our way vigorously

[14]Cf. Latourette, *op. cit.*, p. 77.

toward an ecumenical solution of the knotty practical problems which still block the pathway to this achievement.

We must rise in spiritual stature and transcend our peculiar theological fixations. In penitence we must confess that many of our Protestant groups are still characterized by such fixations. The high churchmen among the Anglican brethren still find it difficult to overcome the long-standing fixation in reference to the historic episcopate. Many Disciples of Christ and Baptists still find it difficult to transcend a fixation that developed among them in regard to the immersionist mode of baptism. Many Baptists are too inclined even yet to construe Christian freedom to mean: let each go his own way, unmolested by the others. This is a distorted concept of liberty, which fails to do justice to the communal quality of the total Christian fellowship. Some Lutherans still encounter difficulty in the ecumenical effort to rise above a fixation which they developed in reference to the doctrine of the "real presence" in the Eucharist. Some Presbyterians still manifest an attitude which indicates a resolve to be loyal to the Presbyterian denomination, ecumenicity or no ecumenicity. In the People's Church in Germany today, there is a resurgence of historic confessionalism which stands in sharp conflict with ecumenical impulses at work there.

Let us humbly confess it: these and similar denominational and confessionalistic fixations are still blocking the way to the growth of greater unity in Christ. There can be no doubt that the immediate goal for greater unity is the challenge thrown down to us by Providence that we transcend these fixations and establish a more forthright and universal practice of mutual recognition and a more vital and organic fellowship with one another. It is high time that all Christian groups remove to the periphera all theological beliefs and all ecclesiastical practices which are blocking the pathway to a forthright and unqualified mutual recognition of the ministries and members of other groups. Until we do so, we scarcely can be said to have freed ourselves from the sin of sectarianism.

The Problem of Developing and Establishing More Meaningfully a Familial Relation Between Different Church Groupings

A more feasible way of finding a higher kind of unity than the way which banks so heavily on a unilateral ecclesiastical form can perhaps be found in the concept of a family of church groups. It is not at all unlikely that Jesus' vision of the unity of his disciples was structured in terms of the concept of the family. For it is undeniable that Jesus used familial relations more than any other analogy to clarify the nature of the kingdom.

In numerous ways, for example, Jesus drew on the analogy of fatherhood to clarify the relation of his followers to God. When they prayed, they were to say, "Our Father who art in heaven."[15] Like a father, God is sympathetic and understanding. One may therefore confidently unburden himself to him "in secret."[16] Like a father's solicitous concern for his children is God's infinite care for man. "Your Father knows what you need before you ask him."[17] Jesus reminded his disciples of the fact that the "heavenly Father" feeds the bird on the wing, and then added: "Are you not of more value than they?"[18] For his followers to allow themselves to get caught in the

[15]Matthew 6:9.
[16]Matthew 6:4, 6, 18.
[17]Matthew 6:8.
[18]Matthew 6:26.

anxious scramble for material things would be to fail in faith and trust in God. Anxiety about material needs was not to find lodgment in their hearts, for "your heavenly Father knows that you need them all."[19]

The wisdom and bounty of God are also illustrated by that of an earthly father. If earthly parents, being evil, know how to bestow good things upon their children, "how much more" will your Father in heaven bestow good things on those who ask in faith.[20] Furthermore, his followers were called upon to be generous, gracious, and lavish in their forgiveness toward others, *especially* their enemies, "that you may be sons of your Father who is in heaven; for he makes his sun rise on the evil and on the good, and sends rain on the just and on the unjust."[21] In fact, they were to be "perfect, as your heavenly Father is perfect."[22]

If God is "our Father," we are related to one another as brothers. The community of those who do the Father's will is comparable to that of brothers and sisters in a family, only on a higher level. "For," said Jesus, "whoever does the will of my Father in heaven is my brother, and sister, and mother."[23] Thus Jesus exhorted his disciples to "call no man your father on earth, for you have one Father who is in heaven." Neither were they to be called "rabbi," for they had one teacher, and they were all brethren.[24]

It is because Jesus made so much of the spirit of "brotherhood" that it became the most outstanding ethical quality of the community of his followers.

---

[19]Matthew 6:32.
[20]Matthew 7:11.
[21]Matthew 5:45.
[22]Matthew 5:48.
[23]Matthew 12:50.
[24]Matthew 23:8-9.

This concept of the family,[25] if applied to the problems of ecumenical unity today, would lead to the formation of *a kind of organic unity* which would allow for variety in ecclesiastical forms of expression. It would, however, be *organic unity,* not mere *federation.*

The concept of federation, implying as it does merely voluntary association, seems inadequate. The New Testament has made Christians aware that the relation between various groups of Christians is more organic and vital than the political analogy of federation suggests.

The unity of a family, however, is something vastly more than a mere federation of its individual members. It is *an organic whole* that pulsates with a spirit which, through all, is seeking the good of each, and through each the good of all. There is infinite variety in a good family. Each member is encouraged to find and realize his own true self, in all of its uniqueness and creativity. Yet such independence and freedom are undergirded and sustained by the dynamic whole. As Van Dusen aptly puts it, the family "is an order which unites the essential meanings of organic and indissolvable kinship and of free and profound common loyalty; an order which conserves both the autonomy of persons and their necessary interdependence for individual and corporate fulfillment."[26]

What now would it mean if we could carry out fully the implications of this kind of relationship between the various church groups of Christendom? It would mean that each church group would gratefully acknowledge itself to be a member of the whole family of God, that it would consider this membership to be primordial in nature, and that it would regard any sectarian separation or split-off from the family to

---

[25] Cf. Van Dusen, *op. cit.,* p. 234.
[26] *Ibid.,* p. 234.

be a sinful denial of its most precious birthright. It would mean that we would strive to extend to *the whole of Christendom* the kind of relationship which now obtains in what is called "the brotherhood." Each church group would regard other church groups in the same way that a congregation of "the brotherhood" regards its sister congregations. One of the signs of the prophetic power of the Christian Spirit is that it is already expanding in this direction.

A fraternal, familial spirit would obtain throughout the entire church, while the decisions of the church family, as a whole, would be made in keeping with the ideal of democratic pluralism. A relationship of mutual reciprocity would prevail. Such an ecumenical church would be obliged to operate by the principle of mutual reciprocity, for a family believes, with its whole heart, in the liberty of its members. Within the church family, ample provision would thus be made for vigorous growth in the church's quest for the full truth of the gospel. The situation would be kept open, in the name of the liberty and dignity of each group member and in humble awareness of the fragmentary character of all human apprehensions of truth.

The ecumenical hope is that the development and expansion of some such familial relationship throughout Christendom might enable us to put a stop, finally, to the seemingly interminable sectarian split-offs which rend asunder the body of Christ. These split-offs have of course stemmed from multiple causes. All too frequently, however, they have resulted from the conflict between new prophetic insights into Christian truth, on the one hand, and the nonfamilial, totalitarian attitude adopted toward such theological novelty by the defenders of the established points of view, on the other. To secure the establishment of the familial spirit would be to put an end to such religious totalitarianism, for it would not only not stifle the prophetic spirit, it would positively encourage new increments of truth, and would happily and humbly adjust its theological position, in the light of the demands of the valid, new insights.

The denominational type of Protestantism is standing under the judgment of God in our day. Whether the members of the churches, which for so long a time have been conditioned by denominational patterns of thought, will be able to respond to the contemporary challenge for unity and throw off the yoke of denominationalism remains to be seen. Their leaders seem able to do so—in ecumenical gatherings. Yet there are numerous disheartening evidences of a lethargic hesitation on the part of denominations to allow the old forms to crumble and disappear, as we follow the call of God to the formation of a higher kind of unity in the whole family of God.

The Problem of Establishing an Undenominational Loyalty to the Church Universal

Throughout this book we have consistently adopted a critical position in our attitude toward denominational Protestantism. Such criticism must not be understood to mean that diversification and variation in different groupings, in man's response to the gospel, are basically wrong. On the contrary, there is quite properly and inevitably a Presbyterian grouping of Christians, a Lutheran grouping, a Disciple grouping, a Methodist grouping, and so forth. It is an error, however, to regard these groupings *as churches,* for there is only one church, the body of Christ, which includes all who respond in faith to the call of God in Jesus Christ, as God gives them to understand this call. The church is one, truly catholic (universal) and holy.

A Christian grouping, in response to the call of God in Christ, becomes a denomination when the loyalty of the individual members to the religious forms of the group is identified absolutely with loyalty to Christ's church. This is *the major error of denominationalism.* It is the root from which there springs an uncharitable heart, a narrow, bigoted, and ungracious spirit.

Let us frankly call such denominationalizing of the faith what it is: a sinful reduction of the church universal to a religious sect or party! It is a part claiming to be the whole. It is religion cursed by the disease of partyism. It is Christianity malformed by the blight of camp consciousness. The success of Christianity is henceforth measured by how many heads can be counted in "our" camp. Forgotten is the criterion of Christ: "By this all men will know that you are my disciples, if you have love for one another."[27] Instead of the New Testament standard which should lead us to test the truth-value of every historical form of Christianity by how much Christlikeness it creates and fosters in the human heart, denominationalism measures Christianity's success by counting heads in a camp. Again and again this camp consciousness has led to a division of the body of Christ and to a neglect of the virtues of Christian love. Oliver S. Tomkins rightly says, "Wherever doctrinaire abstractions distract from the love of souls, there unity is threatened."[28]

[27]John 13:35; for a systematic statement of the basic elements of the sectarian spirit, see Ralph G. Wilburn, "The Sectarian Spirit: An Essay in Definition," in *Christian Education,* Vol. XXXI, No. 3, pp. 198-206.

[28]*Man's Disorder and God's Design,* I, 145.

We are confronted thus with the grand delusion of denominational Christianity: it inspires its members to believe that their group has a priority, if not actually a monopoly, on the truth of the gospel. Hence the spirit of religious pride and complacency; hence denominational snobbery.

We say, then, that those Christians of our day are caught in a contradiction which would be ludicrous were it not tragic, who claim that they stand for undenominational Christianity, yet in the same breath betray an attitude which causes them to feel that their group is absolutely right and all others are wrong. As one minister said recently, speaking to a minister of another group: "Brother, you're wrong; we stand on the book; we've got it." To which the other brother quite appropriately replied: "Brother, you keep it." There is too much "we" protruding in such an attitude to be consistent with the ideal of undenominational Christianity.

Here was a Christian minister claiming to be undenominational in outlook, and in the very next breath claiming to have a monopoly on God's truth; as if he and his group were the *sole authorized dispensers* of religious truth; as if God had chosen *them and them alone* as the *depository* of his truth. Now they *have* it; they think that they actually *possess* God's truth; they can manipulate it as they wish, include and exclude from the kingdom whomsoever they will. This is the cardinal sin of denominational Christianity; it is, in fact, the popery of the Vatican. All Christians who think and speak in this fashion are, in truth, theological descendants of the papal chair.

It is utterly impossible to be true to undenominational, ecumenical Christianity and cling to such sectarian attitudes of bigotry, conceit, and self-righteousness. He who thinks that he and his group are absolutely right and that other groups are wrong is still a victim of the denominational fallacy. He lacks that breadth of spirit and charity of disposition which are essential ingredients in undenominational Christianity.

Undenominational Christianity nourishes in the heart a growing appreciation of all goodness and truth and beauty wherever and whenever found. It is a spirit of joyful appreciation or love, which, said Paul, "does not . . . gloat over the wickedness of other people. On the contrary, it is glad with all good men when Truth prevails."[29]

It is imperative to the cause of ecumenicity that Christians take the demand to transcend denominationalism seriously, and establish and secure genuinely undenominational loyalty to the church universal.

This task is highly problematical, however, precisely because there is no way in which one can become a member of the "one holy catholic church," the church universal, except by being a member of some particular Christian group. One becomes a Christian through identification with a specific Christian group. There is no church invisible apart from the church visible.

Furthermore, one's religious consciousness is strongly conditioned by and attached to the particular group, due to its tangible concrete nature, long before he develops the depth of spiritual maturity requisite for a dominating loyalty to the church universal. Further, the sense of unity with one's own group easily becomes the all-controlling loyalty, for each confession sincerely believes that its tradition is an

[29]1 Corinthians 13:6, Phillips trans.

important witness to the truth of the gospel, and that it is its duty under God to bear this witness, in boldness.

Somehow these two dimensions of one's loyalty to the kingdom must be brought into harmonious relation. Both must find validity in a context which avoids their perversions. But certainly, loyalty to the church universal must, in the last analysis, correct the one-sidedness and errors of the lesser loyalties which are, after all, but broken light of the whole.

It is our hope that the formation and functioning of the World Council of Churches indicate, in some fashion, that the churches *are* at long last beginning to find a saving measure of this higher loyalty to the church universal. Is it too much to interpret the message of the Council as a first meager attempt to express "the common mind of the *Una Sancta*"? Visser 't Hooft argues that the Council can hardly be regarded merely as a conference which discusses the problem of church unity in faith and order, but that it must also be viewed "in some way as an attempt to confess the faith of the churches in the measure of unity already attained."[30]

Another way of stating this dual character of the Christian's loyalty is to put it in terms of the need for combining *freedom* with *unity*. Through the centuries, down to the Reformation, the church knew *a kind* of unity which was achieved and sustained at the expense of individual and congregational freedom. For about half a millennium now Protestantism has gloriously exercised the rights of liberty, but at the expense of unity. The ecumenical movement is an attempt to transcend this age-old dilemma and to find

[30]*Man's Disorder and God's Design*, I, 180.

a kind of unity which is not only *compatible* with freedom, but which *sustains* and *supports* it.

The ecumenical plea is thus reminiscent of an early Protestant slogan: "In essentials unity, in opinions liberty, and in all things charity." The problem of what the "essentials" are, however, is being thought through a bit more critically in our twentieth century. As E. V. Zollars was fond of putting it, when the essentials shall be reduced to "a simple personal faith in a divine personal Savior," the uniting of the children of God in the strong bond of universal fellowship will be attained. The definitive basis of membership in the World Council of Churches, adopted at Amsterdam in 1948, is basically just this simple faith in Christ. The World Council defines itself as a "fellowship of churches which accept our Lord Jesus Christ as God and Savior."

The plea of the free churches for congregational autonomy obviously contains a vital truth, if the ideal of liberty is valid. That there is truth in the principle of autonomy, we have shown throughout this book, as we have pointed out the fallacies of authoritarianism. Yet it must be admitted that the distorted interpretation of congregational autonomy, which turned it into theological and ecclesiastical isolationism, represents a distortion of the value of liberty. This distorted view of autonomy rests on the presupposition of the obsolete, atomistic conception of man of the eighteenth century. The nineteenth-century discovery of the organic interrelatedness of humanity and the more recently discovered awareness of the inevitable involvement of all individuals and groups in world life call for a reinterpretation of the principle of congregational autonomy which will do justice to the values of community, while yet preserving the values of religious liberty. Somehow, congregational liberty must find its place within the framework of the oneness of the whole body of Christ. Angus Dun has aptly warned the free churches that "with this congregationalism there can readily come a spirit of local independence that loses a feeling for the organic quality of the church as indeed 'one body.' "[31] In many Protestant groups of the congregational type, this isolationism has doubtless been all too prevalent.

Congregational autonomy, when rightly construed, however, is indispensable. Which means perhaps, as Karl Barth suggests, that the principle of congregationalism—"the free congregation of the free Word of God"[32]—is indispensable if the ecumenical church is to remain free, and that the ecumenical church itself should be organized along congregationalist lines. Yet the self-government of the congregation is an integral part of the whole body of Christ. The good of the whole family of God must always be the primary, ruling norm.

The Need of Maintaining a Vivid Awareness of the Lordship of Christ as the Dynamic Source and Center of the Church's Oneness

The numerous, knotty organizational and practical aspects of the problem of unity must not detract attention from the most important aspect of true Christian unity: it must find the dynamic source of its being forever in the Lordship of Christ.

If denominational Christianity is asked, "What makes one a good Christian?" it replies, "Belief in and acceptance of the official creed of the group." If ecumenical Christianity is asked, "What is your norm,

---

[31]Angus Dun, *Prospecting for a United Church* (New York: Harper and Brothers, 1948), p. 28.

[32]*Man's Disorder and God's Design,* I, 75.

your authority?" it replies emphatically, "The divine confrontation in Jesus Christ, this and nothing else."

Not belief in a creed, but faith in a person, personal surrender to Christ as Lord, is what makes one a member, in good standing, of the ecumenical church. That this is the normative ground of unity which also prevailed in the church of the New Testament period, there can be no doubt.

This recognition that the vital source of the church's oneness stems from the transcendental realm lies deep also in the heart of prophetic Protestantism. Despite the fact that creedal dogmatism has tended again and again to blur insight into this principle and often threatened even to undo it, Protestantism has, throughout its history, maintained an awareness that a horizontal harmony of wills and groups of selves in the Christian community can be rightly achieved only when the character of the horizontal dimension is determined primarily by the vertical dimension of relation to the living Lord, through faith. One can be in right relation with his fellows only if he is first in right relation to God. To put it more concretely, only the power of creative love, which works mightily through Christ, can break the vicious circle of man's self-centeredness and enable him to determine his relation to others by an attitude of unconditional good will.

It must always be clearly borne in mind that the constitutive principle of the life of the church is the living Word of God, mediated through Jesus Christ. The oneness of the church is therefore rightly understood and realized only when it is seen in organic relation to this dynamic center.

The basic error of the concept of unity that prevails in Roman Catholicism lies in its failure to recognize that the unity of the church is an organic rather than organizational type of oneness, because the vital center of the church's life is the prophetic Word, rather than a visible, absolutistic form. Rome believes that the church is "the body of Christ," but it sees this "body" actualized in the priestly, sacramental institution. Hence our Catholic brethren tend to identify the visible, hierarchical church with the body of Christ. As we have shown repeatedly throughout this book, such a concept of the church represents an idolatrous distortion of the expression and realization of the Word of the gospel.

The oneness of the church is a profoundly spiritual kind of oneness. Luther pointed to this in an impressive way in a sermon which he preached in 1523. Commenting on Paul's eucharistic explanation in 1 Corinthians 10:16-17, Luther said: "And since we are one with Christ, the result is that we become one with one another, . . . as the grains of wheat, when they are ground up, are thoroughly mixed with one another, so that none retains its flour by itself, but rather is mixed with the others until it becomes one thing. So with Christians, none remains to himself alone, but each manifests and spreads himself among his fellows in love."[33]

We must, then, keep clear the distinction between the inner essence of the church's reality, the vital center of which is the Lordship of Christ, and the external forms through which this creative dynamic is actualized and fulfilled. The external forms of expression and realization undergo continuous change, due to the fact that this fulfillment is in history; and history, as such, is a living, changing process. Because the church is constantly being fashioned out of the

[33] "Und so wir denn mit Christo ein kuchen sind, so wirkt das selbige soviel, das wir auch unter einander ein ding werden" (*D. Martin Luthers Werke,* bearbeitet von G. Buchwald, G. Kawerau, P. Pietsch [Weimar: Hermann Böhlaus Nachfolger, 1891], XII, 488). Trans. R. G.W.

life of the world, it is constantly changing, in the succession of believers. Here it is one thing, there another. Yet the church remains always one and the same; for it is the same Spirit of creative love which animates her throughout all the changing forms of her historical career.[34]

This aspect of prophetic Protestantism, which stresses the fact that true unity in Christian community comes down from above, that its source lies in transcendental, unconditional reality, is finding eloquent expression today, in outstanding voices of the cause of ecumenicity.[35]

The Oxford Message of 1937 rightly says, "The source of unity is not the consenting movement of men's wills; it is Jesus Christ whose one life flows through the Body and subdues the many wills to His." And the affirmation of unity adopted by the Conference on Faith and Order at Edinburgh, in the same year, says, "This unity does not consist in the agreement of our minds or the consent of our wills. It is founded in Jesus Christ Himself . . . who through the Holy Spirit dwells in His Church. We are one because we are all the objects of the love and grace of God, and called by Him to witness in all the world to His glorious Gospel."

It is because the church is the body of Christ that the only true unity must be what the author of the Ephesian epistle calls "the unity of the Spirit."[36] All of our attempts to achieve the fulfillment of the prayer of the Johannine Christ for unity must begin and end with a recognition of this fact.

No mere organizational approach to the problem, therefore, can be adequate, since such an approach

[34]Cf. *D. Martin Luthers Werke*, bearbeitet von G. Buchwald & G. Kawerau (Weimar: Hermann Böhlaus, Nachfolger, 1886), IV, 169; cf. also Schleiermacher, *The Christian Faith*, pp. 676 ff.

[35]See *Man's Disorder and God's Design*, I, 63, 185.

[36]Ephesians 4:3.

ignores the important distinction between the internal and external character of the church. For this reason also the concept of unity as a mere federation of church groups, each anxiously concerned about its own sovereignty, is inadequate. The essential spiritual character of the church means that the desired unity must be more than a federation; it must be a *fellowship.* It must be more than a mere combine of sovereign states; it must be a spiritual togetherness in one organic whole, where the only ultimate sovereignty is Christ the Lord, his will, his Spirit, his way of life.

The pathway to ideal Christian unity, then, leads through the valley of humility. Unity can never be primarily our own human achievement. Only God can make us one. Only by drawing closer to him who is the head of his body, the church, can we attain a greater spiritual unity among ourselves. We are united with one another because and to the extent that our lives are "hid with Christ in God."[37]

---

[37]Colossians 3:3.

BIBLIOGRAPHY

Books

Abbott, B. A. *The Disciples, An Interpretation.* St. Louis: The Bethany Press, Christian Board of Publication, 1924.

Adam, Karl. *The Spirit of Catholicism.* Trans. Dom Justin McCann. London: Sheed and Ward, 1939.

Allen, Alexander V. G. *Christian Institutions.* New York: Charles Scribner's Sons, 1897.

Ames, Edward Scribner. *The Disciples of Christ.* Chicago: printed privately, 1943-44.

Amsterdam Assembly Series. *Man's Disorder and God's Design.* Vol. I. New York: Harper & Brothers, 1948.

Ante-Nicene Fathers. Eds. Alexander Roberts and James Donaldson. Vols. I, V. Grand Rapids: William B. Eerdman's, 1950.

Aquinas, Thomas. *Basic Writings of Saint Thomas Aquinas.* Vol. I. Ed. Anton C. Pegis. New York: Random House, 1945.

Baillie, John. *The Interpretation of Religion.* New York: Charles Scribner's Sons, 1928.

Bainton, Roland H. *The Reformation of the Sixteenth Century.* Boston: The Beacon Press, 1952.

Barry, F. R. *Recovery of Man.* New York: Charles Scribner's Sons, 1949.

Barth, Karl. *Die Kirchliche Dogmatik,* Vol. II, 1946, Vol. III, 1948. Zürich: Evangelischer Verlag A. G. Zollikon.

—. *The Word of God and the Word of Man.* Trans. Douglas Horton. The Pilgrim Press, 1928.

Berdyaev, Nicolas. *The Meaning of History.* Goeffry Bles: The Centenary Press, 1945.

Bewkes, Eugene Garrett et al. *Experience, Reason and Faith.* New York: Harper & Brothers, 1940.

Bornkamm, Günther; Bultmann, Rudolf; & Schumann, Friedrich Karl. *Die christliche Hoffnung und das Problem der Entmythologisierung.* Stuttgart: Evangelische Verlagswerk, 1954.

Bornkamm, Heinrich. *Luthers Geistige Welt.* Bielefeld: Ernst Gieseking, Deutscher Heimat Verlag, 1953.

Bowman, John Wick. *The Religion of Maturity.* New York: Abingdon-Cokesbury Press, 1948.

Brandt, Richard B. *The Philosophy of Schleiermacher.* New York: Harper & Brothers, 1941.

Brown, William Adams. *Toward a United Church: Three Decades of Ecumenical Christianity.* New York: Charles Scribner's Sons, 1946.

Brunner, Emil. *Revelation and Reason.* Trans. Olive Wyon. Philadelphia: The Westminster Press, 1946.

—. *Die Mystik und Das Wort.* Tübingen: J. C. B. Mohr, 1924.

—. *The Divine-Human Encounter.* Trans. Amandus W. Loos. Philadelphia: The Westminster Press, 1943.

—. *Natur und Gnade.* Tübingen: J. C. B. Mohr, 1935.

Buber, Martin. *Two Types of Faith.* Trans. Norman P. Goldhawk. New York: The Macmillan Company, 1952.

Bultmann, Rudolf. *The Theology of the New Testament.* Vol. I. Trans. Kendrick Grobel. New York: Charles Scribner's Sons, 1951.

Cairns, David S. *The Image of God in Man.* New York: The Philosophical Library, 1953.

Calhoun, Robert L. *What Is Man?* New York: Association Press, 1939.

Calvin, John. *Commentary on the Gospel According to John.* Trans. William Pringle. Edinburgh: The Calvin Translation Society, 1847.

—. *Institutes of the Christian Religion.* Vol. I. Trans. John Allen. Philadelphia: Presbyterian Board of Christian Education, 7th ed., n.d.

Campbell, Alexander. *The Christian System.* St Louis: The Christian Publishing Company, n.d.

—. *The Evidences of Christianity, A Debate Between Robert Owen and Alexander Campbell.* St. Louis: The Christian Publishing Company, 1906.

Campbell, Thomas. *Declaration and Address.* Indianapolis: International Convention of Disciples of Christ, 1949.

Catholic Encyclopedia. Vols. V, XIII, 1912, and XIV, 1913. New York: The Gilmary Society, 1913.

Channing, William E. *The Works of William E. Channing.* Boston: American Unitarian Association, 1900.

Colwell, Ernest Cadman. *The Study of the Bible.* Chicago: The University of Chicago Press, 1937.

Davies, Rupert Erich. *The Problem of Authority in the Continental Reformers: A Study in Luther, Zwingli, and Calvin.* London: The Epworth Press, 1946.

Denzinger, Heinrich. *Enchiridion Symbolorum.* Edito 29. Barcinone: Herder, Friburgi Brisg., 1946.

Dickie, Edgar P. *Revelation and Response.* New York: Charles Scribner's Sons, 1938.

Dinkler, Erich. *Bibelautorität und Bibelkritik.* Tübingen: J. C. B. Mohr-Paul Siebeck, 1950.

Dun, Angus. *Prospecting for a United Church.* New York: Harper & Brothers, 1948.

Emmons, H. H. (ed.) *Light of Emerson.* Cleveland: The Rex Publishing Company, 1930.

England, Stephen J. *The Apostolic Church.* Eugene: Northwest Christian College, 1946.

Faith and Order. The Report of the Third World Conference at Lund, Sweden, August 15-28, 1952.

Ferré, Nels F. S. *Faith and Reason.* New York: Harper & Brother, 1946.

—. *The Christian Fellowship.* New York: Harper & Brothers, 1940.

Frank, Erich. *Philosophical Understanding and Religious Truth.* New York: Oxford University Press, 1945.

Garnett, A. Campbell. *A Realistic Philosophy of Religion.* New York: Willett, Clark, & Company, 1942.

Garrison, W. E. *An American Religious Movement.* St. Louis: Christian Board of Publication, 1945.

Gogarten, Friedrich. *Entmythologisierung und Kirche.* Zweite Auflage. Stuttgart: Vorwerk-Verlag, 1953.

Grimm, Harold J. *The Reformation Era, 1500-1650.* New York: The Macmillan Company, 1954.

Harnack, Adolf von. *History of Dogma.* Trans. Neil Buchanan. Vol. VII. Boston: Little, Brown, and Company, 1900.

Herrmann, D. W. *Der Begriff der Offenbarung.* Giessen: Verlag von Alfred Töpelmann (vormals J. Ricker), 1908.

Herrmann, Wilhelm. *Ethik.* Tübingen: J. C. B. Mohr, 1913.

Hermelink, Heinrich. *Katholizismus und Protestantismus: im Gespräch um die Una Sancta.* Stuttgart: Ehrenfried Klotz Verlag, 1949.

Hippolytus. *The Apostolic Tradition.* Trans. Burton Scott Easton. Cambridge: The University Press, 1934.

Hocking, William Ernest. *The Meaning of God in Human Experience.* New Haven: Yale University Press, 1924.

—. *Living Religions and A World Faith.* New York: The Macmillan Company, 1940.

Hume, David. *An Inquiry Concerning Human Understanding.* Chicago: The Open Court Publishing Company, 1927.

James, William. *The Varieties of Religious Experience.* New York: Longmans, Green and Company, 1917.

Jenkins, Daniel T. *The Nature of Catholicity.* London: Faber & Faber Ltd., 1942.

Joachimsen, Paul. *Die Reformation als Epoche der Deutschen Geschichte.* München: Chr. Kaiser Verlag von R. Oldenbourg, 1951.

Justin Martyr. "First Apology." *Ante-Nicene Fathers.* Vol. I. Eds. Alexander Roberts and James Donaldson. Grand Rapids: William B. Eerdman's Publishing Company, 1950.

Kidd, B. J. *The Roman Primacy.* London: Society for Promoting Christian Knowledge, 1936.

Kierkegaard, Soren. *The Sickness Unto Death.* Trans. Walter Lowrie. Princeton: Princeton University Press, 1941.

Kirk, Kenneth E. (ed.). *The Apostolic Ministry.* London: Hodder & Stoughton, 1947.

Latourette, Kenneth. *The Emergence of a World Christian Community.* New Haven: Yale University Press, 1949.

Lindsay, Thomas Martin. *A History of the Reformation.* Vol. I. New York: Charles Scribner's Sons, 1906-07.

Locke, John. *Locke Selections.* Ed. Sterling P. Lamprecht. The Modern Student Library Philosophy Series. New York: Charles Scribner's Sons, 1928.

—. *Essay on Human Understanding.* London: George Bell and Sons, 1903.

Luther, Martin. *D. Martin Luthers Tischreden.* Vol. I. Weimar: Hermann Böhlaus, Nachfolger, 1912.

—. *D. Martin Luthers Tischreden.* Vol. II. Weimar: Hermann Böhlaus, Nachfolger, 1913.

—. *D. Martin Luthers Werke.* Vol. I. Bearbeitet von J.K.F. Knaacke. Weimar: Hermann Böhlaus, Nachfolger, 1883.

—. *D. Martin Luthers Werke.* Vol. II. Bearbeitet von J.K.F. Knaacke. Weimar: Hermann Böhlaus, Nachfolger, 1884.

—. *D. Martin Luthers Werke.* Vol. IV. Bearbeitet von G. Buchwald und G. Kawerau. Weimar: Hermann Böhlaus, 1886.

—. *D. Martin Luthers Werke.* Vol. VII. In Nomine Ihesv. M. D. XXI, acta et Res Gestae D. Martini Lutheri, n.d.

—. *D. Martin Luthers Werke.* Vol. VII. Bearbeitet von G. Buchwald, P. Drews, J. K. F. Knaacke, P. Pietsch, E. Thiele, Weimar: Hermann Böhlaus, Nachfolger, 1897.

—. *D. Martin Luthers Werke.* Vol. XII. Bearbeitet von G. Buchwald, G. Kawerau, P. Pietsch. Weimar: Hermann Böhlaus, 1891.

—. *D. Martin Luthers Werke.* Vol. XLIII. Bearbeitet von O. Bremer, K. Drescher, R. Reichert. Weimar: Hermann Böhlaus, Nachfolger, 1912.

—. *D. Martin Luthers Werke.* Vol. XL. Bearbeitet von O. Bremer, K. Drescher, A. Freitag, & J. Luther. Weimar: Hermann Böhlaus, Nachfolger, 1911.

—. *First Principles of the Reformation or the Ninety-five Theses and the Three Primary Works of Dr. Martin Luther.* Ed. and trans. Henry Wace and C. A. Buchheim. Philadelphia: Lutheran Publication Society, 1885.

—. *Works of Martin Luther.* Trans. Henry Eyster Jacobs. Vol. VI. Philadelphia: A. J. Holman Company, 1915-1932.

—. *Table Talk.* Ed. & trans. William Hazlitt. London: H. G. Bohn, 1865.

—. *Works of Martin Luther.* Trans. Henry Eyster Jacobs. Vol. I. Philadelphia: A. J. Holman Company, 1915-32.

Lyman, E. W. *The Experience of God in Modern Life.* New York: Charles Scribner's Sons, 1918.

Manson, T. W. *The Church's Ministry.* Philadelphia: The Westminster Press, 1948.

McGiffert, A. C. *Protestant Thought Before Kant.* New York: Charles Scribner's Sons, 1911.

Moore, George Foot. *A History of Religions.* Vol I. New York: Charles Scribner's Sons, 1941.

Morrison, Charles Clayton. *The Unfinished Reformation.* New York: Harper & Brothers, 1953.

Newman, John Henry. *Apologia Pro Vita Sua.* London: J. M. Dent and Sons Ltd., 1921.

Nicene and Post-Nicene Fathers. Trans. Phillip Schaff & Henry Wace. Vol. I. New York: The Christian Literature Company, 1890.

Niebuhr, H. Richard. *Christ and Culture.* New York: Harper & Brothers, 1951.

—. *The Meaning of Revelation.* New York: The Macmillan Company, 1941.

Niebuhr, Reinhold. *The Nature and Destiny of Man.* Vols. I, II. New York: Charles Scribner's Sons, 1943.

Oman, John. *Grace and Personality.* Cambridge: University Press, 1928.

Oxford Universal Dictionary. Vol. V. Ed. C. T. Onions. Oxford University Press: Doubleday, Doran, and Company, 1937.

Pauck, Wilhelm. *The Heritage of the Reformation.* Boston: Beacon Press, 1950.

Phillips, J. B. *Letters to Young Churches.* New York: The Macmillan Company, 1948.

Rauschenbusch, Walter. *Christianizing the Social Order.* New York: The Macmillan Company, 1919.

—. *Christianity and the Social Crisis.* New York: The Macmillan Company, 1913.

Richardson, Alan. *Christian Apologetics.* New York: Harper & Brothers, 1947.

—. *The Gospel and Modern Thought.* London: Oxford University Press, 1950.

Richardson, Alan and Schweitzer, Wolfgang (eds.). *Biblical Authority for Today.* Philadelphia: The Westminster Press, 1951.

Richardson, R. *Communings in the Sanctuary.* St. Louis: Christian Publishing Company, 1888.

Roberts, David E. and Van Dusen, Henry Pitney (eds.). *Liberal Theology.* New York: Charles Scribner's Sons, 1942.

Ross, Floyd H. *Addressed to Christians: Isolationism vs. World Community.* New York: Harper & Brothers, 1950.

Schaff, Phillip. *The Creeds of Christendom.* Vol. III. New York: Harper & Brothers, 1905.

Schleiermacher, Friedrich. *On Religion.* Trans. John Oman. London: Kegan Paul, Trench, Trübner and Company Ltd., 1893.

—. *Sämmtliche Werke.* Erste Abteilung zur Theologie, Zweiter Band. Berlin: G. Reimer, 1836.

—. *The Christian Faith.* Trans. H. R. Mackintosh and J. S. Stewart. Edinburgh: T. & T. Clark, 1928.

Scott, E. F. *The New Testament Idea of Revelation.* New York: Charles Scribner's Sons, 1935.

Seeberg, Erich von D. *Luthers Theologie in Ihren Grundzügen.* Zweite Auflage. Stuttgart: W. Kohlhammer Verlag, 1950.

Smith, George D. (ed.). *The Teaching of the Catholic Church.* Vol. I. New York: The Macmillan Company, 1949.
Spann, J. Richard (ed.). *The Christian Faith and Secularism.* New York: Abingdon-Cokesbury Press, 1948.
Sweet, William Warren. *The Story of Religion in America.* New York: Harper & Brother, 1930.
Temple, William. *Nature, Man and God.* London: The Macmillan Company Ltd., 1934.
—. *The Universality of Christ.* New York: George H. Doran Company, 1922.
Thatcher, Oliver J. & McNeal, Edgar H. *A Source Book for Medieval History.* New York: Charles Scribner's Sons, 1905.
Tillich, Paul. *The Protestant Era.* Trans. James Luther Adams. Chicago: The University of Chicago Press, 1948.
—. *The Shaking of the Foundations.* New York: Charles Scribner's Sons, 1948.
—. *Systematic Theology.* Vol. I. Chicago: University of Chicago Press, 1951.
Van Dusen, Henry Pitney. *World Christianity.* New York: Abingdon-Cokesbury, 1947.
West, Robert Frederick. *Alexander Campbell and Natural Religion.* New Haven: Yale University Press, 1948.
Whitehead, Alfred North. *Process and Reality.* New York: The Macmillan Company, 1930.
—. *Adventures of Ideas.* New York: The Macmillan Company, 1933.
Wilburn, Ralph G. *Christianity vs. Legalism.* Los Angeles: Associated Publishers, 1949.
Williams, Daniel Day. *God's Grace and Man's Hope.* New York: Harper & Brothers, 1949.
—. *What Present-Day Theologians Are Thinking.* New York: Harper & Brothers, 1952.
Zollars, E. V. *The King of Kings.* Cincinnati: The Standard Publishing Company, 1911.

ARTICLES

Aubrey, E. E. "The Present Status of Liberalism." *Crozier Quarterly.* Vol. XXV. No. 1.
Brunner, Peter. "Umrisse einer Lehre von der Autorität der Heiligen Schrift." *Evangelisch-Lutherische Kirchenzeitung.* 9 Jahrgang. Nr. 9. May 1, 1955. Herausg. Richard Eckstein, Berlin.

Campbell, Alexander (ed.). *The Millennial Harbinger.* I (New Series, 1837).

Christian-Evangelist, The. Vol. 89, No. 48.

Garnett, A. Campbell. "The Impact of Modern Scholarship on Christianity." *Journal of Bible and Religion.* Vol. XXI. No. 3.

Hocking, William Ernest. "Reconception Reconsidered." *The Christian Century.* Vol. LXXII. No. 9. March 2, 1955.

Schumacher, Frederick T. "The Word of God as Event." *Journal of Bible and Religion.* Vol. XX. No. 4.

Wilburn, Ralph G. "The Sectarian Spirit." *Christian Education.* Vol. XXXI. No. 3.

—. "The Skeptically Religious Student." *Christian Education.* Vol. XXX. No. 3.

INDEX